TOURISM MARKETING

TOURISM MARKETING

Ravindra Verma

CENTRUM PRESS
NEW DELHI-110002 (INDIA)

CENTRUM PRESS
H.O.: 4360/4, Ansari Road, Daryaganj,
New Delhi-110002 (India)
Tel: 23278000, 23261597, 23255577, 23286875
B.O.: No. 1015, Ist Main Road, BSK IIIrd Stage,
IIIrd Phase, IIIrd Block, Bangalore-560085 (INDIA)
Tel: 080-41723429
Email: centrumpress@gmail.com
Visit us at: www.centrumpress.com

Tourism Marketing

First Edition, 2010

ISBN 978-93-80540-07-8

PRINTED IN INDIA

Printed at Mehra Offset Press, Delhi

Contents

Contents

Preface

People hold a variety of misconceptions about marketing. Most common is its confusion with selling and advertising. Selling and advertising are actually types of promotion which is only a component of marketing. Marketing involves much more, including product/ service development, place (location and distribution), and pricing. It requires information about people, especially those interested in what you have to offer (your "market"), such as what they like, where they buy and how much they spend. Its role is to match the right product or service with the right market or audience. Marketing, as you will see, is an art and a science. According to the American Marketing Association, marketing is "the process of planning and executing the conception, pricing, promotion, and distribution of ideas, goods, and services to create exchanges that satisfy individual and organizational objectives." Simply stated it is creating and promoting a product (ideas, goods or services) that satisfies a customer's need or desire and is available at a desirable price and place. Earlier it was mentioned that a product can be "ideas, goods, or services." Since tourism is primarily a service based industry, the principal products provided by recreation/ tourism (R/T) businesses are recreational experiences and hospitality. These are intangible products and more difficult to market than tangible products such as automobiles. The intangible nature of services makes quality control difficult but crucial. It also makes it more difficult for potential customers to evaluate and compare service offerings. In addition, instead of moving the product to the customer, the customer must travel to the product (area/community). Travel is a significant portion of the time and money spent in association with recreational and tourism experiences and is a major factor in people's decisions on whether or not to visit your business or community.

As an industry, tourism has many components comprising the overall "travel experience." Along with transportation, it includes such things as accommodations, food and beverage services, shops, entertainment, aesthetics and special events. It is rare for one business to provide the variety of activities or facilities tourists need or desire. This adds to the difficulty of maintaining and controlling the quality of the experience. To overcome this hurdle, tourism related businesses, agencies, and organizations need to work together to package and promote tourism opportunities in their areas and align their efforts to assure consistency in product quality.

Globalisation and Liberalisation is gaining growing attention as a strategy for survival, competition and growth. The limitations of national markets, the diversity and unevenness of resource endowments of different nations, complexity of technological developments, differences in the levels of development and demand patterns, differences in production costs and efficiencies, technological revolution in communication and other fields etc., mandate globalisation. The concept of marketing is a dynamic concept. It has changed altogether with the passage of time. Such changes have far reaching effects on production and distribution. This book contains papers on marketing management, practices, policies and emerging trends in global business.

—Ravindra Verma

1

Tourism Marketing

Marketing is indispensable part of any substantive tourism enterprise. As the market is expanding, the role of marketing as a driving force in a business endeavour is also being recognized. With growing competition, organisations in tourism business have no option but to do organised and targeted marketing. An organised approach to marketing always helps, whether it is on the tour operator end or at destinations. Guides, escorts, restaurants, hotels, transporters, shops etc. compete one another to stay ahead. A proper tourism marketing strategy calls for close cooperation between the government, tourism industry and the local population.

Evolution of Marketing

Marketing as a concept has evolved in the last 30 years. Development of marketing has three distinct stages: Production Era, Sales Era and Marketing Era. Marketing era arrived when organizations began producing what they could sell rather than trying to sell what they manufactured. While planning and designing a product, customers' needs, tastes and satisfaction were considered. Growth of competition prompted organisations to frame marketing techniques.

Change in travelling trends also made it necessary to adopt new approach. The emergence of long haul traveller prompted the need for marketing research which studied market trends, consumer behaviour and ascertained procedure to make products which satisfied the users of tourism products. Gradual social and economic development culminated in segmentation of mass market into specialized target markets. Tackling these markets needed an approach which was in tune with new times.

Selling and Marketing

Selling and Marketing are different concepts. Selling focuses on the needs of the seller while marketing concentrates on buyers' needs. A marketing oriented organisation focuses on customer needs and earns profits through customer satisfaction. Several organizations in tourism field are product oriented. They emphasise on the available services of products but ignore consumers' requirements. A marketing oriented tourist organisation has a completely different approach. They offer services around the tourists' needs.

Travel Lean and Green: Ecotourism Today

The new trend in travel is ecotourism these days, or ecological tourism to give it its full name. In a world where more and more people are looking at ways and means to save the environment as a result of environmental degradation. As a result, ecotourism has been around for years, since the 1980s to be exact. It has only been the last few years that it has really caught the attention of travellers everywhere though.

Ecotourism is perfect for individuals that are interested in the natural world. It is all about getting back to nature and valuing everything around us. As a result, ecotourism is incredible and can really make you feel like you are alive. The one thing that puts most individuals off is that it sounds expensive, but if you know where to look and take the hints and tips given to you, then it need not be expensive at all.

There are many countries all over the world that have very active ecotourism resorts, and the majority of them have received rave reviews from individuals that have already experienced them. Costa Rica, India, Ecuador and Kenya are the most popular destinations that support ecotourism at the moment, but there are others that seem to fly under the radar and these may be the best picks for individuals or couples wanting to experience it first-hand in a remote location.

New Zealand is one such country supporting ecotourism, as is Australia. Both countries have not publicised this fact because they are relatively new to the world of ecological tourism and are developing their resorts as we speak. The variety of ecotourism there and the sheer beauty of the landscape is definitely worth a trip for, but you can actually turn it into a tour of the region and spend a month or so there if you so wish. If you do want a successful trip of the ecotourism variety then you should research the area first to find out what the customs and values of that country actually are because it is quite easy to undo all of the good work in ecological areas by making one of several mistakes. The list below will help you to distinguish between what you can and cannot do:

1. The first is obviously to do your homework. The areas that individuals visit in eco-tourist trips are finely balanced and usually value more natural ways life. If you do not know those values then it is easy to damage the equilibrium of the area. In fact, you can actually cause more harm than you realise by just acting as you would in a Western First World country.
2. Try not to give things away to those in need. This may sound harsh to begin with, but ecotourism is all about helping individuals work their way out of poverty and giving things away simply encourages begging, which is exactly what the country is trying to avoid by setting up ecotourism.
3. Don't barter with the locals if it is not in their culture for you to do so. The items that they are selling usually help them to live and cost just pence back home. The whole point of ecotourism is outlined above and this applies here as well.
4. Avoid buying souvenirs that are made out of flora or fauna from the local area because the likelihood is that this is going against the principles of ecotourism. It is about using local materials, but that does not include animals and plants.
5. Be wary of where you take photos because it may offend some people if they are actually snapped without giving their consent. This is just common decency. They are not there to be made a show of, just simply to do their job.

Southeast Tourism Policy Council

This charter establishes a general framework of organization for cooperation between private sector tourism interests and multiple Federal and State agencies in the southeastern United States. The parties defined herein propose to work together in support of the resolution passed by the Southeast Tourism Society at the September 6, 2002 Federal-State Tourism Summit in Louisville, Kentucky, to establish a Southeast Tourism Policy Council (STPC). The parties further propose to coordinate and support the development and implementation of a strategy that encourages travel and tourism by serving as a forum for travel and tourism related issues of public policy and opinion in the Southeast United States. The charter recognizes that the vitality of tourism in the southeast states is dependent upon providing opportunities to develop and enhance the management of travel and tourism activities in balance with sustainable management practices that keep the environment in a sound state, and prevent the exploitation, destruction, or neglect of the natural, historical, and cultural resources, and the national patrimony of the southeast.

In order to assure equity in representation, the STPC shall be structured in such manner that no party will have more than one representative on the governing board and no party will have more than one vote in policy and governance issues considered by the council.

Mission Statement

The mission of the Southeast Tourism Policy Council to provide leadership that insures broad representation of tourism interests in the southeast, encourage partnerships between public and private sectors of tourism and advocate for sustainable economic growth in an environmentally responsible way.

Vision Statement

By 2008, the Southeast Tourism Policy Council will lead the travel and tourism industry in identifying and analysing travel and tourism issues and serve as a forum to affect public policy and legislation for the sustainability growth industry in the southeast.

STPC Philosophy

It is the philosophy of the STPC that the tourism industry in the southeast has a responsibility to be an advocate for the future of treasured public lands by acting as a spokesman on issues of sustainable tourism in the region. Further, the STPC believes that partnerships should be forged that recognize conserving and sustaining our valuable natural, cultural, and historic resources can coexist with supporting the economic vitality of tourism interests and communities that serve visitors.

Goals and Objectives

In order to achieve the STPC mission its members embrace and encourage tourism goals that:

* Enrich the visitor experience by providing opportunities to appreciate and enjoy the rich heritage of the southeast.
* Optimize understanding of the contributions of tourism to the quality of life and intercultural appreciation of the southeast's natural and human resources, history and ethnicity.
* Support the economic viability of tourism interests and communities.
* Conserve and otherwise protect the natural, cultural and historic resources that are the cornerstone for travel and tourism.
* Promote the integrity and authenticity of tourism related sites and activities and showing respect for the values of the people of the southeast.

Goals

Generally Stated, the Goals of the STPC Shall Be:

* Sustainable Use-Because tourism is the cleanest and perhaps most sustainable industry in the world, it makes economic sense to explore ways in which federal and state agencies can work together with the tourism industry to create sustainable environments that foster sustainable industry.
* Resource Conservation-Natural, historic, cultural, and recreation resources administered by federal and state agencies must adhere to commonly accepted conservation and management practices if the integrity and use of resources is to be sustained and of continuing value to the community and the public.

  It will be increasingly important to conserve, and, where appropriate restore, the natural, cultural, historical, and recreation resources that serve as the basis for travel and tourism.
* Economic Development/Diversification-Tourism is an essential economic diversification tool. It is not the total answer to prosperity planning and development, nor to economic improvement for most communities. Federal and state agencies can help the private sector provide necessary and profitable services inside and outside site boundaries. This government commitment must be made, furthered by a commitment to have local vendors and providers under government contracts perform on a competitive basis for tourism services. Provide

skill and expertise in developing strategic plans and visions. The private sector can assist public lands/communities in the proper development, use, and enjoyment of those treasures thereby infusing local economies with those dollars.

* Quality of Life Enhancement and Personal Growth-Enrichment of surroundings grows from personal learning, appreciation, and commitment to provide best management practices and decisions on lands inside and outside federal and state site boundaries. The quality of life near or adjacent to federal or state administered properties should come from an appreciation for their value and a desire to sustain them for the future as something of inestimable worth to society. It is also important that whatever approaches are taken to increase the health and viability of tourism, that the STPC respect the needs and values of the constituents it purports to serve.
* Enhancement of Visitor Experiences-By advancing public awareness of travel and tourism opportunities and improving the quality and value of service to the public, visitors to the southeast states will have quality life enriching experiences in order to maximize tourism revenue.

Objectives

* Mobilize public and private tourism interests to educate elected officials about the value of public lands and sustainable tourism.
* Identify and advocate for issues of public policy and legislation affecting travel and tourism in the southeast and nationally.
* Promote public lands stewardship as part of an on-going educational curricula.
* Create opportunities for continuing dialogue between public and private tourism to sustain mutual understanding of their respective roles and responsibilities.
* Advocate for a unified effort for the restoration of a national tourism office to enhance the domestic and foreign tourism market.

Guiding Principles

The following principles will guide our collective efforts and agency to industry relationships. We will:

* Treat all parties with respect and dignity;

orest Service (FS).

* Recognize and respect differing perspectives and mandates while building on common interests;
* Increase communication and learning to overcome challenges resulting from differing perspectives and mandates; ensure responsive coordinated processes and decision making, thereby demonstrating a high standard for public and industry policy that produces better overall results for citizens and the environment;
* To the maximum extent possible, resolve issues within the STPC sphere of influence;
* Seek to integrate agency programs, resources, and capabilities with those of the tourism industry to maximize our collective responsiveness; and
* Lead, coordinate, and innovate to produce more effective outcomes with greater efficiency.

Governance

The STPC shall be managed by the Southeast Tourism Society (STS) under the authority of the STS Board of Directors. The Board shall designate an Executive Committee to provide management oversight over the STPC composed of the current Board Chair, the immediate past Board Chair, the President and CEO, the Board Secretary, and one other member at large. This charter further defines the establishment of an Interim Leadership Council overseen by the Executive Committee that will formalize the organization of the STPC. The interim leadership council will remain intact until such time as the full council is fully operational and has determined its officers, organizational structure, policies, procedures, and administrative decorum. The Interim Leadership Council shall elect its own Board and officers and shall meet as often as necessary to conduct business.

Once formally established the STPC will meet quarterly, one meeting being held in conjunction with the Southeast Tourism Society Congressional Summit in Washington, D.C. Meetings of STPC officers may be held at other times and locations as dictated by issues under consideration.

It is further stipulated that the STPC shall consist of nine designated classes of membership:

(1) Federal Agencies.
(2) State Travel Offices.
(3) State Resource Agencies.
(4) Economic Development Agencies & Organizations.
(5) Industry Associations.
(6) Private Tourism Interests.
(7) Elected Officials.
(8) STS Board of Directors Representatives.
(9) Marketing Organizations.

Additional classes of membership may be added by the STPC from time to time as necessary for the conduct of business. In like manner, admission of additional agencies, offices, associations, interests, and officials may be added by petition to and approval of the STPC.

Failure of any agency, office, association, interest, or official to execute its responsibilities to the STPC shall be cause for removal of the representative from the council.

No agency, organization, association, or individual interest shall have more than one representative except that the STS Board of Directors shall have five representatives. No agency, organization, association, or individual interest shall have more than one vote on matters deliberated and acted upon by the STPC.

General administration and day-to-day office management shall be the responsibility of the Southeast Tourism Society. Funding of/for the STPC may be derived from a number of sources recruited and coordinated by the STPC Board and the Board of Directors of the Southeast Tourism Society. Funds will be managed by the STS as the fiduciary agent for the STPC.

Definitions

Federal Agencies-Federal agencies are bureaus of the Executive Departments of the United States government that provide information resources, access, resource protection, education, and recreation activities to the public. Variously designated, these Federal agencies include, but are not limited to:

* Department of Agriculture.

- Forest Service (FS).

- Natural Resource Conservation Service (NRCS).

* Department of Defence.

- Army Corps of Engineers (USCOE).

* Department of the Interior.

- Bureau of Indian Affairs (BIA).
- Fish and Wildlife Service (USFWS).
- National Park Service (NPS).
- Advisory Council on Historic Preservation.

* Department of Transportation.

- Federal Highway Administration (FHWA).

* Department of Commerce.

- Environmental Protection Agency (EPA).
- Tennessee Valley Authority (TVA).

State Travel Offices-State Travel Offices are offices operated by the eleven southeast states that provide for the development, marketing, and travel information services of the states. Generally, the State Travel Directors will represent State Travel Offices.

State Resource Agencies and Economic Development Offices: These agencies are defined as those dedicated to the management and conservation of natural and cultural resources and to the management and operation of State park systems. Examples of such agencies include: Departments of Natural Resources, Forestry, Fish and Wildlife, State Park Systems, and State Historic Preservation Offices.

Economic Development Agencies and Organizations: Variously defined, these agencies provide services related to industrial development, small and minority businesses, financial incentives (such as enterprise zoning programs, grants, direct loans, and tax incentives), and business and entrepreneurial development. These organizations may include economic development districts and multi-county economic development corporations.

Industry Associations: Tourism industry associations are those consortiums, and incorporated profit, not for profit, and non-profit organizations engaged in the business of tourism. Examples of such organizations are: National Tour Organization, International Association of Convention and Visitors Bureaus, National Association of State Park Directors, and American Recreation Coalition.

Private Tourism Interests-Private tourism interests include, but are not limited to individual profit, not for profit, and non-profit businesses engaged in the business of tourism. Such interests may or may not be incorporated under the laws of the various states. Examples of such interests include: destination management organizations, convention and visitors bureaus, attractions, hotels/lodging, airlines, car rental companies, advertisers, and media providers.

Elected Officials-Elected officials are individuals elected by their various constituents to serve the public interest, and who are sworn to uphold the laws, policies, and regulations of their jurisdictions. Elected officials serving on the council must have demonstrated interest in and support for travel and tourism in the southeast.

Statement of Mutual Interest

The STPC recognizes that visitors to the southeast states will be better served when STPC members work together toward mutually developed goals and objectives. STPC objectives will contribute to the economically sustainable growth and health of communities through conservation and wise management of the public land heritage and through the complimentary development and promotion of public and private destinations.

The cooperating federal agencies responsible for the management of federal resources and lands are dedicated to the wise development and use of natural and cultural resources in the southeast. By becoming members of the STPC, they agree to assist in increasing the public's knowledge, awareness, and appreciation of these resources and their management. They will encourage travel and tourism on these lands as an appropriate way of extending the benefits of their designation to the larger community they serve, both domestically and internationally. The public sector will offer expertise to the private sector in terms of knowing how and what to help with when developing resources for tourism interests.

STPC private sector members recognize they have a beneficial role in helping carry out activities that facilitate development of sustainable projects that support and which are compatible with the mandates of the various federal agencies. They agree to provide assistance to the federal agencies in their efforts to plan, develop, market, and manage travel and tourism on public lands, assist in travel and public and private tourism projects, and in resource assessments related to travel and tourism and its value in rural development.

In executing their mutual interests, members further recognize their obligation to define the information needs of the travel and tourism industry and how best to deliver educational and informational material.

This charter in no way restricts STPC members from participating in similar activities or agreements with other public or private interests.

Nothing in this charter or the associated Memorandum of Understanding shall obligate Federal or State agencies to expend appropriations or to enter into any contracts or other obligations.

It is mutually understood that the legal mechanism for Federal agency participation in the STPC is a properly executed Memorandum of Agreement, signed by bureau officials or their designees having delegated signature authority.

Applicable Laws

By agreeing to this charter, STPC members further agree that any and all actions shall be undertaken in accordance with applicable Federal, State and local laws. Unless otherwise provided by law, all contract work undertaken by the STPC shall be authorized by the STS Board of Directors and shall be performed in accordance with Federal and State procurement and claims laws, regulations, procedures and policies.

Federal Agency Exclusions

Federal agency representatives agree to comply with all conflict of interest policies and regulations set forth by the United States Code or by specific departmental or agency policies. The STPC understands that although the agencies agree to cooperate and participate in the actions and decisions of the STPC, Federal and state representatives are excluded from voting or otherwise engaging in the financial management unless such exclusion is waived by the appropriate federal officials having jurisdiction.

Officials Not to Profit

It is understood that STPC members individually nor collectively shall directly profit from the business and undertakings of the STPC. It is further understood that unless specifically authorized by the STS and/or STPC no specific businesses, companies, enterprises, attractions, interests, or products will be endorsed by the STPC or its members. Unless otherwise authorized by the STS and/or the STPC, members will assume responsibility for their own travel and expenses related to meetings and business of the STPC. Travel expenses of federal members funded by the STS or STPC shall be in conformance with established laws, regulations, and policies of their respective departments and agencies.

Non-Discrimination Clause

During the performance of this Charter Agreement, the participants agree to abide by all applicable civil rights laws, regulations, and certifications. Participants will not discriminate against any person because of race, colour, religion, sex, or national origin. Participants will take affirmative action to ensure that applicants for any positions on or related to the STPC are employed without regard to their race, colour, religion, sex, or national origin.

Charter Agreement

Notwithstanding the execution of a Memorandum of Understanding between the Federal and state agencies and the STPC, by affixing signatures hereto, all parties agree to this charter as the principle governing policy of the STPC. It is further agreed that this charter shall remain in effect until or unless modified by the STPC in agreement with the Board of Directors of the Southeast Tourism Society.

Marketing of Tourism Services in India

A Study With Special Reference to Orissa their workers, have contributed a lot in infusing interest to look around to a place for an annual or biannual visit with family members. Even though India has a very meager share amounting to 0.38 percent of tourists and 0.51 percent of the amount of world tourism trade in 2001, it has the hope for attracting more and more foreign tourists by exploiting her unexploited tourist spots of the country. Mostly tourists from North America, Central and South America, Africa, Australia, Western Europe, Eastern Europe, West Asia, South Asia, South East Asia and East Asia are visiting India as foreign tourists.

Out of these the share of North America, Western Europe, West and South Asia occupies a major share in increasing Indian tourism trade. India accounts for four out of five tourists to South Asia.

Another healthy trend in the foreign tourism in India since 1991 is the conspicuous increase in business travels with its spin off effects in upgradation of accommodation and introduction of new technology in communications and other services. On an average, a foreign tourist stays for about 27 days in India which is an important indicator of increase of the foreign exchange earned by the country.

Tourism in India has vast employment potential, much of which still awaits exploitation. At present about 8.5 million persons are directly employed by hospitality services. This is about 2.4 percent of the total work force of the country. In addition, the industry provides indirect employment to about 30 million persons. Further it is interesting to note that the employment generation in proportion to investment is very high in tourism industry. According to an estimate, an investment of Rs.10 lakh creates 89 jobs in hotels and restaurants sector as against 44.7 jobs in agriculture and 12.6 in manufacturing industry. Another important aspect of employment in tourism is that it employs a large number of women in hotels, airlines services, travel agencies, handicrafts making and marketing and cultural activity centres. As per 1983-84 indices the employment output ratio in tourism was 71, whereas in leather 51, textiles 27, electricity 14, beverages 12 and cement 6. Generally the visit of a foreign tourist to India provides employment to one person and 6.5 domestic tourists generate one job. Hotel sector is the key segment of tourism industry to earn foreign exchange. Realising the importance of hotel segment the government has taken initiatives to encourage hotel industry by providing tax benefits and other incentives. Foreign investment and collaboration are now facilitated under new economic policy. The hotel industry has shown a spectacular growth during the last one and half decades. The number of hotel rooms has increased from 30200 in 1986 to 57386 in 1995 and to 62000 in 1996 and to 68000 in 2001. In the approved list of Department of Tourism the classified hotels are 125 in One Star, 286 Two Star, 274 Three Star, 73 Four Star, 56 Five Star, 42 Five Star Deluxe, and 41 of heritage hotel category.

Inspite of rapid strides made by the hotel industry since last one decade or so, the hotel accommodation falls short of the requirement of growing inflow of the tourists. Assuming a modest growth rate of 7 to 8 percent per annum, the requirement to hotel rooms is expected to rise to 91,000 by 2002-03 and to 1.125 lakh rooms by 2005. Besides a large number of budget hotels will be required for about 200 million strong middle class Indian tourists also. Places of tourist interest are so numerous and of varied nature that it is not easy to describe these places comprehensively.

These include mostly the Himalayan Region, the great plain of north India, the peninsular plateau and coastal plains. In general the tourist spots are counted more like Buddhist sites, Shrines, Forts, places of historical importance, hot springs, Jain monasteries, lakes and birds, sanctuaries, religious centres, science spots, sea beaches, summer resorts, water falls and wild lives etc. In this context, a reference can be drawn for Orissa that all above kinds of spots are richly available to attract more and more foreign as well as domestic tourists. About 25 lakh of domestic tourists and 30000 foreign tourists visit Orissa annually. The share for South Orissa is 30 percent of the total tourist arrival to Orissa. Orissa has several important nationally and internationally famous tourists' centres like Puri, Bhubaneswar, Konark, Cuttack, Chilika Lake, Chandipur, Gopalpur, Beach etc.

The other places are Baripada, Khiching, Baud, Koraput, Bolangir, Jeypore and Udayagiri etc. The area remains unexplored because of want of infrastructural development, more comfortable modes of transport, accommodation etc. Although India has progressed a lot since the fifties with respect to tourism, she is still way behind the developed, even the developing countries. India earns one seventh of China, one fourth of Indonesia and less than half of Philippines from tourism in comparison. The development of tourism depends upon the development of an integrated infrastructure of national and international highways, railways, ports, civil aviation, telecommunication, hotel accommodation and allied services. Inadequacies of such infrastructural facilities adversely affect tourism. The sluggish growth of Indian tourism arises from India's inability to sell effectively her rich tourist potential.

India should market itself as a value added tourism destination stressing its variety and cost effectiveness. Satisfaction of the tourist should be the top priority of the tourist industry. Apart from infrastructural development, tourism requires an environment of peace and stability where the tourist is sure of his safety and security. Political unrest and fear of violence is a death knell to tourist industry. Unfortunately, one part or the other of the country is hit by *bandhs*, strikes, ethnic clashes and insurgency which adversely affect our tourism service marketing. Epidemics, such as plague, AIDS and dengue fever are also detrimental to the growth of tourism.

It is surprising that some small countries like Malaysia, Indonesia, Hongkong and get Singapore have been able to attract more tourists and better receipts than India. Even in terms of quality, the diminutives like Maldives and Bhutan present an appreciable model of sustainable tourism. In this context, in order to give a philip to the tourism trade the Central Government as well as the State Government should come forward to develop some of the newly unexploited and selected tourist places, diversify some of the culture oriented tourism to holiday and leisure tourism, develop trekking, winter sports, wild life, beach resorts tourism, launching, key markets near tourist centres, provide inexpensive accommodation and to improve service efficiency. India still hopes better to improve the tourism marketing services and to take an equal and more challenging steps with her competitors in the field more vigoursly.

Promoting Private Sector of Tourism in Jammu and Kashmir

Tourism is considered to be the largest export industry in the world. However, this industry can have an impact on the economy only when it has the motivational force of the Private Sector. Being a service oriented industry it requires professionalism and dedication which are generally lacking in the Public Sector especially in our part of the world. In the initial stages when tourism was just picking up, the state had to intervene. Private capital would be hesitant in investing without being sure of returns. To give a push to the activity it was essential for the government to go for infrastructure development. A lead was given to the industry and the public sector activities were in fact started totally as part of the department of tourism. It was like facilitating and motivating the private entrepreneurs to take up this activity. The annual expenditure on maintenance of various establishments run by the government in the shape of huts and tourist bungalows was over Rs.1.50 crores but the total revenue generated was hardly Rs.30 lakhs per year. These establishments were also run as a healthy competition to private sector to keep the prices of these services in check.

The greatest mistake was turning over all these establishments in one go to state run tourism development corporation. In almost all major tourist destinations, the infrastructure for accommodation, food, transport, and recreation is run by the private sector. The government has only to take care of the very basic infrastructure such as road connectivity, power, water, and communications. It has been proved everywhere that any commercial venture run by the government invariably ends in the red. There are many reasons for this. Firstly, the government service is taken more or less as social security. Employees cannot be fired even if their contribution is zero. The hire and fire system cannot be enforced in government due to a number of reasons. On the contrary in the private sector one has more flexibility both in the selection of the professional staff and policy of hire and fire can be enforced with some minimum guarantees. Apart from tourism, almost all other government corporations are in red. If we have to aim for development of international tourism, we have to promote private sector in a big way. In fact, the state sector organisations should also be gradually disinvested. To begin with some of the lucrative properties should be put up for joint ventures.

Many attempts have been made in the past in this regard but most of these have failed as only loss making properties were offered for joint ventures or outright disinvestment. In addition, the procedures were made so complicated that every enterprising investor got fed up and ran away. The government has to take a conscious decision and plan it properly. Something like a golden handshake has to be worked out for the staff and their consent obtained. Any ad hoc measure is bound to recoil. These days specialist agencies are available for such jobs. Once it has been sincerely decided that the private sector has to be promoted, a number of substantive incentives have to be provided to attract investment. The present incentive rules initiated in mid nineties do not come up to the mark. At the time of declaring these incentives the main motive was to accede to the popular demand of declaring tourism as an industry. This was done with least financial commitment in view of the bad financial position of the state at that time.

Even though tourism was declared to be a priority industry yet the important incentives such as on power were not made available to this sector. It was declared an industry in name only. The first requirement would be to revise these incentive rules and make investment in tourism related infrastructure most attractive for both local as well as international investors. Not many people know that there are already a host of incentives available as part of the central industrial policy for various tourism projects. Most of the incentives are for Eco-Tourism projects, which is the most suitable activity for our state having a fragile environment. Lack of knowledge among the members of the trade as well as the administrators is making the local entrepreneurs lose these incentives by default! All tourism ventures should be given a complete tax holiday at least for ten years to motivate the private sector. There should be no bar on the location of these units provided these are in conformity with all local laws. Preference should be given to joint ventures involving local entrepreneurs and also ensuring substantial local employment in such projects. One often hears about single window clearance but it is never implemented on ground.

People coming for investments in any field have to spend months and sometimes years to obtain various clearances. The ideal situation can be setting up of a Tourism Investment Board with private/public sector participation to ensure clearance of projects at an accelerated pace. The areas for investment are extensive. To begin with is the world class accommodation in the major cities like Srinagar and Jammu. Many global hotel chains can be motivated for giving local franchise with government facilitation and if necessary, a counter guarantee in view of the prevailing circumstances.

In fact, totally new resorts can be developed by professional developers and made available for sale among locals who have enough resources for making sizeable investments in this field. Next comes transport. We are nowhere near the minimum world standards. Avis and other rent a car brands which are already in some metros have yet to arrive here. We do not have luxury cars and coaches for sight seeing. Even though over last couple of years locals have taken some initiatives in regard to cars, yet the coaches of the Volvo brand are missing from Kashmir.

There has always been a persistent complaint about lack of recreational and entertainment facilities. We need not always go for night clubs and casinos but there are plenty of other recreational facilities which are missing. These could include bowling alleys, indoor ice and roller skating rinks, amusement parks, cable cars with mountain top panoramic restaurants, theatres, standard art galleries, and museums. There are umpteen other possibilities for decent avenues of entertainment. Unfortunately, instead of promoting private investment, the government is itself venturing into these projects thereby creating some more liabilities for future. It is the right time for both the industry as well as the government to wake up and prepare jointly a comprehensive tourism policy especially in regard to participation of private sector. The only involvement of the government apart from facilitation and motivation should be monitoring and regulation. We need very strong and upright set ups involving a panel of experts from various related fields of hospitality industry to over see all these developments in regard to tourism. They should adopt international standards and ensure adherence to these by all concerned.

There should also be a fool proof redressal mechanism. It is possible to have these things under the existing legislation in the tourism field by incorporating amendments keeping in view global standards. In addition, various players in the industry need to streamline their own organisations by establishing some sort of ethics committees and setting up reasonable standards of service with continued adherence for allowing membership to these bodies. Defaulters should be automatically thrown out to maintain credibility of standards. Given all the above inputs our motto for future development in tourism should be, "Private Sector, Private Sector, and Only Private Sector"!

2

Framing a Travel Strategy

Travel policies aren't designed just to keep costs down. You also need to consider your team's needs, the system's ease of use, and convenient locations and schedules.

If you've been to the supermarket or the drug store lately, you've likely learned the basic rule of purchasing: Frequent customers get the best prices and the best service. American Airlines first invented a frequent shopper's program when it launched Advantage to encourage travellers to bring all their business to one supplier.

Thirty years later, even small firms and their clients can save money and make taking to the road a little easier for their travellers by applying this basic rule of purchasing. This edition of Transit Authority will outline the nine components of a corporate travel program that small and midsize firms can institute for their own employees and partners or recommend to their clients. Our goal: finding the delicate balance that keeps travel costs down and road warriors happy.

At companies with larger travel spends (where the annual travel tabs run over $100 million), managing the travel program is a serious business handled by a dedicated staff. When travelling for the firm, their employees are urged — or even ordered — to book their trips through a designated travel agency or Internet travel site, using airlines and hotels with which the firm has negotiated discounts. Travellers charge their tickets to a single charge card, drive cars from the firm's designated car-rental company, bring their meetings to preferred hotels, file their expense reports online. The best practices of their corporate travel programs can be adapted on a smaller scale by companies and firms of every size.

Optimizing travel comes down to making decisions about nine things: the corporate travel policy; the manager of the program; the type of travel agency that will serve as your intermediary to suppliers; the airlines, hotels, car-rental, charge-card and online travel-booking companies with whom you will partner; and the system you will use for tracking and reporting spending data. We'll look at and offer best practices for each piece of the puzzle, with a focus on small and midsize companies and their business customers.

Start the Journey With a Map

Whether your employees are travelling on firm business or billing every charge back to a client, they are only human. Everyone likes to fly first class — and will, unless someone sets clear limits. Every firm and company should have a travel policy outlining the basic rules, signed off on by top management and distributed to every employee who travels. Keep in mind, however, that buying travel is not like buying paper clips; flying far from home is a stressful and emotional business, and the time of executives is a valuable commodity not to be wasted. A bus may be the cheapest option for getting from Chicago to New York, but odds are good that Southwest Airlines will be the better value in terms of time and effort saved.

While travel policy should come from the top, be sure to include a broad contingency in the discussion, including at least one of the most frequent travellers and the assistants who will make the actual reservations. Many firms also consider a two-tier policy, one for road warriors, senior partners, and executives, and a second for those who travel only to an occasional conference. Keep the policy concise and clear, covering the basic goals and guidelines for each of the nine major components.

Building a Framework

Companies have two options for selecting the framework for the travel management function: whether to handle it internally or to outsource it to a travel agency. Unless your annual travel budget is over $1 million and your office is open 24/7, the best practice usually is to contract with a professional travel agency. Keep in mind, though, that while you can outsource the tasks involved in making reservations, providing customer service, collecting spending data and negotiating contracts with suppliers, you cannot outsource management functions.

It's imperative, therefore, to designate an employee of your own to oversee the program, manage the relationship with the travel agency, insure best practices in pricing and execution, and negotiate some deals of your own.

Consolidating all travel through a single travel agency is the best way to collect data, provide 24-hour service to travellers on the road, and rarely cause for objection by travellers themselves. In the not-so-distant past many firms had travel agents physically sit in their buildings, but rising personnel costs make that unfeasible today, and technology makes it unnecessary; travel agency call centres provide excellent service to small firms and companies at a fair price.

Even less costly is the option of booking travel online, through dedicated small-business programs offered by the major online travel agencies: Expedia, Travelocity, Travelport, and Orbitz. All four systems produce monthly spending reports for your firm or company and can be configured so that when travellers say they need a hotel in Phoenix, for example, the Hyatt with which you have a negotiated discount will be highlighted. Shifting traveller behaviour so that they book their own trips online instead of calling Mary at the agency down the block may take some doing, however. A clear policy from top management is imperative; even then, expect about 50% compliance unless your top executives are prepared to not reimburse travellers unless they comply.

Beyond the fees you can save, letting travellers self-serve by making their own reservations invariably results in lower costs. Perhaps the biggest surprise travel managers have realized from online booking is that when travellers are offered a wide range of options on their computer screen, a surprisingly high number do the right thing and change their plans slightly to take advantage of lower-priced options. In fact, if we had to offer a single piece of advice for cutting travel costs, it would be this: Get as many travellers as you can to book their travel online as fast as you can.

Note that many small companies report that they are being inundated by offers from Southwest Airlines' SWABiz program. The savings there are real, as travellers are entering their own information directly into Southwest's computer system and saving the agency transaction fees. But, travellers will see only flights and fares for one carrier, and lose the ability to comparative shop.

The travel industry is built on discounts and market share bonuses. No matter what agency or online system you are using, opt to pay them flat fees for services rendered and have any discounts you earn flow back to your firm. The point is to underline to both the agency and the suppliers that your firm is the customer here, not the travel agency.

Trains, Planes, and Automobiles

While larger companies are often best served by pushing all their travellers to use one airline and then negotiating discounted rates, small companies generally fare better allowing travellers to just pick the airline or hotel with the lowest fare on each trip. Remember that every dollar not spent falls right to your bottom line; saving a few thousand dollars in expenses may be as valuable as ten times as much in additional sales.No matter how hard you try, though the need for some high-end travel will not go away. These are where the airlines derive their biggest profit margins. Track them and try to negotiate a discount for all first- and business-class tickets with a single major airline that offers frequent flights from your home city. Virtually every airline, hotel and car-rental company offers discounts to business customers; make it someone's formal responsibility to negotiate on your behalf and then to nudge travellers to use these vendors. Airline programs typically offer small-business programs that yield free tickets with the purchase of a given number; take advantage of them. Beware the prepaid miles programs, however, which generally cost about 53 cents per mile; firms that let travellers choose their own low-cost flights online report that they average about 22 cents a mile. When employees are travelling on client business and billing their expenses back, there is a fiduciary responsibility to travel at the same level as the client would. Many firms follow client travel policies in such cases, and sometimes use the client's travel agency as well. Be careful about how you handle negotiated discounts in such cases; KPMG and Price water house Coopers in 2004 paid $17 million and $54.5 million, respectively, to settle a class-action lawsuit that charged them with billing clients for full fares and then keeping corporate discounts they got back from travel suppliers.

Checking in with a Hotel Program

While it's possible to push your travellers to use one or two major airlines without inconveniencing them much, hotels are a different story. Location really does make a difference. Staying in a particular hotel often offers tangible and intangible benefits: saving cab fares and wear and tear, keeping you close to the action at a conference or meeting, and allowing for mingling with important contacts or potential new customers. Rather than insist that everyone always stays at a Marriott or a Holiday Inn, a best practice is to focus on the five or six cities to which your firm travels most frequently, and negotiate discounts with a hotel or two in each. If your travellers or their assistants are using a corporate Internet site, set the system up so that these properties appear first and are highlighted as your preferred properties.

Maximize your business at these properties by requiring employees to register any meetings they will be holding with the travel manager, who in turn can encourage them to use the same properties as much as possible. Managing meetings is politically sensitive, as many meeting planners receive gifts and rewards from the hotels to which they bring business. Like every purchasing decision, though, it's important to base the choice of a meeting location on what's best for the firm, not the individual doing the buying. Centralizing and managing your meeting spend is likely the biggest single remaining opportunity for travel management for smaller companies.

Other Pieces of the Puzzle

Of all the pieces of the travel framework, moving travellers to a single car-rental supplier is the easiest. The issue here, again, is cost vs. Convenience; in general, on-airport companies cost more, off-airport companies cost less. But any preferred car-rental program brings one important advantage: free insurance. With car-rental companies typically charging $9-14 a day, and the average rental lasting 2.5 days, the savings from directing your travellers to just one are compelling.

The most important piece of the travel program, though, is a single corporate charge card to which all travel expenses must be billed. This is a relatively easy step to enforce; mandate that charges not booked on the credit card will not be reimbursed. Charge cards (like the American Express or Diner's Club corporate cards, which are not "credit cards" as they must be paid off every money)-capture the data that shows what your travellers actually bought, and are the key to rebates, discounts, and enhanced services. When dealing with the data, don't allow the sheer magnitude to overwhelm you. Pick out the key items or objectives that matter most and track those. Some companies have developed a dashboard or scorecard of key travel program measurements they track quarterly: percent of compliance to travel policy for air, car, hotel; average airline cost per mile through the agency and through online booking sites; rate of online booking adoption; average hotel room rate in key cities. Those are your fundamentals. Establish the parameters for success for each key measure and work toward achieving those. When you get there, develop new measures.

Passenger Space Travel and the Wright Brothers' Vision

It is a great pleasure and a great privilege to be invited to contribute to the Centenary celebration of one of the truly world-changing inventions of the 20th century — Orville and Wilbur Wright's development of controlled, powered flight. It is also a particular pleasure to speak at the session on space tourism, of which I am confident the theme will be recognised in coming years as the most significant at this Symposium. The topic I was invited to discuss is the market demand and transportation infrastructure for space tourism, but it seems only appropriate to begin by giving some thought to the relation of this subject, passenger space travel, to the Wright brothers' achievement and vision. If the word genius has any value, then we can certainly say that Orville and Wilbur Wright were engineering geniuses, not in the popular sense of being able to solve incomprehensible mathematical problems, but in having the rare combination of different abilities that enabled them to do something important that no-one else at that time was able to do. It seems reasonable to guess that if the Wright brothers were alive today, they would be working to realise passenger space travel and the future developments to which it will lead. So we might ask: "If the Wright brothers were alive today, what would they think of progress in space travel so far?" Well, if we look at their own experience in developing air travel, and at the present situation in space travel, I think we have to conclude that they would be *shocked and appalled*.

To see the truth of this we need to remember the treatment the Wright brothers received from the U.S. Government. At the same time as they were pursuing flight as a hobby, Professor Samuel Langley, secretary of the Smithsonian Institution, was funded by the U.S. Army to develop what he called an "aerodrome". Though Langley was a fine researcher, he did *not* make the conceptual breakthroughs necessary to achieve flight. However, the Smithsonian supported Langley, even years after his death, and refused to recognise the Wrights' achievement. It even collaborated in 1914 with Glenn Curtiss in flying a modified variant of one of Langley's failed attempts at an aeroplane — whereupon they claimed that this proved that Langley was the co-inventor of flight with the Wright brothers.

Orville and Wilbur could not accept such dishonesty — and so the Smithsonian refused to recognise their invention. It was not until *44 years* after the Wright brothers' first flight, 1947, that the government-funded Smithsonian finally acknowledged what everyone else in the world already knew — that the Wright Brothers alone invented flight.

This may have been the most shameful episode in the Smithsonian's history. So it would be comforting to believe that its shockingly dishonest mistreatment of the Wright brothers — who contributed perhaps more to U.S. technological prowess and prestige than anyone else in the 20th century — was a unique aberration. However, we have to face the fact that such self-serving behaviour is not anomalous; it is typical of governments everywhere, including particularly "democratic" ones, as they act to protect the interests of economically powerful groups within the economy against others, notably newcomers and the general public. It is indeed quite similar to the British government's decades-long refusal to award the "Longitude Prize" to John Harrison, the genius inventor of the chronometer.

The defining feature of governments is that they employ force to achieve their purposes, and controlling this force to work for the public good, instead of for the benefit of the people comprising the government, is the central problem that humans face in trying to create and maintain free and fair societies. In this context it is relevant to refer to the work of another American genius, Professor James Buchanan, who received the Novel Prize in 1986 for his work on the economic analysis of governments' behaviour and how to control it. The basic assumption of the field of economics concerns human psychology — it that humans are intelligent animals who use their brains to improve their situation. Adam Smith, the father of economics, analysed the implications of assuming that people act in their own self-interest in the case of business people and their customers; however, although he also noted that government officials "...have generally an interest to deceive and even oppress the public", he did not analyse the implications of this in detail. Buchanan and the colleagues with whom he pioneered the field of Public Choice economics analysed its implications for the behaviour of politicians and bureaucrats, and for the formal constraints needed on government. Niskanen extended this work, showing that in order to constrain government organisations, or "bureaus", to act in the public interest, their activities need to be the subject of close scrutiny not by politicians but by large numbers of the general public.

It is widely recognised that the USA has an exemplary Constitution, designed both to ensure the provision of the services that only government can provide, and also to protect the people from government's inexorable tendency to become tyrannical. However, governments become more tyrannical the larger they grow, and the U.S. government is surely no exception to this, despite the Constitution. In order to appreciate this we do not need to consider anything controversial such as foreign policy; we need only consider the case of Prohibition when the U.S. government imposed a disastrous law invasive of private liberty and against the wishes of an enormous number of its own population — or the fact that the U.S. government today keeps a larger proportion of the national population imprisoned than any other government in the world. So the shockingly dishonest mistreatment of two of the nation's greatest geniuses, whom we are celebrating at this symposium, by a government organisation should not be thought of as an aberration, but as typical. Every government system is different in innumerable details, and the 44 years that it took the U.S. government to finally admit what everyone else in the world already knew can perhaps be seen as the "cycle time" of the U.S. Federal government system in correcting an error.

This digression brings us directly back to our main topic — since it is now 42 years since Alan Shepard performed the first space flight by a U.S. Citizen. Of course Shepard was a government employee — it's as if the U.S. Army-funded Langley had succeeded in developing controlled, powered flight. It is therefore *extremely striking* that no private US citizen has yet been permitted to travel to space, but only a tiny number of government employees and related invites selected by the U.S. Government's 45-year old monopoly space agency, Nasa. In addition, despite having spent an astonishing $1 trillion of taxpayers' money on nominally civilian space activities (that is, nearly $1,000/second for 40 years, measured in 2003$), the U.S. Government *has not reduced the cost of travelling to space at all.*

So if we were to ask the Wright brothers what they thought of space flight today, perhaps in such terms as: "Don't you think our space agencies are doing a wonderful job?" they would not be impressed — they would surely laugh bitterly: "Are you joking? What did you expect? You left it to the U.S. Government. *Look how they treated us!*

The U.S. Government's 45-year old monopoly space agency, Nasa currently has a travelling exhibition called "Starship 2040" which includes a mock-up of a small module which it suggests might be feasible for tourism by 2040 — which would be *79 years* after Alan Shepard. Based on this we can perhaps guess what would have happened if Langley had indeed invented flight: at the rate of development of space travel proposed by the U.S. Government, passenger air travel would have started in 1982. In fact, by that date private passenger air travel, as initiated by the Wright brothers, already exceeded 1/2 billion people/year, or 1.5 million passengers/day! Fortunately, 44 years seems to be a better estimate than Nasa's estimate of 79 years. For it is surely not unrealistic to hope to see private suborbital space flights — that is, short trips of just a few minutes like that made by Alan Shepard himself — starting by 2005. If they do start then, it seems likely to be with little or no help from government space agencies, which continue to spend $20 billion/year of taxpayers' money on non-science space activities of little economic value, as discussed in Aviation pioneered by the Wright brothers contrasts sharply with space flight pioneered by governments, most notably in providing transportation services to the general public whereas space agencies provide no such services to the public, for whom their activities are largely incomprehensible. In terms of cost-performance the results are predictably disastrous: despite Nasa's use of $1 trillion of taxpayers' money, the first private U.S. Citizen to pay for a space flight, Dennis Tito, had to fly on the 1,657th Soyuz rocket— essentially the same vehicle that carried Yuri Gagarin 40 years earlier in 1961! Tito also faced public abuse from the then Nasa administrator. If that $1 trillion had been used as productively as the cumulative investment in the civil aviation industry launched by the Wright brothers, we would have a nearly $1 trillion/year space travel industry today. This failure of "space" to follow in the economically successful footsteps of "aero" represents a massive hiatus in "aerospace" development in the U.S.A. Due largely to the influence of the cold war. As a consequence, the U.S. Government decided to compete with the Soviet Union on its own terms in space, and established a monopoly agency which quickly developed self-serving habits, such as holding invitation-only press events (paid for by taxpayers), which are extremely effective in minimising critical media scrutiny. If the Wright brothers were developing passenger space travel today — well, obviously they would develop services that the public want to buy. Government space agencies periodically pay for surveys of public support for their budgets; but what they have never done — except finally, grudgingly, in just the last two years, with a tiny budget, and with minimal publicity — is ask the public what they want, and specifically whether they would like to travel to space.

Passenger Demand

In a paper presented at the 1986 IAF Congress, a colleague and I wrote: "Great interest must therefore attach to any detailed market surveys that are performed to determine the likely level of demand for space tourism services of various kinds". At that time the idea of space tourism was not considered a serious topic within the space industry, and the proposal was met with silence — which is the first point to be made about passenger demand for space travel.

Lack of Data

Surely the most striking feature of the data on the demand for passenger space travel is *how very little data there is*. In view of the fact that Nasa is required by U.S. Federal law "to encourage to the maximum extent possible the fullest commercial use of space", and other government agencies such as Esa, Nasda and the BNSC have similar responsibilities, it is clearly wrong for them to ignore a potentially major new market for space transportation. Such a decision might be acceptable if the agencies were achieving great success in their preferred activities, but the economic performance of the non-science activities in which they have collectively invested $1 trillion is disastrous: the resulting commercial turnover is about 1/50 of what ordinary companies would have achieved with the same investment.

However, this behaviour is in close agreement with Niskanen's analysis of the economic behaviour of bureaucratic organisations, in which, as he explains succinctly, individual officials "have no incentive to know or seek to know the public good, nor to work for the public good". It is particularly striking that space agencies continue to rigidly ignore the passenger market even in the early years of the 21st century while the space industry is shrinking drastically for lack of demand: U.S. aerospace employment has fallen to its lowest level for 5 years, and both the European monopoly launch supplier, Arianespace, and the remaining European monopoly manufacturer of large satellites, EADS, are cutting staff by a further 30%.

Prior to the first market research data published in 1994, "guesstimates" had been published by Ehricke, Citron and the author. As part of a Nasa study of future launch markets, some more detailed "guesstimates" were also published in 1994. In view of the growing evidence that tourism is the only activity capable of growing large enough to develop space economically, it seems clear that having relied on government monopoly organisations for access to space has greatly delayed its realisation. Indeed, in view of the growing interest in suborbital space travel services, which could easily have started during the 1970s, this delay caused by space agencies has reached decades already.

Worldwide Demand

The second very striking feature of the data on the demand for passenger space travel is that it is hugely positive, across all categories— age, sex, income-level and country — everywhere and every time that people have been surveyed. In 1993 I was finally able to use a small budget to perform the first ever market research on the subject, as a Science & Technology Agency Fellow in Japan; with a number of colleagues I distributed a pamphlet and questionnaire to 3030 people selected quasi-randomly from all age-groups, and roughly nationwide. As Figure 1 shows, a substantial majority of the general population, both men and women, said they wished to travel to space: the youngest were the most keen, but even many older people also said they would like to buy such a service.

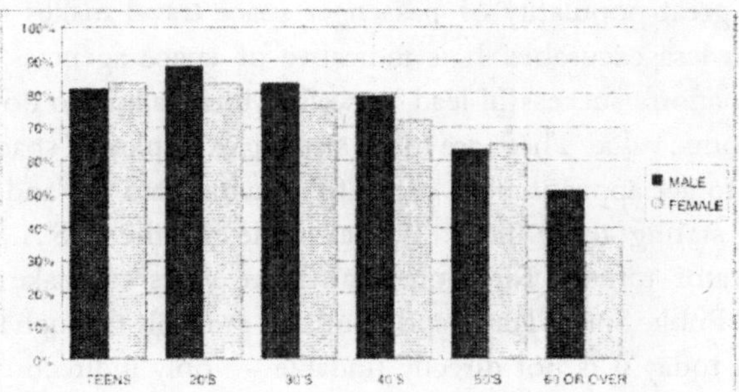

Figure 1: Wish to travel to space by age-group, Japan

Figure 2 shows the response to the same questionnaire delivered by telephone in the U.S.A. The main difference is that U.S. women are somewhat less enthusiastic than men, which is presumably due to the military connection and more "macho/techno" image of space flight in the U.S.A. than in Japan.

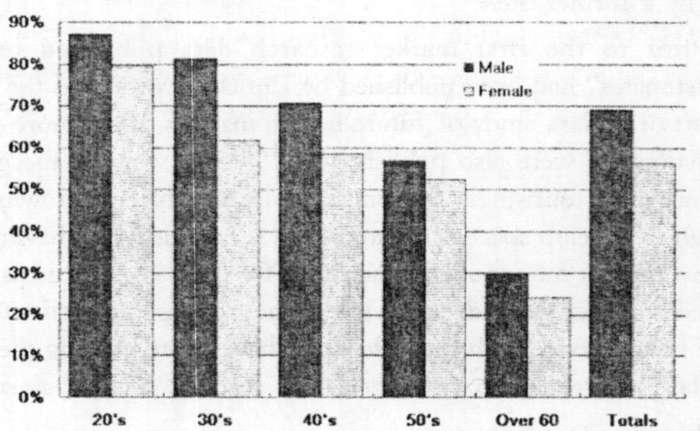

Figure 2: Wish to travel to space by age-group

In response to the question "How many months' salary would you pay for a space flight?", some 70% of those wishing to travel to space in Japan, North America and Germany said they would pay several months' salary, and in each country a few percent said they would pay even 1 year's salary or more. Bekey usefully surveyed various different studies as of 1998, as Crouch did in 2001. More recently Kelly Space & Technology Inc and Futron Inc, in studying potential markets for reusable launch vehicles for Nasa, surveyed the potential demand for space tourism — using Nasa funds for this purpose for the first time. Both studies concluded that passenger travel offers the most promising market for space transportation.

The great popularity of passenger space travel makes the lack of data even less excusable. It is indicative of space agencies' failure to follow aviation's successful lead, as well as their failure to do work that has economic value. There are many striking examples of space agencies refusing to act appropriately, even after having paid for and published research stating these facts. For example, in the U.S.A. the Nasa administrator refused for more than three years to make its report "General Public Space Travel and Tourism" available through its website, and even today it is not directly findable — only indirectly through a link to another site. In Japan, the director of planning at the government's National Aerospace Laboratory (NAL), even after having paid $4,000 for a survey in the U.S.A., and having co-authored four papers including statements such as "the demand apparently has the potential to grow to many times the most optimistic projections for existing commercial space activities", stopped all work on the subject, while continuing to spend hundreds of millions of dollars/year on activities with little economic value, for six years — until it was decided to merge the NAL with other research organisations.

These examples are sadly typical of space industry officials who feel no pressure to contribute to economic growth. At a time when commercial demand for space transportation (i.e. satellite launch) has been shrinking progressively, and the U.S. and Japanese economies are in their worst crises for 50 years *due precisely to the lack of investment in commercially promising new businesses*, this deeply irresponsible attitude has been disastrous for taxpayers.

In summary, it is now recognised worldwide that there is a potentially very large market for passenger space travel services. There remains a great need for more market research, as discussed in. This should be performed in collaboration with aviation and other travel-related organisations, of which the thinking is based on supplying passenger services.

This matches the facts that the most vigorous advocate of passenger space travel within the U.S. Government is the FAA's Associate Director for Commercial Space Transportation (AST), and the main organisation working for it in Japan is the Japanese Aeronautical Association (JAA). However, it is important that the need for more market research on space tourism should not be used as an excuse for further delaying work towards its realisation; it should rather be widened to include research on a range of related matters. These include the planning of many aspects of passenger space flight services as seen from the point of view of passengers, including vehicle specifications, passenger cabin interior design, orbital accommodation facilities and thence to the entire range of infrastructure needed.

Transportation Infrastructure

In trying to envisage the details of the future development of passenger space travel services, and what vehicles and other infrastructure will be needed, the historical development of passenger air travel offers a useful precedent. In combination with elements of the hotel industry and the cruise-liner industry, civil aviation seems to offer a fairly complete model for passenger space travel services. For the regulatory aspects, in addition to aviation and other safety regulations there will be a need for traffic rules, police services, specialised pilot services (as on difficult-to-navigate waterways), and possibly an equivalent of coastguard services. However, what we may expect to see a few decades in the future depends both on what is technically possible, and on how much is invested in coming years to realise passenger space travel.

Technical Possibilities

Very similar to the situation concerning demand, there is strikingly little information on the technical possibilities for passenger space travel, but all the information that does exist is positive. The lack of data is due to government space agencies — never having commisioned a feasibility study of a dedicated passenger launch vehicle in more than 40 years.

In order to understand the potential it is perhaps useful first to dispel the remains of a very widespread myth — that in order to provide space travel services a vehicle like the U.S. Government's "space shuttle" is needed. From this it is commonly concluded that, since that vehicle costs about $100 million/passenger/flight, space tourism is therefore a fantasy, or at least conceivable only in the far future after several more decades of government-funded space technology. The most important point to note is that the "space shuttle" was designed to military specifications; its hypothetical cost/passenger is therefore of no more relevance to space tourism than the cost of carrying passengers in a bomber aeroplane would have to commercial air travel. Hence the only relevant data are those relating specifically to dedicated passenger vehicle design studies. Over the past decade or more, a number of such studies have been published based on varying degrees of effort. However, they show considerable consensus about the cost of developing a fully reusable passenger-carrying launch vehicle capable of repeated flights to and from low Earth orbit, with most estimates clustered around $10 billion.

Designs of single-stage, vertical takeoff and landing (VTOL) rockets include Pacific American Launch Systems' " Phoenix", a passenger-carrying variant of the German " Beta", and the " Kankoh-maru" designed as part of the Japanese Rocket Society's (JRS) space tourism research program started in 1993. Designs of two-stage horizontal takeoff and landing (HTOL) vehicles include the "Spacecab", "Spacebus" and precursor vehicles proposed by Bristol Spaceplanes Ltd., several designs studied by Penn and Lindley at the Aerospace Corporation, and a recent study done at Boeing. Development and operating costs for several configurations are usefully tabulated by Bekey in. The estimated development costs in these studies range from a few billion dollars to about $16 billion.

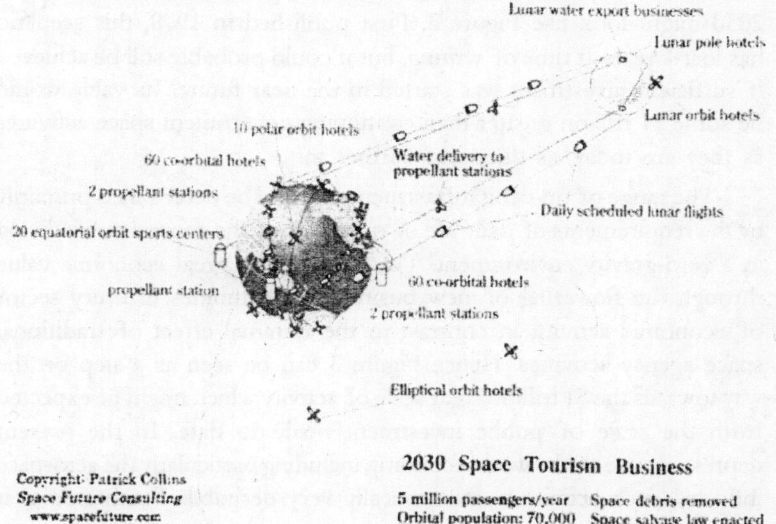

Figure 3: Transportation infrastructure required for space tourism

What is perhaps most striking about these figures is that even the largest is less than one year of G7 space agencies' current spending on non-science activities — which have little economic value in terms of generating commercial space revenues. Thus such an investment could be funded by using about 5% of space agencies' annual budgets over a decade, which would clearly not be a significant burden to taxpayers. Indeed, if planned government space projects' funding were reduced by 5%, and their timetables extended a little, the vast majority of the general public would not even be aware of the change — but at the end of the period, space activities would enter a new era with the start of low-cost, reliable access to orbit.

If the actual cost of developing the transportation infrastructure required for passenger space travel was even ten times higher, this would be only of the same order of magnitude as the international space station (ISS), which has little measurable economic value (particularly since its future depends on an unreliable transportation system). Consequently developing a passenger vehicle would be greatly preferable. How best to achieve the desired result organisationally is a different issue discussed further below. The estimated timetable to reach initial passenger service is about 10 years, if the resources were provided without interruptions. In that case the transportation infrastructure in 2030 might look like Figure 3. First published in 1999, this scenario has lost 4 years at time of writing, but it could probably still be achieved if sufficient investment was started in the near future. Its value would be some $1 trillion greater than continuing government space activities as they are today, as discussed further in.

The range of on-orbit infrastructure would be determined primarily by the requirements of daily life of members of the general public living in a zero-gravity environment. This would have great economic value through the flowering of new business opportunities in every sector of economic activity, in contrast to the minimal effect of traditional space agency activities. Hence Figure 3 can be seen as a step on the way towards the $1 trillion/year scale of activity which might be expected from the scale of public investment made to date. In the present depressed state of the world economy, including particularly the aerospace industry, such activity is economically very desirable. Furthermore, it is the *only way* of achieving commensurate economic benefit for taxpayers from the public investment in developing space capabilities to date.

Actual Progress

How much progress we will actually make towards the future illustrated in Figure 3 depends of course on how much is invested in achieving passenger space travel, how soon it is invested, and how effectively it is invested. This particularly includes achieving efficient, complementary roles for both government organisations and private companies. Unfortunately it is currently unclear how much space agencies are capable of contributing to this very desirable outcome, due to their inappropriate organisational structures. This problem can be seen from the orders of magnitude difference in cost between G7 space agencies' procedures, and what can be taken as a proxy for commercial "best practice" today. This was put into sharp focus recently when it was stated that the Russian company NPO-Energia builds Soyuz crew vehicles for $12 million, Progress cargo craft for a little more than $6 million, and Soyuz launch vehicles for about $16 million. By contrast, Nasa estimates the cost of developing a 4-to-6-person "orbital space plane" (OSP) to be launched on an existing expendable rocket by 2010 at $13 billion or more. Even after allowing for the fact that the OSP is intended to be reusable, and ignoring the higher cost of U.S. expendable rockets, it is clear that its cost/flight would not approach that of Soyuz in even 1,000 flights. When the difference in reliability between the two systems Soyuz having made nearly 2,000 flights, including hundreds of successful manned flights are taken into account, it is clear that Nasa's technical capabilities are of little economic value. Indeed, at the time of writing, the latest news is that Nasas proposed Orbital Space Plane may actually be a non-reusable capsule, which closes the circle: Nasa is now proposing to use $13 billion of taxpayers money to redevelop an Apollo capsule 40 years after the original.

Some people might conclude, puzzled, that the US space industry cannot compete with 50 year old Russian technology! But this is not so. Even despite the Soyuz's advantages of having low labour costs and development costs written off long ago, if given a free hand US companies can get at least close to the same costs, as can be seen from a single example. HMX Inc proposed its reusable XV cargo carrier in 2000 for Nasas Alternate Access to Space program (AAS). Total program costs for four XV launches carrying 300 lb payloads were estimated at $145 million.

If produced, the first flight would have been in 2003; this would have been invaluable after the loss of the space shuttle Columbia, and would save US taxpayers billions of dollars. However, the AAS program was imposed on Nasa by the Office of Management and Budget (OMB) and the Congress in an attempt to get value for money for U.S. taxpayers; consequently, out of $62.7 million that Congress provided for the AAS program in 2003, Nasa brazenly redirected $40 million to its favoured OSP program, and announced that AAS will not continue in 2004 !

Why is AAS resisted by Nasa in favour of OSP? The answer is plainly because it is not in the short-term economic interest of Nasa and its client companies to permit such a simple low-cost solution to their requirements. Unfortunately, as Niskanen also explains, nor would it be in the short-term interest of the politicians who nominally "oversee" Nasa and its budget. One might paraphrase Winston Churchills famous description of Russia as a riddle wrapped in a mystery inside an enigma by saying that G7 space agency cost estimates are a scandal wrapped in a sham inside a farce.

In truth, Nasa's own cost estimates in this case are economically meaningless. Quite apart from being undependable and prone to balloon, they refer to the development of a service for which there is no demand except from Nasa itself, devised in a "sui generis" manner and hence under no pressure to be an economically competitive or "best-practice" result, and following no agreed standard so that the resulting service cannot be judged. An aviation expert involved in the JRS space tourism study programme accurately described the difference between civil aviation and space industry practice in vehicle development by saying that the latter are like children making model aeroplanes: they make up rules as they go along, deciding what is acceptable (to themselves) on an "ad hoc" basis rather than following agreed rules derived from accumulated experience, and designed to achieve a target level of performance.

That is, after more than 40 years, governments' role in space activities is still at the same stage as the early days of aviation when government aircraft development projects suffered repeated disasters from which the fundamental lesson was learned that the three roles of customer, manufacturer and safety regulator must be performed by independent organisations. If they are not, the conflicts of interest that arise between political and commercial objectives ensure failure. This is well illustrated in the book " Slide Rule", which describes the simultaneous development of the successful, company-developed R100 and the disastrous, government-developed R101 airship projects. As a result of experience, governments (reluctantly) corrected their role in aviation from (disastrously) developing aircraft directly, to (successfully) supporting the development of commercial aviation. U.S. government actions such as the 1925 Airmail Act privatising the air mail, and the 1926 Air Commerce Act giving the Department of Commerce responsibility to promote aviation, were in much the same vein.

In order to make progress in this situation, the single most important step for the space industry is to collaborate with the civil aviation industry, as discussed in. As Antunano has described, the "aviation approach", its fundamental way of thinking, is the opposite of space agencies: the objective of aviation authorities is to enable as many people as possible to enjoy the services they wish. Consequently instead of government defining rules for selecting candidates for space flight, passengers select themselves, and it is necessary only to advise them of possible risks.

However, space agencies currently have no plans to even study the feasibility of passenger travel services, let alone initiate the fundamental rethinking needed to generate economic value for taxpayers in this way from their massive investment in space technology development. The huge cost to taxpayers' of permitting the present economically wasteful situation to continue, that is the cost of governments' continuing failure to amend their mistaken approach to space development contrary to what they did successfully in aviation is discussed next.

Economic Cost of Delay

As described in Section 3.1 above, the development of passenger space travel services is economically very desirable. As a corollary, delaying this development represents a very large economic cost to taxpayers, which can be considered as comprising four components, namely the direct cost of $1 trillion to date plus $20 billion/year spent on non-science space activities with little economic value, and the economic, social and macroeconomic costs of the lost potential value of new economic activities, as discussed further in. In the following we consider the economic cost of not benefiting from the commercial space activities that could have been generated. In addition to space agencies' investment of $1 trillion over recent decades, G7 governments have spent some $2 trillion on nuclear power and ten times this on economically unproductive military activities. Using these funds for political purposes instead of for taxpayers' economic benefit hinders the innovation which is vital for the continuation of economic growth. These three fields also employ a very significant fraction of all engineers; employing these highly skilled people in economically unprofitable work greatly reduces the economic value of technological progress — to the point that it becomes a threat to the stability of the economic system.

Each individual decision to use taxpayers' money for purposes other than to create wealth by developing services for which there is potential demand, is made in the belief that there will always be another year's budget from the "golden goose" of government. Collectively, however, these economically damaging decisions have nearly killed the golden goose, by gradually choking off the possibilities for growth. These cumulative wasteful actions have contributed greatly to the present situation of spiralling government debts, collapsing corporate profits, and ever-rising unemployment — in the USA as well as in Japan, and elsewhere. Indeed, this cost has now reached such a scale that it is causing serious dislocation of not only the US economy but the world economy as a whole, which is in serious distress due to excess capacity in many older industries and lack of new industries, leading to the highest level of unemployment for decades in almost every country today. G7 space agencies have contributed their share to this problem, by adding to taxpayers' debt burden by $20 billion/year while refusing, year after year after year, even to study the possibility of developing a new service that the public are known to want to buy. The potential being wasted in this way is illustrated in the following fictional analogy:

"After the invention of the camera, government established the National Camera Science & Applications Administration (NACSAA) which grew rapidly to employ many thousands of researchers developing camera technology. Highly trained "cameranauts" used the resulting government cameras, which cost many millions each, to take photographs of specially chosen subjects "for the benefit of the people". NACSAA prepared voluminous educational materials describing NACSAA's history and activities, and urged members of the general public to take more interest in camera technology. The possibility of developing cheaper cameras as consumer products was said by the leaders of NACSAA and the "camera industry" to require decades more government-funded technology development. Surveys showing a widespread wish among ordinary people to use cameras and own photographs themselves were publicly criticised as "unpatriotic", and said to show lack of respect for NACSAA history and for NACSAA's "cameranaut heroes". However, in response, NACSAA started a Photographic Commercialisation Initiative (PCI) which provided a range of new services to the public, including discount sales of government photographs, rental of government cameras to selected members of the public who underwent training at NACSAA in "non-cameranautic photography", and a travelling exhibition to widen access to NACSAA photographs and NACSAA history....."

It is clear that, in such a hypothetical situation, the existence of NACSAA and its political and economic interest group would have created enormous resistance to the development of a genuinely commercial, consumer-oriented camera and photographic industry. This would have imposed a very large economic cost on the public due to not having the benefits of the innovations that have in reality arisen in the absence of NACSAA's repressive influence.

In order to appreciate the scale of this "invisible cost", we need only consider the century-long, true "gale of creative destruction" that has in fact been brought about successively by the invention, development and commercialisation of cinematography, colour photography, instant photography, photocopiers, fax systems, television, video, highspeed photography, Schlieren photography, X-ray photography, holography, IMAX, cineplexes, laser discs, laser printing, disposable cameras, video-conferences, digital cameras, digital film standards, Internet graphic protocols, computer graphics, data compression algorithms, DVDs, colour faxes, mobile-phone cameras, video e-mail, and many other actual developments in imaging technology, many of which have already gone through several generations of technology.

All of this astounding creativity, which has had enormous economic value and created millions of well-paid jobs, is driven by *demand from the general public*, from the "mere consumers" whom NACSAA — and government space agencies — spurn. The growth of passenger space travel, which is finally being grudgingly recognised as the only activity which can energise the stagnating space industry, through the power of consumer demand, can surely be expected to generate at least as great a profusion of innovative and profitable new activities as photography. That is, Figure 3 barely scratches the surface of what will be done by private citizens once they have access to space.

It is important to recognise also that the cost of not benefiting from innovation would have been invisible to those living in the world of NACSAA, and the existence of such a cost would have been vociferously denied by the leaders and political supporters of NACSAA, who would have been eloquent in their praise of its wealth of accumulated experience, the excellence of its staff, the importance of its historic achievement, and so on. Like the hypothetical NACSAA, G7 space agencies' use of US$1 trillion over 45 years — *without having improved on the access to space provided by the Soyuz launch vehicle* — represents an extreme miscalculation of taxpayers' money. The fact that, during the first four decades of their history, the agencies never even investigated whether the taxpayers for whom they supposedly work would like to visit space, further illustrates how far space agencies are from being "servants of the people": *They do not even want to know what the public wants*— precisely as Niskanen describes.

In the Wright brothers' centenary year it is time to face the fact that, as presently constituted, government space agencies are not only not capable of developing space economically, they are actively preventing it from happening. They do this by spending hugely on activities that have minimal economic value, while confusing the public about what is worth doing in space, and obscuring the truth about the enormous economic potential of developing passenger space travel. Unlike government expenditure on nuclear power and military activities, the development of space technology has created capabilities which have the potential to contribute greatly to economic growth by supplying a wealth of popular new consumer services. It is therefore economically very desirable to redirect government space activities so as to achieve greater economic benefit from the technological capabilities developed to date by supplying passenger space travel services.

Conclusions-Where Next?

Once the need to change the present situation is acknowledged, we must face the question how to realise the productive and profitable institutional and political reform that is required, which is discussed elsewhere, including in. Fundamentally it is necessary to follow the Wright brothers' lead, and provide services which the public want to buy. In order to do this economic policy-makers must be made aware of the enormous cost of the present disfunctionality of government space funding; the value of the goal of passenger space travel must be recognised officially; the public must be educated about its feasibility (undoing space agencies' cumulative influence in spreading the false idea that only statistically unusual people can survive the "rigours of space flight"); and detailed collaboration must be established with aviation organisations, of which the spontaneous inclination is to develop popular passenger services. This collaboration must be carried out in such a way as to aid the private sector, as air-mail contracts did in the early days of flight. The development of suborbital passenger vehicles and related services should also be encouraged.

However, these changes will not be easy to achieve, due to the continuing influence of those with vested interests in preserving the status quo. Unfortunately, as Public Choice economics explains, governments are very slow to change, and frequently do so only in the face of crisis. We must hope that the government of a country with the required capabilities will take the initiative before the condition of the world economy deteriorates much further; the benefits of doing so are potentially very large. At a time when overproduction in older industries and lack of new ones is reaching crisis level, it is alarming that there is a faction within government arguing that this situation is unavoidable; that war is a means of "economic stimulus" (as well as social control); and that rich countries should take control of the world's "dwindling resources" to maintain their living standards far above the average. Such narrow-minded blindness is tragically mistaken; in truth the future is a cornucopia — there is almost no limit to the potential availability to humans of any known resource. The false belief in a "closed world" rests ultimately on meaningless cost estimates made by G7 space agencies. We can be sure that the Wright brothers would not have been taken in for a moment.

Among other components of the present unusually severe recession, civil aviation is suffering down-sizing, bankruptcies and overall shrinkage within the richer countries. The failure of space to contribute to the economy in any way commensurately to the massive public investment which it has received is because it has systematically put short-term political and corporate interests ahead of the wishes of the general public. The result is sadly predictable: unlike aviation, the space industry supplies almost no services that the public want to buy.

In order to achieve the limitless possibilities for peaceful, plentiful growth that can only be realised through passenger space travel opening space to economic development, the public must learn the hard lesson of the Wright brothers' own harsh experience at the hands of government— and design institutions and rules that ensure that governments' investment in space benefits the general public. Above all, this requires that the goal of space investment is changed to follow aviation's lead and ensure successful development of commercial passenger travel services. The contrast between the histories of aviation and space is key: space must learn from aviation that the only road to real growth is to supply services that the public want to buy. This must be recognised as the most valuable goal of space development. It is so simple and obvious that the only possible resistance is from those with vested interests in preserving existing arrangements. Space agencies' continuing silence on the matter testifies to their recognition that they cannot justify their long-standing negative stance in open debate; they're "hunkered down", hoping the golden goose will continue to lay. In recent years the most economically important new products have been personal computers and mobile telephones (together with the internet protocols which link them all together), of which sales revenues have reached hundreds of $ billions/year. Both the worldwide boom in sales and the still-continuing rapid technological improvements seen in these two industries were unpredicted, indeed seemed almost unthinkable, even just a few years before they began. Both arose and continue because *they provide products and services that most of the general public wish to buy*. There can be little doubt that the development of passenger space travel has the potential to create an economic boom that will grow far larger than either of these two, and continue far longer. This is because these new services are not only known to be extremely popular among the general population — giving the potential to emulate the "Lindbergh Boom" in aviation — but they also involve opening access to new territory, which has itself been the stimulus for major booms in history. This probability is a further reason why governments mired in a global recession should urgently study the possibility in depth.

It was the Wright brothers' vision and achievement to give the human race access to the sky, thereby fulfilling millenia of dreams. The true continuation of their vision is unquestionably to give humans access beyond the sky, which is collectively our ultimate dream. It is now clear that this requires reorganising governments' role in space development to follow the hugely successful model of civil aviation that the Wright brothers pioneered, rather than continuing the economically unsuccessful model of government monopoly space agencies.

As described in Section 1, for reasons clearly explained in the field of Public Choice economics, government space agencies are not capable of putting the economic interest of the general public ahead of their own contrary interests. The centenary of the Wright brothers' world-changing first flight, which is also the 42nd anniversary of the first space flight (but only the second anniversary of the first private passenger space flight), is high time for governments to face this, and take urgent steps to ensure the further flowering of the Wright brothers' vision, to the immense benefit of us all.

3

Half-century Delay in Space Travel Development

"We have proved rocket propulsion practicable for space travel. This 3rd day of October, 1942, is the first of a new era in transportation, that of space travel."-Walter Dornberger, having achieved controlled space flight for the first time.

If the German engineers developing rocket-propelled vehicles had continued in peacetime as Dornberger hoped, the V2 (of which a winged version was flown to Mach 4) and the Me163 piloted rocket-plane projects would between them have surely led to the start of suborbital passenger space flights by 1950. In this case, orbital passenger space travel services would presumably have started by the mid-1960s. Instead, rocket development was "highjacked" by the cold war competition between the USA and USSR, so that launch vehicles were derived from long-range missiles, rather than being designed ab initio as passenger vehicles. Government space agencies have continued to develop expendable rockets, of which the safety and cost/passenger are inevitably much closer to those of missiles than to passenger vehicles. (The space shuttle, as well as being partly expendable, was designed primarily to fulfil a military requirement, not to achieve low-cost space travel.)

Suborbital passenger space flight services are due to start in 2010. There has thus been more than a half-century delay in developing passenger space travel. To understand the implications of this delay, and the cost to society, it is useful to note that the world population when space travel could have started was 1/2 what it is today, while the use of energy and other resources, and the production of pollution were all 1/4 of what they are today. Air travel safety was 100 times lower than today, and the general public were correspondingly less risk-averse in general. Thus, in many respects it would have been easier to develop space tourism at that time than it is today. On the other hand, cumulative engineering capabilities and experience are far greater in every field today, and there is also great pent-up demand for passenger space travel. Consequently, when this industry finally starts, it can in principle grow much faster today than it would have during the 1950s.

Considering the question how different would world conditions be today if passenger space travel services had started as early as they could have during the 1950s, the answer depends on the scale to which passenger space travel might have grown by today. Cost estimates by the Japanese Rocket Society, Bristol Spaceplanes, Bekey and others, corroborated by the very low cost of "Space Ship One", indicate that once space travel grows to 1 million passengers/year, prices could fall to 5,000 Euros for Suborbital flights, and 20,000 Euros for orbital flights. The latter is approximately 200 Euros/kg or about 1% of launch costs today. We can estimate that if Suborbital passenger travel had started in 1950, orbital travel could have grown to perhaps several million passengers/year by 2000, as shown in Figure 1.

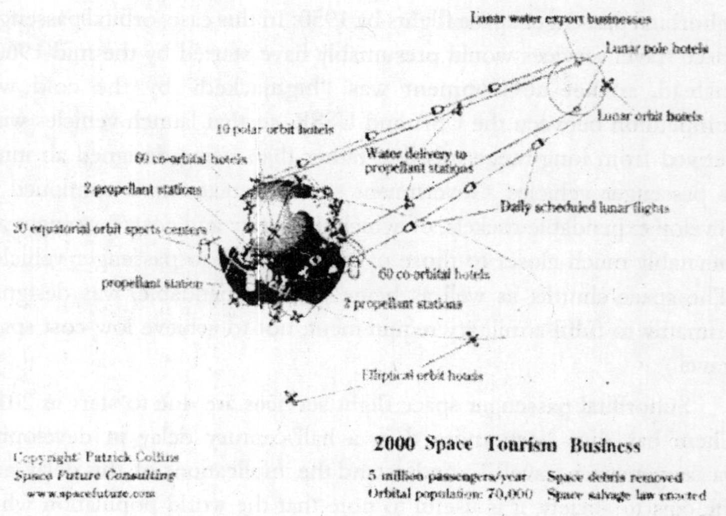

Figure 1: Year 2000 Space Tourism industry if Suborbital tourism had started in 1950

Cost estimates for the development of low-cost orbital passenger transportation systems are of the order of 10 billion Euros. Even 10 times this amount would be less than 5 years of space agencies' current budgets. The economic benefits would greatly outweigh such a cost, due to the much larger commercial markets that would be created as a result, in contrast to the very small markets created with 1 trillion Euro-equivalents invested in satellite and launch vehicle manufacturing to date.

Starting from today, in order to achieve the scale of activity shown in Figure 1 over the next 30 years, government funding equivalent to about 10% of space agencies' budgets, or some 2 billion Euros/year would probably suffice to stimulate private investment in reusable orbital passenger vehicle manufacturing and operations. Thereafter most of the funding could come from private companies, just as airlines and hotel chains today finance their own growth.

Implications of Launch Cost Reduction

Reducing the cost of space travel to 1% of existing launch vehicles' costs, in combination with the growth of a new consumer service market in space, would greatly aid the growth of many commercial space activities, thereby creating numerous new business opportunities both on Earth and in space. This process is already at work on a small scale in relation to Suborbital flight services: in addition to a large number of travel companies acting as agents for Suborbital flights (including JTB, the largest travel company in Japan), Zero-G Corporation supplies parabolic flight services, Bigelow Aerospace is developing the first space hotel, Spaceport Associates advises on spaceport design, Orbital Outfitters Inc supplies customised flight suits, and so on. All of this activity is occurring some years before the first high-priced services even start, so a much wider range of different space travel-related businesses are sure to grow in future.

In the case of orbital services there will be an even wider range of companies with much larger revenues, including companies supplying various services to orbiting hotels. These will include services which terrestrial hotels purchase today, plus such additional services as space-based window maintenance services, air supply, solar-generated electricity, water supply, waste disposal services and others.

As activities in orbit expand progressively, they could grow to include use of materials extracted from the Moon and near-Earth asteroids and cometoids, of which the potential has been researched for decades. Due to the much higher cost of activities in orbit than on the surface of the Earth, the first market for non-terrestrial materials like ice, water, oxygen and hydrogen, is likely to be orbital hotels, as discussed in.

Another potentially major space-based industry, which has been held back for 40 years by high launch costs, is the supply of space-based solar power (SSP) to Earth. Although the potential of this system was recognised in studies by the US Department of Energy in the late 1970s, and confirmed in the 1990s, total funding has remained minimal. However, progress could be rapid once launch costs fall to a few percent of ELV costs. Hence, as passenger space travel activities expand to large scale, a growing range of manufacturing activities in Earth orbit, on the lunar surface and elsewhere, are likely to develop spontaneously. These will open the door to large-scale activities in space, as described in. The growth of orbital passenger space travel to several million passengers/year within a few decades would represent a direct commercial turnover of some 100 billion Euros/year. In such a scenario of rapid growth, annual investment in new facilities, research and development might add the same amount again. Indeed, having reached such a scale, there would be no foreseeable limit to further growth-in particular it need not be constrained, like terrestrial activities, by environmental or social stresses. Quite apart from the numerous opportunities which such a scenario offers for growth of the space industry, it also offers great potential benefits for humanity, in several different fields, as discussed in turn in the following.

Employment

In most countries, most of the population do not have economically significant land holdings, and so employment is the economic basis of social life, providing income and enabling people to have stable family lives. The high level of unemployment in most countries today is therefore not only wasteful, it also causes widespread poverty and unhappiness, and is socially damaging, creating further problems for the future. One reason for investing in the development of passenger space travel, therefore, is that it could create major new fields of employment, capable of growing as far into the future as we can see.

The passenger air travel industry, including airlines, airports, hotels and other tourism-related work enabled by air travel, employs about 20 times the number of people employed in aircraft manufacturing alone, about 50 million people today. Likewise, passenger space travel could create employment many times that of expendable launch vehicles-in vehicle operations and maintenance, at spaceports, in orbiting accommodation, in many companies supplying these, in services such as staff training, certification and insurance, and in a growing range of related businesses.

This is important because high unemployment, both in richer and poorer countries, has been the major economic problem throughout the world for decades. Consequently the growth of such a major new market for advanced aerospace technology and services is highly desirable. By contrast, in recent years employment in the traditional space industry in USA and Europe has been shrinking fast: a 2003 report by the US Federal Aviation Administration stated that employment in launch vehicle manufacturing and services fell from 28,617 in 1999 to 4,828 in 2002, while employment in satellite manufacturing fell from 57,372 to 31,262. Likewise, European space industry employment fell by 20% from 1995 to 2005; the major space engineering company Astrium cut 3,300 staff from 2003 through 2006; and in 2005 alone, European prime contractors cut 13.5% of their staff or some 2,400 people. Unfortunately, the probability of space industry employment recovering soon is low, because satellite manufacturing and launch services face both low demand and rapidly growing competition from India and China where costs are significantly lower.

It is therefore positively bizarre that government policy makers have declined to even discuss the subject of investing in the development of passenger space travel services, and have permitted no significant investment to date out of the nearly 20 billion Euro-equivalents which space agencies spend every year! This is despite the very positive 1998 Nasa report "General Public Space Travel and Tourism", and a 2002 Nasa-funded study which concluded that Suborbital travel services in the USA alone might grow several times larger than the commercial satellite industry.

In the capitalist system, companies compete to reduce costs since this directly increases their profits. However, reducing the number of employees through improving productivity raises unemployment, except to the extent that new jobs are created in new and growing industries. In an economy with a lack of *new industries*, increasing so-called "economic efficiency" creates unemployment, which is a social cost. In this situation, under governments concerned for public welfare, either the rate of creation of new industries must be increased, and/or the reduction of jobs should be slowed, at least until the growth of new industries revives, or other desirable social arrangements are introduced. These include more leisure time, job-sharing, and other policies designed to prevent the growth of a permanent "under-class" of unemployed and "working poor" – a development which would pose a major threat to western civilisation.

One of the many ill effects of high unemployment is that it weakens governments against pressure from corporate interests. For example, increased restrictions on such activities as arms exports, unfair trade, environmental damage, corporate tax evasion, business concentration, advertising targeted at children, and antisocial corporate-drafted legislation such as the "codex alimentarus" and "tort reform" are socially desirable. However, when unemployment is high, corporations' arguments that government intervention would "increase unemployment" have greater influence on governments.

As outlined above, the opening of near-Earth space to large-scale economic development promises to create millions of jobs, with no obvious limits to future growth. At a time when high unemployment is the most serious economic problem throughout the world, developing this family of new industries as fast as possible should be a priority for employment policy. To continue economic "rationalisation" and "globalization" while not developing space travel is self-contradictory, and is both economically and socially extremely damaging.

Economic Growth

The continuation of human civilisation requires a growing world economy, with access to increasing resources. This is because competing groups in society can all improve their situation and reasonable fairness can be achieved, enabling social ethics to survive, only if the overall "economic pie" is growing. Unfortunately, societies are much less robust if the "pie" is shrinking, when ethical growth becomes nearly impossible, as competing groups try to improve their own situation at the expense of other groups. Continued growth of civilisation requires continual ethical evolution, but this will be possible only if resources are sufficient to assure comfort, health, education and fair employment for all members of society. The world economy is under great stress recently for a number of reasons, a fundamental one being the lack of opportunities for profitable investment-as exemplified by Japan's unprecedented decade of zero interest-rates. This lack of productive investment opportunities has led a large amount of funds in the rich countries to "churn" around in the world economy, causing ever greater financial instability, thereby further harming economic growth and widening the gap between rich and poor.

Increasing the opportunities for profitable, stable investment requires continual creation of new industries. Governments today typically express expectations for employment growth in such fields as information technology, energy, robotics, medical services, tourism and leisure. However, there are also sceptical voices pointing out that many of these activities too are already being outsourced to low-cost countries. Most of the net new jobs created in the USA during the 21st century so far have been low-paid service work, while the number of US manufacturing jobs has shrunk rapidly. The decades-long delay in developing space travel has contributed greatly to this lack of new industries.

The rapid economic development of China and India offers great promise, but creates a serious challenge for the already rich countries which need to accelerate the growth of new industries if they are to benefit from these countries' lower costs without creating an impoverished underclass in their own societies-the long-term cost of which would greatly outweigh the short-term benefits of low-cost imports. The development of India and China also creates dangers because the demands of 6 billion people are now approaching the limits of the resources of planet Earth. As these limits are approached, governments become increasingly repressive, thereby adding major social costs to the direct costs of environmental damage. Consequently the decades-long delay in starting to use the resources of the solar system has caused heavy, self-inflicted damage to our economic development, and must be urgently overcome.

Popular Demand is the Basis of Economic Growth

The continuing heavy dependence of the space industry on taxpayer funding, despite cumulative investment to date of some 1 trillion Euro-equivalents, is due to the simple fact that those directing the industry have chosen not to supply services which large numbers of the general public wish to buy. Yet it is elementary that only by doing this can the space industry grow into a normal commercial activity. Doing this will create a new industry which raises private investment to develop newer and larger facilities in order to sell better services to more customers-in the familiar "virtuous circle" of business growth. Eventually this activity may even reach a scale sufficient to repay the public investment to date. In successful companies, investment is skillfully judged so as to produce goods and services for which there will be large commercial (i.e. non-governmental) demand. If this earns sufficient profits, then the activity will continue to grow spontaneously for decades or more, like manufacturing of cars or airliners. If, instead, funds intended for investment are spent on developing non-commercial products, such as surveillance satellites or a space station for which the only significant customer is government, then clearly the space industry is doomed to remain forever a small, taxpayer-funded activity-a hindrance rather than a help to economic growth.

Economic policy makers responsible for deciding the public budget for space development must no longer rely on the advice of the space industry itself, which ever since its origin has had different objectives than the economic benefit of the general public. That is, economic policy makers, who are responsible for trillions of Euros of activity, must take the initiative and fund the development of passenger space travel systems as soon as possible-a policy level well above what is called "space policy", which is responsible for less than 1% of this. Among other steps, this will require the important institutional innovation of collaboration between civil aviation and civil space activities. Since, even with today's knowledge, researchers foresee the possibility of economic development in space growing to a scale similar to terrestrial industry, it must be considered as having the potential to become a major new axis for economic growth-but with minimal environmental impact, as discussed below-and therefore deserving of the most serious and urgent attention by economic policy makers.

Environmental Protection

Economic development in space based on low launch costs could contribute greatly, even definitively, to solving world environmental problems. As a first step, substantially reducing the cost of space travel will reduce the cost of environment-monitoring satellites, improving climate research and environmental policy making.

Space-based Solar Power Supply

A second possibility, which has been researched for several decades but has not yet received a budget to enable testing in orbit, is the delivery of continuous solar-generated power from space to Earth. Researchers believe that such space-based solar power (SSP) could supply clean, low-cost energy on a large scale, which is a prerequisite for economic development of poorer countries while avoiding damaging pollution and climate change. However, realisation of SSP requires much lower launch costs, which only passenger space travel could achieve. Hence the development of orbital tourism could provide the key to realising SSP economically.

Carbon-neutral Space Travel

Clean energy produced by SSP could eliminate the environmental impact of space travel, and even make it "carbon neutral" if this is considered desirable. Moreover, SSP has a much shorter energy payback time than terrestrial solar energy, due to the almost continuous supply of power which it can generate, rather than only in daytime during clear weather. Some critics claim that Suborbital space travel will become a significant environmental burden. However, while superficially correct in the short term, this is the opposite of the truth over the longer term. It would be a dangerous error to prevent the growth of space tourism in order to avoid its initial, minor environmental impact, since this would prevent a range of major benefits in the future, including the supply of low-cost, carbon-neutral SSP, and other space-based industry.

Space-based Industry

If orbital travel grows to a scale of millions of passengers/year-as it could by the 2030s, with vigorous investment-it will stimulate the spontaneous growth of numerous businesses in space. These will grow progressively from simple activities such as maintenance of orbiting hotels, to industrial use of asteroidal minerals. For example, the development of SSP would lead to a range of industrial processes using the advantages of space, including low-cost electricity, high vacuum, weightlessness and minerals in shallow gravitational wells. If SSP grows to supply a significant share of the terrestrial energy market, more and more industry would operate outside the Earth's ecological system. While most industries cause growing damage to the Earth's environment as they grow in scale, industrial activities which are outside the Earth's ecosystem need not cause any such damage. Hence the growth of space-based industry to large scale offers the longer-term possibility of decoupling economic growth from the limits of the terrestrial environment. Indeed, it has been argued that only the use of space resources, including especially SSP, offers the possibility of protecting the Earth's environment while enabling sufficient economic growth to preserve civilised society.

Global Cooling

As a measure of the uncertainty about climate change there is a significant group of climatologists who, while acknowledging the physical mechanism of the "greenhouse effect", argue that it is outweighed by other natural influences, including the global cooling trend which is heading towards the next Ice Age. With a period of tens of thousands of years, the last Ice Age saw much of Northern Europe covered by ice 1 kilometre deep!

In the face of such a threat, it is notable that SSP satellites with area of tens of square kilometres, whether transmitting microwave power or sunlight reflected with large orbiting mirrors, could uniquely help to counteract Ice Age cooling by melting snow and ice over large areas. This could prevent the vicious circle of accelerating cooling due to increased reflection of sunlight from snow-covered areas. Direct weather modification is a new field with many uncertainties, but it may be the only way to prevent the destruction of civilisation by the next Ice Age. Thus, from the point of view of risk management, it is a major attraction of SSP that it could help to mitigate climate change, whether due to global warming, as CO_2-free electric power supply, or global cooling, by directly warming the Earth's surface.

Ethical Consumption

Passenger space travel and its numerous spin-off activities have the important potential to escape the limitations of the "consumerism" which governments in the rich countries have encouraged in recent decades in order to stimulate economic growth, defined as GDP. This is resulting in "excess consumption" which causes unnecessary environmental damage, while reducing rather than increasing public satisfaction. "First world" citizens are increasingly trapped in a culturally impoverished "consumer" lifestyle which reduces social capital, social cohesion and happiness. By contrast, expenditure on the unique experience of space travel promises to play a more positive role in the economy and society, enriching customers culturally without requiring mass production of consumer goods.

Education

The educational value of space activities is well known: children and young people find the subject of space and space travel uniquely fascinating. A number of space-based, science-fiction films and television series have achieved extraordinary popularity, extending over decades. As a result, various organisations have created space-related educational programmes involving satellite design, small rockets and simulation of space flights. Unfortunately, while these activities are popular with the participants, it has to be recognised that they are not effective in increasing young people's scientific education overall, which continues to decline in most countries. That is, children who enjoy science classes find satellite projects inspiring, but these classes do not prevent the "flight from science" seen in rich countries, which is so dangerous for the successful continuation of civilisation.

However, the possibility of being able to travel to space oneself is of much greater interest to young people than watching videos of other people travelling to space, or than simulating travelling to space. Hence the start of low-cost passenger space travel services holds unique promise for education in fields related to space travel. In particular, the expectation that the price of a Suborbital flight could fall as low as 5,000 Euros as the service grows to millions of passengers/year offers the possibility of almost all children being able to take a flight sometime. This possibility can be used as a uniquely stimulating teaching tool. In addition, the scenario shown in Figure 1 will employ tens of thousands of staff in orbit – a uniquely exciting goal for young people.

Culture

The history and artefacts of the European Renaissance are still the subject of worldwide admiration today. One reason for this unique flowering-such as in 14th century to 16th century Firenze-was that there was a social ethic whereby the successful and wealthy had a sufficiently strong sense of civic duty that they used part of their wealth to enrich the community, particularly by building inspiring civic spaces-libraries, galleries, palazzi and other buildings-and by commissioning works of art and scholarship, with results which still inspire us 600 years later. Such an ethic requires that those who are materially successful, however "self-made" and praiseworthy they may be, recognise that they are also all beneficiaries of good fortune-to have been born in a country, an era, a locale, and a family in which they have opportunities to learn language and manners, to accumulate formative experiences, to obtain useful knowledge, and then opportunities to exercise their talents and grow into a great career. In a successful society, people who are blessed with such good fortune accept that they have a social duty to repay this-by creating a similarly nurturing environment for future generations. The enduring popularity of the achievements of the Renaissance surely illustrates the enormous value of such an ethical sense in society.

Need for a New Worldwide Renaissance

By contrast, as societies became richer over the following centuries, they were increasingly disfigured by becoming more materialistic, a trend accompanied by more and more brutal and destructive wars, including the horrific "world wars" and communist revolutions. This trend has continued with the recent shocking decline in ethics of the US and UK governments openly flouting national and international law-and even the Geneva Conventions, once seen as a bulwark of European civilisation (by making war less inhumane through banning torture and the killing of civilians).

The way of thinking of Renaissance leaders is strikingly different from today when the wealthy are encouraged to follow the rubric: "If you've got it, flaunt it", or appear to follow the frankly psychopathic: "Everything for us-and nothing for anyone else." The futility of such an attitude is well-known throughout the ages, as expressed in such sayings as: "You cannot take it with you when you die," or "There are no pockets in a shroud". The great universalist religions of Buddhism, Christianity and Islam are in agreement that material wealth is transient and acquisitiveness is not the path to happiness: to the contrary, having gratitude for good fortune, and making efforts to help others less fortunate than oneself are extolled. The reason why these teachings have lasted for millenia is because they help people to live satisfying lives, to raise healthy children, and to maintain stable, resilient societies.

They are the basis of humane culture and true civilisation. Thus it is clear that, while societies have grown far richer since the Renaissance, the way of thinking of the rich today is far poorer. Despite almost unlimited opportunities for creativity and cultural contribution, most of the rich today leave behind little or nothing worth remembering. At best they typically use their money to buy large numbers of possessions, which are redistributed on their death. Of course many people, including the wealthy, give to charitable organizations, many of which do very good work. However, much of this work does little more than offset some of the worst effects of the policies followed by the rich countries which widen the gap between rich and poor worldwide.

We can judge this behaviour: the great benefactors of the Renaissance were more admirable human beings. Unless corrected soon, this futile materialism will destroy civilisation. Yet under "neo-liberal" or "neo-con" dogma, instead of using the opportunity provided by wealth to contribute culturally to society, the already rich exert pressure on governments to reduce their taxes further, to remove remaining restraints on monopolies and illegal surveillance of the general public, while falsely blaming already deteriorating welfare systems for government's fiscal crisis. The lack of new industries described above weakens governments against such pressures. Such psychopathic greed and dishonesty among the upper levels of a society are the prelude to its destruction, and represent the most serious challenge to western civilisation. A new, worldwide Renaissance is urgently needed.

"The Earth is Not Sick – She's Pregnant"

Healthy societies can revitalise themselves. An interesting explanation of the potential of space travel and its offshoots to revitalise human civilisation is expressed in the idea that "The Earth is not sick: she's pregnant". Although this idea may seem strange at first hearing, it is a surpisingly useful analogy for understanding humans' current predicament. According to the "Pregnant Earth" analogy, the darkening prospect before humanity is due to humans' terrestrial civilisation being "pregnant"-and indeed dangerously overdue-with an extra-terrestrial offspring. Once humans' space civilisation is safely born, the current stresses within the mother civilisation will be cured, and the new life may eventually even surpass it's parent. This idea not only illuminates many aspects of humans' present problems, it also provides detailed directions for how to solve these problems, and explains convincingly how successfully aiding this birth will lead to a far better condition than before the pregnancy. A young couple may be happy in each other's company, but their joy is increased by the birth of children and life with them, from which many new possibilities arise.

Likewise, the birth of humans' coming extra-terrestrial civilisation will lead to a wide range of activities outside our planet's precious ecosystem. This evolution will solve not only humans' material problems, by making the vast resources of near-Earth space accessible, but it will also help to cure the emptiness of so-called "modern" commercial culture – including the "dumbing down" by monopolistic media, the falling educational standards, passification by television, obesity, ever-growing consumption of alcohol, decline in public morality, narcotics, pornography, falling social capital, rising divorce rates, and youths' lack of challenge and lack of "dreams". It will do this by raising humans' sights to the stars, and showing that the door to them is unlocked, and has been for decades-we have only to make a small effort to push it open forever.

Reopening a true geographical frontier, with all its challenges, will in itself be of inestimable value for the cultural growth of modern civilisation. The widespread sense that we live in a closed world which is getting more and more crowded will be replaced by an open-ended, optimistic vision of an unlimited future. Access to the cornucopia of space resources that await humans' exploitation can clearly make a unique contribution to this. To the extent that leaders of major industries are motivated by ambition in business competition, they will welcome this opportunity to extend their activities to new fields in the far wider arena of space; to the extent that they are motivated by the attempt to achieve monopolistic control and profits, they may try to hinder development in space, even at the cost of preventing its wide benefits, since this will be more profitable to them. However, implementing the "Pregnant Earth" agenda can stop this cultural regression and start a true worldwide Renaissance, an unprecedented flowering of civilisation of which human culture has been in need ever since the inspiration of the Italian Renaissance was followed by a decline into progressive materialism and warmongering.

World Peace and Preservation of Human Civilisation

The major source of social friction, including international friction, has surely always been unequal access to resources. People fight to control the valuable resources on and under the land, and in and under the sea. The natural resources of Earth are limited in quantity, and economically accessible resources even more so. As the population grows, and demand grows for a higher material standard of living, industrial activity grows exponentially. The threat of resources becoming scarce has led to the concept of "Resource Wars". Having begun long ago with wars to control the gold and diamonds of Africa and South America, and oil in the Middle East, the current phase is at centre stage of world events today.

A particular danger of "resource wars" is that, if the general public can be persuaded to support them, they may become impossible to stop as resources become increasingly scarce. Many commentators have noted the similarity of the language of US and UK government advocates of "war on terror" to the language of the novel "1984" which describes a dystopian future of endless, fraudulent war in which citizens are reduced to slaves.

As an alternative to the "resource wars" already devastating many countries today, opening access to the unlimited resources of near-Earth space could clearly facilitate world peace and security. This is acknowledged by the U.S. National Space Security Office, which started its 2007 report on the potential of space-based solar power: "Expanding human populations and declining natural resources are potential sources of local and strategic conflict in the 21st Century, and many see energy as the foremost threat to national security". It ended the report: "Considering the timescales that are involved, and the exponential growth of population and resource pressures within that same strategic period, it is imperative that this work for "drilling up" vs. drilling down for energy security begins immediately".

Although the use of extra-terrestrial resources on a substantial scale may still be some decades away, it is important to recognise that simply acknowledging its feasibility using known technology is the surest way of ending the threat of resource wars. That is, if it is assumed that the resources available for human use are limited to those on Earth, then it can be argued that resource wars are inescapable. If, by contrast, it is assumed that the resources of space are economically accessible, this not only eliminates the need for resource wars, it can also preserve the benefits of civilisation which are being eroded today by "resource war-mongers", most notably the governments of the "Anglo-Saxon" countries and their "neo-con" advisers. It is also worth noting that the $1 trillion that these have already committed to the Iraq war is *far more* than the investment needed to access space resources.

Industrial and financial groups which profit from monopolistic control of terrestrial supplies of various natural resources, like those which profit from wars, have an economic interest in protecting their profitable situation. However, these groups' continuing profits are justified neither by capitalism nor by democracy: they could be preserved only by maintaining the pretence that use of space resources is not feasible, and by preventing the development of low-cost space travel.

Once the feasibility of low-cost space travel is understood, "resource wars" are clearly idiotic as well as tragic. A visiting extra-terrestrial would be pityingly amused at the foolish antics of homo sapiens using long-range rockets to fight each other over dwindling terrestrial resources-rather than using the same rockets to travel in space and have all the resources they need!

High Return in Safety from Extra-terrestrial Settlement

Investment in orbital access and other space infrastructure will facilitate the establishment of settlements on the Moon, Mars, asteroids and in man-made space structures. In the first phase, development of new regulatory infrastructure in various Earth orbits, including property/usufruct rights, real estate, mortgage financing and insurance, traffic management, plotting, policing and other services will enable the population living in Earth orbits to grow very large. Such activities aimed at making near-Earth space habitable are the logical extension of humans' historical spread over the surface of the Earth. As trade spreads through near-Earth space, settlements are sure to follow, of which the inhabitants will add to the wealth of different cultures which humans have created in the many different environments in which they live. The success of such extra-terrestrial settlements will have the additional benefit of reducing the danger of human extinction due to planet-wide or cosmic accidents. These horrors include both man-made disasters such as nuclear war, plagues or climate change, and natural disasters such as super-volcanoes or asteroid impact.

It is hard to think of any objective that is more important than preserving peace. Weapons developed in recent decades are so destructive, and have such horrific, long-term side-effects that their use should be discouraged as strongly as possible by the international community. Hence, reducing the incentive to use weapons by rapidly developing the ability to use space-based resources on a large scale is surely equally important. The achievement of this depends on the low space travel costs which, at the present time, appear to be achievable only through the development of a vigorous space tourism industry.

Summary

As discussed above, if space travel services had started during the 1950s when they first could, the space industry would be enormously more developed than it is today. Hence the failure to develop passenger space travel has seriously distorted the path taken by humans' technological and economic development since WW2, away from the path which would have been followed if capitalism and democracy operated as intended. Technological know-how which could have been used to supply services which are known to be very popular with a large proportion of the general public has not been used for that purpose, while suffering due to the unemployment and environmental damage caused by the resulting lack of new industries have increased.

In response, policies should be implemented urgently to correct this error, and to catch up with the possibilities for industrial and economic growth that have been ignored for so long. This policy renewal is urgent because of the growing danger of unemployment, economic stagnation, climate change, educational and cultural decline, resource wars and loss of civil liberties which face civilisation today. In order to achieve the necessary progress there is a particular need for collaboration between those working in the two fields of civil aviation and civil space. Although the word "aerospace" is widely used, it is largely a misnomer since these two fields are in practice quite separate. True "aerospace" collaboration to realise passenger space travel will develop the wonderful profusion of possibilities outlined above.

Humans' Urgent Choice: Heaven or Hell on Earth?

As discussed above, the claim that resources are running out can be used to justify wars which may never end: present-day rhetoric about "the long war" or "100 years war" in Iraq are current examples. If political leaders do not change their viewpoint, the recent aggression by the rich, "Anglo-Saxon" countries and their cutting back of traditional civil liberties are ominous for the future. However, this "hellish" vision of endless war is based on an assumption about a single number – the future cost of travel to orbit – about which a different assumption leads to a literally "heavenly" vision of peace and ever-rising living standards for everyone forever. If this cost stays above 10,000 Euros/kg, where it has been unchanged for nearly 50 years, the prospects for humanity are bleak. But if humans make the necessary effort, and use the tiny amount of resources needed to develop passenger space vehicles, then this cost will fall to 100 Euros/kg, the use of extra-terrestrial resources will become economic, and arguments for resource wars will evaporate entirely. This is not a decision for the far future or the 22nd Century. It has to be made very soon if humans are to have a reasonable future.

The main reason why this step has not been taken yet seems to be lack of understanding by investors and policy-makers of the myriad opportunities that space travel will create. Now that the potential to catch up half a century's delay in the growth of space travel is becoming understood, continuing to spend 20 billion Euro equivalents/year on government space activities while continuing to invest nothing in developing passenger space travel would be a gross failure of economic policy, and strongly contrary to the economic and social interests of the public.

As this policy error is corrected, and investment in profitable space projects grows rapidly in coming years, we can look forward to a growing worldwide boom. Viewed as a whole, humans' industrial growth has been seriously underperforming for decades, due to the failure to exploit these immensely promising fields of activity. The tens of thousands of unemployed space engineers in Russia, America and Europe alone are a huge waste. The millions of disappointed young people who have been taught that they cannot travel in space are another enormous wasted resource. The potential manpower in rapidly developing India and China is clearly vast. Correcting this error, even after such a costly delay, is going to ameliorate many problems in the world today.

We do not know for certain when the above scenario will be realised. However, it could have such enormous value that considerable expenditure is justified in order to study its feasibility in detail. At the very least, vigorous investment by both private and public sectors in a range of different suborbital passenger vehicle projects and related businesses is highly desirable. Fortunately, the ambitious and rapid investment by the Indian and Chinese governments in growing space capabilities may finally jolt the space industries of Russia, America, Europe and even Japan out of their long economic stagnation, and induce them to apply their accumulated know-how to economically valuable activities – notably supplying widely popular travel services to the general public

General Public Space Travel and Tourism

The travel and tourism business is among the largest in the world. In the United States alone, travel and tourism generate sales of more than $400 billion per year. This translates into jobs: the travel and tourism business is the second largest employer in the U.S.

Recently, the idea of extending travel and tourism beyond the surface of the Earth has been increasingly suggested — trips by ordinary people to space, not as scientists or technologists, but for personal reasons including adventure, recreation and business. This idea is not a new one; it has been examined several times in the past 30 years and some initial abortive attempts to commence actual travel and tourism businesses took place in the U.S. a dozen years ago. Early in this decade the Japanese Rocket Society encouraged the conduct of broad space tourism studies, including market studies. In 1994, the (then) six major U.S. aerospace firms concluded in their Commercial Space Transportation Study (CSTS) that general public space travel and tourism had the potential to become a very large market if space transportation safety and reliability could be sharply increased, and per passenger costs could be reduced, substantially.

The latest professional space travel and tourism market survey — one conducted in the United States by non-space interests — clearly suggests that very many (tens of millions) "average" American adults can envision themselves taking a trip to space (as they imagine, today, what such a future trip would be like) and, altogether, paying a great sum to do so. However, substantial obstacles remain that prevent the immediate creation of a large scale business.

Today, the cost of access to space for people using currently operational vehicles remains very high; a half-dozen astronauts can accompany the delivery of payloads to space on Shuttle trips that cost some $400 million each. In addition, the safety and reliability of operational space transportation vehicles is presently far too low: a risk of some 1-in-100 of failure involving fatalities may be acceptable today for government missions and for a few adventure travellers, but not for airline-like general public passenger-carrying operations which will have to be safer by several factors of ten.

Finally, there has been a persistent lack of credibility because now it is generally thought that only NASA and the Russian government can send people to space and that they must be highly trained professional astronauts. This so-called giggle factor is especially prevalent among some experienced aerospace systems engineers unfamiliar with potential new capabilities that are inherent in recent technological advances and the increased insistence of the Congress that public spending in space result in greater economic growth, especially in the human spaceflight area. And they may not recall the enormous strides made in commercial aviation over just a few decades. The general public is actually more accepting of the idea of public space travel than these engineers.

Fortunately, critical advances have been made during the past decade in many of the technologies that can enable non-astronaut human space travel to become both technically and economically feasible, and more are foreseen. As a result, the potential exists for the creation, in the next very few decades, of a $10-20 billion... per year "general public space travel and tourism" business.

Too, initial steps can be taken at the surface, then in the atmosphere and later in space so that early profitability and experience, and credibility-creating activities, can begin prior to full orbital trips and long-term stays there.

During 1996-1997, the Space Transportation Association (STA) and the National Aeronautics and Space Administration (NASA) have, through a cooperative Space Act agreement, conducted a study of the potential for future general public space travel and tourism businesses. Several important findings were made. In their light, suggestions concerning what must be done to surmount the barriers to this business creation have been formulated.

Although several significant issues were identified, consensus grew within this study that the aerospace industry and travel and tourism interests, working in partnership with each other and with the Federal government where appropriate, could overcome all identified obstacles and that a viable, and potentially very large, general public space travel and tourism business could begin to be created over the next decade or so.

The basic objective of the NASA-STA study was to determine the feasibility of a commercially viable, general public space travel and tourism business being created in the U.S. through private initiatives with private resources, along with government encouragement, cooperation, and key scientific research and technology development investments.

As indicated, it is believed that such a business could grow to have great benefits for the U.S. economy while, at the same time, substantially increasing public interest in space activities generally. For, once the sharply increased safety and reliability, and sharply decreased unit costs required for large scale space tourism businesses to succeed have been achieved, many other things could then be done in space using such markedly advanced space capabilities.

A General Public Space Travel and Tourism National Steering Group for the NASA-STA study was formed in the Fall of 1996. This Group conducted a preliminary assessment of the opportunities and problems faced by those who could be interested in forming space travel and tourism businesses, and it found that the former are inviting and, in principle, the latter are tractable. The Steering Group outlined a framework for a General Public Space Travel and Tourism Workshop, and many of its members participated personally therein. Finally, a draft of this Report was provided to the Steering Group by the STA-NASA study leaders and members of the Steering Group participated in its editing.

The General Public Space Travel and Tourism

To develop the concept of general public space travel and tourism further, and to bring together representatives from our space-related government and university interests, the travel and tourism business, the financial community and the aerospace industry, a Workshop was held during February 19-21, 1997. The primary purpose of this Workshop, which was held at the Georgetown University's Thomas and Dorothy Leavey Centre, was to define what must be done in order to allow this new and potentially large space-related market to develop and to generate preliminary strategic concepts, milestones and organizational constructs toward that end. The Workshop was planned to have a relaxed, working atmosphere to encourage the flow of ideas.

Participants worked in teams to discuss the following topics:

* Space Transportation and Destination Facilities.
* Passengers, Crew, Life Support and Insurance Considerations.
* Regulation, Certification, Legislation, Policy and Environmental Issues.
* Financial, Economic, Business Planning and Market Considerations.
* Initial Ground Facilities, Space Tourism Theme Parks and other Orbital Trip "Precursor" Considerations.
* Research and Technology Development Requirements, and Use of Existing Space Assets.

Participants included:

* Travel and tourism business leaders.
* Hotel architect, airline and business leaders.
* Insurance interests.
* Aerospace entrepreneurs.
* Aerospace technical experts.
* Space health and medical experts.

The objectives of each of the several working sessions were: (a) to develop a detailed statement of the topic, (b) to identify key issues associated with general public space travel and tourism, (c) to identify opportunities to eliminate barriers, and (d) to make recommendations for future action. By the end of the Workshop, each of the teams formulated a series of findings which were captured in both a presentation to the Workshop as a whole and in white papers provided to the NASA-STA study leaders. These results were integrated with other information sources by these leaders to form the kernel of this NASA-STA study final Report.

The strong consensus view of the Workshop was that there is a very real potential for a large, profitable, commercially-driven general public space travel and tourism business to begin to develop beginning a very few years from now.

The Prospects for General Public Space Travel and Tourism

Space Transportation and Destination Facilities Considerations

Getting into and back from space safely and reliably, and for an acceptable price and in reasonable comfort, and having somewhere to go there, are fundamental to the concept of general public space travel and tourism. Areas for consideration are far-ranging, and include space transportation vehicles and their operation (both opportunities to use existing vehicles and the development of specialized transports) and space "habitats" and other facilities in space which will eventually serve as destinations. Some kinds of initial space transportation vehicles would likely also serve as habitats in short duration trips, while space residences would eventually develop to support longer term stays, much as in earthbound travel. Appropriate passenger-carrying Earth-Orbit transport vehicles are clearly essential. These may well be feasible in the relatively near future but, depending upon their size and the overall length and sophistication of the trips, required investment costs could be high — in extreme cases, very high. At present, there are several Federal government-aerospace industry and several purely private sector programs underway that, to various extents, can be visualized as providing some initial space travel and tourism capability. Dramatic advances in propulsion systems and structures are needed to see the lowest unit cost vehicle and largest service market develop. The probable costs to develop these systems will be high and government R&D co-investments are needed.

Validation of the real market for general public space travel and tourism is going to be an essential step. A central issue will be: is it possible to get that validation with current vehicles? In principle, the Shuttle fleet and small-scale trips using vehicles now under development could explore the market incrementally.

A notional — but not at all improbable — concurrent market and system-service development sequence might follow a path such as:

* Enlarged terrestrial space-related travel and tourism businesses.
* Increasingly higher altitude adventure tourist suborbital trips.
* Global suborbital space plane package delivery and passenger-carrying services.
* Short duration adventure tourist orbital trips.

* Longer duration orbital trips, including stays at Low Earth Orbit destinations.

Eventually, supra-LEO trips would be taken, but this study is limited to the consideration of trips to no higher altitudes than LEO.

Although services could be initiated with passengers living in the transport vehicle (as current astronauts do in the Space Shuttle), destination residential facilities will eventually have to be developed. In both cases zero-gravity "sickness" problems must be solved, generally, or artificial gravity provided. Fortunately, there is much attention being paid to the former and studies have shown that the latter is possible.

LEO residential facilities will be sophisticated and expensive undertakings compared to those on the surface. Ultimately, providing levels of comfort and privacy that are comparable to very large and successful terrestrial ocean cruise lines will be a very strong driver for the acquisition of improved in-space infrastructure.

As is often the case in the creation of a new kind of business, issues and arguments tend to be circular: both markets and financing are dependent on each other already being in place. Some use of such government facilities as the Shuttle and the U.S. portion of the International Space Station (ISS) is very highly desirable inasmuch as (a) general public passenger R&D is required, (b) key technologies and subsystems operations must be demonstrated, and (c) general public merchandising demonstrations would be invaluable. Too, having the ISS close by and cooperating with early residential facility use could be comforting to architects, builders, operators and guests.

Passengers, Crew, Life Support and Insurance Considerations

The "human" issues and problems associated with public space travel and tourism are no less important than the technological challenges of getting them to/from space. There is the need to identify the accommodations that will be required to support the general public; the need for experienced crew and attendants and their likely functions; the need for life support equipment that will be required in passenger vehicles and habitats; space sickness, its effects, and its countermeasures and their implications; flight and hull insurance — all, hopefully, at an early moment. Numerous issues must be resolved and actions taken before safe, large scale, comfortable and routine general public space travel and tourism can begin.

There appear to be a variety of options called for beyond terrestrial, and lower atmosphere space travel and tourism, including varying costs, accommodations, and levels of preparedness and acceptable risk-taking by various kinds of future passengers.

These could include:

* Suborbital trips (lasting less than 1 hr; all in the space transportation vehicle).
* Three orbit trips (lasting up to 5 hours; all in the space transportation vehicle).
* Three day trips (possibly including a LEO facility).
* Resort packages (with stays of 1-2 weeks at a LEO facility and possibly even extra-facility activities).

For any of these cases, the transport vehicle and any in-space facility must provide accommodations with certain minimal personal and social standards. These include: safety, privacy, baggage handling, entertainment, training and exercise facilities, and easy to operate toilets, showers, eating-drinking facilities, and medical capabilities (in situ plus telemedicine). For instance, gravity loads during launch and re-entry should be limited to some 2 times that of surface gravity.

One of the major issues concerning general public space travel and tourism (especially during early, relatively short duration trips) is the prevention and/or the amelioration of space sickness in "zero gravity". Nearly half of all people who have gone into space have experienced nausea and become ill because of the lack of gravity. Untreated, nausea and other effects can last for period ranging from a few hours to several days.

However, there are steps that can be taken. First, medication exists which will help almost all individual travellers. Although this medication is inappropriate for a Space Shuttle pilot because of its side effect of drowsiness, there is no present reason to believe that it cannot provide relief to many/most passengers. In addition, for longer term stays, techniques exist by which artificial gravity could be created which would prevent essentially all space sickness. For the latter case, technological-operational approaches range from spinning centrifuges or turntables operating inside an otherwise "zero-gravity" habitat for short stays, all the way to large-scale rotating habitats that could provide as much as Earth-normal gravity on long stays.

Overall, the issue of accommodations, life support and other amenities provided for the paying clients of a space travel and tourism business requires careful consideration. These can be expected to vary in scale and type depending upon the character and expectations of the travellers (especially the ones who could be identified as "adventure tourists") and on the duration of an individual's stay in space.

Another important consideration will be the size and skills of the crew providing support and personal services to the passengers. (Reflecting upon the early days of commercial aviation's passenger service accommodations could be helpful.) In order to assure confidence in comfort and safety a relatively large crew will probably be needed. Members of such crews will need exceptional people skills to handle the situations that are bound to arise in such an "alien" situation — informing without alarming, and calming without isolating when there are problems. Some or all crew members must also have appropriate medical training. In addition, adequate medical facilities must be provided locally, commensurate with the duration of the particular services being provided. Also, for longer duration trips and where a greater degree of physical exertion may be expected (such as in-space sports) an appropriately trained and experienced physician must be available.

Appropriate and thorough passenger preparation will be essential. This may very well include specialized training in some cases. For example, a working familiarity with the systems on board the residential facility might be a useful aspect of assuring health and safety. Rather than being a burden, it may well prove that preparation activities are a valued part of the overall public space travel and tourism experience (perhaps like attending a space camp). Broad experience in the preparation process itself could well become a terrestrial revenue-generating element of an overall general public space travel and tourism business.

Even after the technologies needed to make travel and tourism service affordable have matured and the systems have been developed, tested and deployed, uncertainties and risks will remain.

This will be true for in-space facilities, but it will be especially true for EO transports. Passenger, crew and vehicle insurance could become available, but would be expensive until transports are proven to be reliable by repeated usage over time. The "third party" liability issue must be addressed by both the vehicle developers and operators, and the Federal government, and this matter is now receiving increased attention. Practices similar to those employed on other so-called "adventure travel" trips, such as mountain climbing in the Himalayas where tourists sign a waiver of liability and proceed at their own risk, may be applicable in this case as well.

Again, both transports and hotels must be designed, developed and operated with basic general public physical, psychological and social considerations in mind.

Regulation, Certification, Legislation, Policy and Environmental Considerations

A myriad of legal and regulatory aspects of public space travel and tourism must be resolved before viable large scale businesses can emerge. This is especially true of those public agencies with the responsibility to regulate in the interest of public safety. This includes identification of public policies and/or laws that exist or must be enacted to enable business formation, licensing, certification and approval processes for both passengers and vehicles, clearance and over-flight considerations, and environmental and safety issues including atmospheric pollution, solar radiation (flares) and orbital debris.

National and international regulatory issues will affect general public space travel and tourism significantly. It will be crucial to assure both the Congress and the general public that this new business is considered to be safe by reasonable standards and acceptable by those who would take space trips. For example, it might be reasonable to expect that the earliest services will be safe by the standards of sky-diving, but not by the standards of today's commercial aviation; recall that the latter required improvement over decades to reach its present high level. Whatever standards are applied, it will be important to streamline regulatory processes and to establish uniformity in those standards and their application.

The ability to start viable businesses that offer diverse services of various scales and prices will be the ultimate test for the realization of the concept of general public space travel and tourism. Financial planning, capital needs and sources, and the creation of viable business plans are fundamental to creating a sound new business area.

This study is not recommending any specific ventures inasmuch as these remain the purview of the private sector and its judgment regarding business opportunities, but it does identify general issues and classes of opportunities. For instance, the early years of space tourism flights should be in vehicles whose operations are licensed under the existing authority of the Associate Administrator for Commercial Space Transportation in the FAA-DOT. This office already licenses space cargo launches, and has the statutory authority to closely monitor the safety related policies, procedures, and operations and equipment of launch operators.

After some years of experience with various vehicle types and potential failure modes, the Federal government then could formulate standards for certification of passenger spaceships. This evolution to certification would free spaceship operators of the need for specific approval for each trip that is required under the licensing regime.

Major uncertainties that will affect the initiation of general public space travel and tourism business startups include: market demand and elasticity; transport vehicle acquisition and O&M costs; trip price; trip safety, reliability and comfort; and insurance and regulatory burdens. Notional business models suggest that profitability of eventually truly large scale service operation will depend on per orbital trip costs of not more than about $1-2 Million (roughly 100 times less than Space Shuttle costs and 10 times less than today's Reusable Launch Vehicle program goal). In addition, an overall safety of 0.9999+ (roughly 100 times better than Shuttle) will be needed. Vehicles should be designed able to return to Earth and land safely if required by any space trip emergency. Finally, high utilization of the space transportation vehicles will be critical — including turnaround times of some 24 hours (roughly 100 times shorter than today's individual Shuttle experience).

As these technical-operational goals are achieved, the price per ticket could drop below $50,000 per passenger, and might eventually reach the range of $10,000-$20,000. (By that time, if U.S. economic growth continues at the same rate as the past decade, in effect prices, in 1997 dollars, could be reduced by a factor of some 1.5X, and over 10 million households could have incomes, in 1997 dollars, of over $100,000 per year.) Market forecasts all suggest large real markets, but vary significantly in their predictions of market elasticity. However, with ticket prices well below $50,000, it is believed that there could be the order of 500,000 space trip passengers/year. (Transporting these many people/year would require the carrying to/from space of hundreds of millions of pounds of payload per year — roughly 1,000 times more

than today's total U.S. civil, commercial and industry annual space trip payload, but still many factors of ten less than is carried by commercial airlines.)

Some notional business models that have been constructed suggest that, then, high annual internal rates of return may be achievable. However, it is recognized that such results are crucially dependent upon market elasticity surveys and space transportation service cost estimates that are at early stages of development. They each have major uncertainties and the general public's present trip expectations could change over a decade's time; therefore, such economic feasibility projections could be in substantial error and they should be updated every few years.

As a part of the business start-up process, incremental business formation involving niche markets will be vital. For example, poll data indicate that some people would go on very expensive "space adventure trips" now — even at prices approaching $1 million per ticket and with substantial physical risk. As part of this process, a carefully planned public relations and merchandising campaign is needed to improve public awareness of this opportunity and to change public perceptions of risks and viability. This is essential not just from the standpoint of informing eventual clients, but also from that of satisfying the concerns of potential investors.

The perceived level of risk and uncertainty in a general public space travel and tourism venture will, of course, have a direct bearing on the availability and cost of money for that venture.

Overall, the assessment to date suggests that if EO transportation system-services can be developed that demonstrate acceptable safety, reliability, comfort and affordability, and are sized to serve large enough markets, financially viable general public space travel and tourism businesses can be created by the private sector.

And it is judged that, once public in-space trips of any character commence and continue with regularity, today's terrestrial space tourism businesses would flourish.

Initial Ground Facilities, Space Tourism Theme Parks and Other Orbital Trip "Precursor" Considerations

A variety of ground facilities and activities may be called into play to support successful formation of general public space travel and tourism enterprises, especially including businesses that are formed to exploit the latent market demand even before actual in-space trips are available to the public. These facilities could include theme parks, trip training facilities, and other such public quasi-entertainment facilities that could develop around future general public space travel and tourism launch/recovery sites, and whose function it would be both to prepare the public for the space experience and simultaneously to profit from the undertaking. The success of these businesses could be crucial in raising both public awareness and large amounts of capital for the actual public in-space travel and tourism to follow. Again, these activities would also serve as transition activities for the present terrestrial travel and tourism businesses.

As noted above, Earth-based space travel and tourism already exists and is flourishing. However, to serve as an effective "precursor" to public in-space travel, terrestrial space travel and tourism must enlarge its marketing focus from children and adolescents of the "Star Wars" approach so as to emphasize average, typically very successful, professional adults. Private business may make a lot of money on these types of facilities and entertainment activities, including those around a future commercial spaceport, as well as through training camps, space camps, theme parks, space-related merchandise, etc. Such activities may begin well before actual in-space trips occur, and they could continue growing once in-space trips become available.

A variety of information-oriented "precursor" activities will probably be needed to engender the rapid creation of a general public space travel and tourism business. For example, greatly expanded communications efforts are needed to develop space travel and tourism groups and to promote entertainment in such related applications as movies, prizes, CDs, and books. In addition, using motion picture and/or other media personalities to promote public space trips may be a sound strategy. Private, non-profit, organizations (such as the newly created Space Tourism Society) could lead these information-oriented activities and assist in the building of a consensus on various issues. This would be an important step.

For instance, a virtual reality experience could be offered — one in which, on the surface, a person led by an astronaut could experience to some degree the characteristics of human spaceflight. Such experiences can be expected to whet the general public's appetite for "the real thing". Too, it is now time for a few senior Federal officials who have responsibility for our civil and private sector space interests to consider taking trips to orbit. Their fundamental domain of responsibility is space itself, not the Earth's surface, and their doing so could be a graphic signal to the Country that space trips are no longer to be confined to astronauts. Certainly their personal participation in opening up space to the general public is as important as sending probes throughout the solar system. In so doing, they would simply replicate the trips of such Federal officials as the President and the Secretaries of Defence and State, who oftentimes visit dangerous areas around the globe to ensure that our Country's interests are well understood and supported.

Finally, it will be important that "precursor" activities provide early revenues to nascent general public space travel and tourism businesses and create a new public understanding that human spaceflight activities can be separate and distinct from those of NASA's.

Research and Technology Development Requirements, and Use of Existing Space Assets

There are several appropriate research and technology development activities that the Federal Government should undertake to allow the future creation of privately-funded general public space travel and tourism businesses. These include any technology developments or demonstrations that are too risky or too long term for the private sector to undertake under novel market circumstances, and any research programs, such as in life sciences — all of which are traditional government undertakings. The Government's role in advancing our satellite communications and remote sensing business interests continues to be a useful precedent. Government-owned space assets, such as the Space Shuttle and the U.S. segment of the International Space Station should be used for the conduct of scientific, technological and operational inquiries and, as well, for market-stimulation and initial private citizen trips. National policy regarding Shuttle fleet operations should be examined in anticipation of the desirability of allowing this latter use. The privatization of the Shuttle is proceeding well with initial operations now being conducted by the private sector — the United Space Alliance. Analogous privatization of ISS operations should also be seriously studied.

EO transport vehicles based on current technologies and operating methods are not sufficiently safe or reliable for widespread general public transport, and they cost too much to operate. For example, a space travel and tourism business that used a current NASA Space Shuttle configured to carry 50 people would have to charge some $10 million per ticket just to cover operations and maintenance costs. In the relatively near term, improvements to the Shuttle vehicles and their enlarged operations might enable a 2-4 times reduction in these levels. At such prices, it might be possible to start a business, but it would be one which could only accommodate a few people each year at best.

To ensure that the use of costly public assets are used in a fundamentally egalitarian fashion, private sector interests could explore the use of a national lottery and/or auction with government cooperation.

A lottery would provide funds needed to work out the procedures for training and supporting nonprofessional space travellers. The purpose of an auction would be to determine at what price private trip services might be able to sell their initial tickets; the answer would significantly reduce the uncertainty about the initial market for space tourism, and thus improve the ability of commercial space travel companies to secure financing for private spaceships. The lottery and auction would be conducted only twice each, with a lottery and auction for Shuttle trips and again for combined Shuttle-Space Station trips. After these tests, space tourism would be conducted solely by private entities. It should be noted that the Department of State's Immigration and Naturalization Service now conducts an international visa lottery and the Federal Communications Commission (FCC) has auctioned off use of portions of the electromagnetic spectrum — interesting and encouraging precedents.

In general, the Space Shuttle is suitable for R&D purposes, modest initial "adventure travel" public uses, and fundamental educational and merchandising activities. While some additional R&D could be conducted on the International Space Station its capability should be augmented by a private sector tourist module. Access to these systems would be very helpful in the development of general public space travel and tourism businesses.

R&D programs are underway to reduce the unit cost of space access. For example, the NASA/Lockheed Martin X-33 technology development and demonstration project — a part of the Reusable

Launch Vehicle (RLV) program— is investing in both new technologies and operations approaches. This investment could enable the beginning of more businesses by driving the cost per ticket down to the order of $100,000 each. However, this level is still too high for the development of a truly "mass market". Perhaps a lower "loss leader" price could be charged for Shuttle and/or RLV trips with an acceptable overall profit being obtained by including that from trip-related surface business activities.

Through the Advanced Space Transportation (AST) program NASA is also pursuing the development of technologies which, eventually, could reduce ticket prices to under $50,000.

The program includes:

* Highly reusable engines and vehicles.
* Combination and/or combined cycle propulsion.
* Off-board energy for launch assist or elimination of most propellants.
* Advanced manufacturing, operations (including automation and robotics), and thrust augmentation systems (including upper stages).
* Advanced operations that enable further, dramatic, reductions in the number of ground and trip personnel.

The validation of these technologies should be pursued in future successors to the X-33 technology demonstration program.

Staying at an orbital residence for as little as a week would increase the cost of this kind of general public space travel and tourism significantly. Acceptable unit costs would require more advanced technology and operating concepts than those being used for the International Space Station, and the government should initiate R&D activities to lower such infrastructure costs.

Summary of Findings and Recommendations

The opening of the frontier of space — not just to government missions and astronauts, but now to private individuals and private sector businesses — is a space challenge of overarching importance. It is especially important for the democratic United States of America. This study should play an important role in beginning, in earnest, the process of United States government and business interests recognizing and overcoming the barriers to large-scale general public access to space in the early years of the next century. This fundamentally new human experience could be much closer to being realized than most people now imagine.

The following are the specific Findings and Recommendations of the study that are expected to help make this happen.

Findings

The NASA-STA study found that:

* Professional space tourism studies have been conducted in the United Kingdom, Germany and, especially, Japan. Japanese studies have included conceptual designs for vehicles that would carry large numbers of tourists.
* In a very real sense, "space tourism" already exists in the United States. It exists in the form of millions of visitors each year to space-oriented museums, to space launch/recovery sites and space research and development centres, to a space camp, and in space-related activities generally. And zero-gravity aircraft trips are becoming available.
* Polls consistently find that public interest in actually going to space continues to be large, real and widespread. However, very few realize that it is possible (given appropriate actions) that soon ordinary people, not just highly-trained and government-paid astronauts, could be able to take a space trip — as only a very few have since the beginning of the space age.
* Immediate steps can and should be taken to enlarge today's terrestrial space travel and tourism businesses. In addition, small scale enterprises may be able to get started using very near-term vehicles and/or technologies.
* For instance, two new companies have announced publicly that they are organized to provide space-related terrestrial and atmospheric trips and to position themselves to offer 100 kilometre altitude trips within 5 years; other companies are known to be considering offering similar space tourism services.
* Public communications and merchandising can make a significant difference in raising the level of this awareness.

High profile public figures and senior space-responsible Federal officials could play a very effective role in promotion and education campaigns relating to general public space travel and tourism.

* Economic return on investment could be sufficiently high to attract capital for large-scale ventures. But the initial problems to be solved focus upon creating profitable businesses that serve small markets at high prices. As business moves to do so are successful, and if major issues are satisfactorily addressed, then the creation of financially viable high volume-low price businesses could commence.
* As a result, general public space travel and tourism has the potential to emerge as a large and growing commercial business in the early decades of the next century. Our positive economic experience in the large and rapidly growing private sector satellite communications, navigation/position-fixing and remote sensing business areas should encourage this prospect.
* The cost of a Shuttle trip to/from orbit for a half-dozen people (and upwards of 40,000 pounds of cargo) now approximates $400 million, the individual Shuttle trip turnaround time is about a half-year, and the possibility of a fatal accident about 1%. These spaceflight characteristics can be reduced by roughly a factor of ten times with a next generation of technology, and roughly another factor of ten times in a following generation, i.e., following the pattern that underlies the success of commercial aviation.
* However, to enable the development of broadly-accessible, "mass markets" for public space travel and tourism, new, much lower-cost and much higher safety/reliability transport vehicles are needed, and relatively large-scale and continuing space industry and government programs will be needed to acquire them.
* The DOD-NASA DC-X/"Clipper Graham" technology development and maturation programs, and the ongoing cooperative private sector/Federal government X-33 and X-34 programs, are most encouraging steps forward.
* NASA's 1998 Strategic Plan (NASA Policy Directive (NPD-

1000-1000.1)) moves in the correct direction when it asks in its " Administrator's Strategic Outlook" section: "How can we enable revolutionary technological advances to provide... space travel for anyone, anytime...?"

* We must learn how to reduce, if not eliminate, general public passenger space sickness discomfort.
* Very many more rocket launches will heighten concern about launch site noise and atmospheric pollution, and heighten concern regarding space debris collisions. These concerns must be realistically addressed.
* And recent Mir experience emphasizes the need for space hotel fire detection and suppression characteristics among other safety enhancement needs.
* The $ multi-billion per year NASA and DoD space transportation market should be looked to, as well as the satellite communications market, in considering the required rapid and confident amortization of acquisition costs of new passenger-carrying vehicle-fleets.
* Limiting the in-space experience to the transportation vehicle is acceptable for initial business. In this vein, early suborbital trips should become initial stepping stones to later orbital flights.
* However, to enable large-scale market expansion, orbital residential facilities will be needed. The technologies being developed today represent a good starting point, but clearly more work is needed to reduce the cost of human habitation in space by a large factor.
* Regulatory, policy, legislative/statutory and insurance questions must be addressed with an eye toward balancing public safety with making higher risk adventure travel start-up businesses possible. These discussions should include several organizations within the government.
* Creation of the United Space Alliance to operate the Shuttle fleet, which should lead to the fleet's use for private as well as public use, is an important and positive institutional change. It could well become the precursor, in the human spaceflight area, of our aerospace industry looking, entrepreneurially, to

the private sector marketplace as well as the Federal government, for the large new human spaceflight business opportunities.

* Long distance, very high speed suborbital passenger and cargo transport prospects are also emerging, and would be enhanced by any conceptually related Defence vehicle and operations development programs. These could well furnish the earliest means for expansion into large-scale space travel.
* Both existing and new non-profit organizations outside the government could play important roles in enabling public space access to develop as a major new business activity.
* It should be appreciated by all civil space leaders that a large-scale private sector space travel and tourism business would strengthen the general public constituency for the conduct of civil space science and exploration activities, which otherwise will continue to be increasingly constrained by eroding general public financial support.
* It must be appreciated that widespread space tourism services will become available only as the marketplace is positively judged by our free enterprise business community, not our Federal government, and it should also be appreciated that the realization of a large general public travel and tourism business could take longer than otherwise if one or more of the following happen(s):

a. Another Challenger-like space accident involving loss of life;

b. A marked and prolonged turndown in our Country's economic circumstances;

and/or

c. Insufficient appreciation of the true economic dimension of the business by related aerospace, travel and tourism, and government interests.

Recommendations

In order to facilitate the development of a general public space travel and tourism business, the following steps are recommended:

* Our national space policy should be examined with an eye toward actively encouraging the creation of a large general public space travel and tourism business.

* In the near term, expansion of our terrestrial space travel and tourism businesses should be encouraged; theme and virtual reality space parks; space camps; training, production and launch recovery facilities; and other money-making "precursors" to in-space trips should be considered.
* Space industry companies, space-related financing and insurance interests, theme park developers, airline and cruise ship operators, hotel architects and operators, adventure tour operators,..., all should begin to inform themselves of general public space travel and tourism business prospects to determine their self interests therein.
* In pursuing these recommendations, it is now most important that a complete spectrum of people and businesses become engaged: financial, airline, cruise, hotel, terrestrial tourism and travel, and aerospace. Encouraging the involvement of small businesses and entrepreneurs is especially important.
* The assistance of existing and/or the creation of new not-for profit, non-government, organizations (such as a Space Travel and Tourism Association) should be sought to play a role in the needed communications efforts.
* The Aerospace Industries Association (AIA), the American Institute of Aeronautics and Astronautics (AIAA), the Institute of Electrical and Electronics Engineers (IEEE) and the Travel Industry Association of America (TIAA) should now begin to give increased business and professional attention to space travel and tourism.
* Universities that offer travel and tourism educational programs should now begin to consider terrestrial, in-atmosphere and in-space, trips and businesses.
* The Department of Commerce should focus upon coordinating general public space travel and tourism matters with those of the Departments of Transportation and Defence, NASA, and our presently evolving space travel and tourism businesses, so that the Federal civil space program will adequately encourage and support travel and tourism business interests. The Departments and NASA should also consider how to address this new and potentially large space business prospect.

* The Federal government's role should be that of cooperating closely with our private sector to reduce the latter's initial technological, operational and market risk, much as it has, with laudable success, in aviation, satellite communications and space remote sensing business development. It should:

a. As it does now for our private sector aviation interests, develop and demonstrate technology that would increase space trip safety, reliability and comfort, and decrease unit costs — all by factors of ten; learn how to deal with high rocket launch rate noise, atmospheric pollution and debris collision concerns; learn how to provide low cost human habilitation facilities in orbit; and learn how to ameliorate general public passenger space sickness discomfort;

b. Following on to the NASA Reduced Gravity Student Flight Opportunity Program precedent (in which college students performed experiments under microgravity conditions aboard a NASA KC-135 aircraft) allow the use of such public space assets as the Shuttle fleet and the U.S. portion of the International Space Station (augmented by a private module) to conduct general public tourist R&D and initial fundamental "demonstration" merchandising activities — much as it continues to do, effectively, for the satellite communications business area;

c. Use its own space transportation needs, costing $ multi-billions per year, imaginatively, as a market to assist the private sector to amortize, confidently, its large initial vehicle-fleet acquisition costs;

d. inform the general public about space travel and tourism possibilities; such communications should focus on the idea that ordinary people— not just astronauts — should be able to go on a space trip in the relatively near future as a result of government-private sector cooperation;

e. See senior Federal officials responsible for our civil and business space interests consider taking the lead in "opening up space to the general public" by taking trips to space themselves;

f. balance, prudently, between regulating for public safety and encouraging business success under novel operational circumstances; and

g. Cooperate in holding an annual General Public Space Travel and Tourism Conference.

* Government-sponsored R&D investments should specifically address:

  a. Driving the per flight costs of space transportation down by 10-100 times in order to allow lower trip prices to be charged, in particular by developing and maturing technologies — including particularly rocket engines — that would be needed for low cost and high safety, reliability and comfortable transport vehicles;
  b. Driving down the costs of longer duration visits to LEO dramatically, i.e., for human space habitation, by developing and maturing high safety, low cost and high reliability technologies;
  c. Demonstrating ways to reduce the effects of space sickness to levels acceptable to the general public;
  d. Assuring that high quality, high reliability, "human support" capabilities (such as emergency rescue and in-space health care) can become available; and
  e. Environmental concerns, generally.

* Our X-33 and X-34 cooperative space industry-NASA program leaders should give specific attention to the prospects of general public space travel and tourism, as should the private sector space transportation activities of such companies as AeroAstro, Boeing, Kelly Space, Kistler, Lockheed Martin, Pioneer Rocketplane, Rotary Rocket, Vela Technology, and others.
* Private sector interests should consider the possibility of using lotteries and/or auctions to see that early R&D and merchandising trips involving the general public, especially those that use public assets, are conducted in an egalitarian fashion and paid for with the private funds that it/they could provide.

4

Meeting the Needs of the New Millennium

Introduction: Need for Global Economic Development

The theme of the 2001 IAF Congress was "Meeting the Needs of the New Millennium", reflecting the fact that humans' most urgent need at the start of the 21st century is undoubtedly the continuation of economic growth. This is the only means by which the great majority of the world population can lift themselves out of the poverty in which they live.

The conventional definition of economic growth has been justly criticised. In order to be more useful it needs to be improved by including the preparation of national balance sheets and government accounts according to standard accounting principles, the use of factors to measure 'quality of life', the valuation of unpaid domestic and child-rearing work, accounting for environmental destruction, adjustment of market exchange rates to allow for 'purchasing power parity', and other improvements. New measures such as the "Genuine Progress Indicator" (GPI) are being developed, but they require further work before they can be relied upon.

Although economic measures may not yet be a satisfactorily precise definition of the standard of living, large-scale differences such as that between 'G7' countries with average incomes of about $20 000/yr and developing countries with average incomes of $1000 or less per year are undeniable. As a result of worldwide economic growth to date, more people live at higher standards of living than ever before; middle-class populations in many previously impoverished countries are growing rapidly; and average life spans have grown rapidly in every country in the world over the past two decades. However, this is not a cause for complacency since, thanks to unequal distribution of income and population growth, very large numbers of people still live in poverty.

The long-term effects of economic growth are impressive: in round figures, growth at 2 3% per year raises incomes by 100% in 25-35 yr, and by 1000% per century. Poorer countries growing at 7% per year can double their average incomes in just 10 yr, and grow by nearly 1000% in a single generation. However, achieving continuing economic growth in the world economy requires appropriate policies in both poorer and richer countries. Unfortunately, governments in both democratic and non-democratic countries are continually tempted to follow policies that hinder economic growth, as analysed in depth in recent decades in the field of 'Public Choice' economics. In particular, politicians in democratic countries can often win electoral popularity by implementing policies to 'protect' companies in difficulties. The economic effect of such policies is strongly negative: instead of flowing to new activities with good growth prospects, resources are wasted preserving economically incompetent companies that should be reorganized-thereby delaying needed restructuring of the economy.

This problem has been particularly notable in Japan where, during the 1990s, the government borrowed more than $1 trillion to support a large number of unprofitable companies. As a result there is substantial overcapacity in 'mature' industries such as construction, department stores, real estate, retail banking, car-making, steel-making, shipbuilding, distribution and others, while the number of new companies has declined substantially since 1990. Predictably, this has aggravated the recession caused by the bursting of the economic 'bubble' of the late 1980s to become the worst recession in 50 yr-with continuing deflation, shrinking of the economy and ever-rising unemployment. In order to understand what policies would be more effective in sustaining economic growth, it is useful to understand the pattern of global economic development.

Pattern of Global Economic Development

While there are many details that are the subjects of ongoing research, the large-scale pattern of business and economic development through the 20th century is not the subject of significant dispute. One of the most fundamental underlying trends is that as poorer countries develop economically they progressively 'take over' industries in which low labour costs are a significant advantage, and export their products to richer countries. Employment in these relatively low-productivity activities is thereby lost from the rich countries. In parallel, the familiar processes of automation and improving business practices continually reduce the number of employees needed to produce a given quantity of goods and services. However, these trends have not caused rising unemployment overall because the displaced employees are reemployed in new industries which are continually being created.

The process of global economic development is thus one of continuous change, involving the decline and failure of companies as well as the birth and growth of new ones. As a consequence, for most people it is not possible to improve their standard of living without accepting change in their working lives. In addition, the timing of economic booms and recessions depends on many factors including chance discoveries leading to innovation, the whims of entrepreneurs and the vagaries of political decisions. Although economic growth can be hindered by government policies, the underlying process cannot be stopped-at least not without preventing people from trying to improve their standard of living which is not desirable. In the simplest terms, some people use their heads to work out ways of achieving the same results with less effort. This human creativity, specifically in inventing machines improving business practices (including expanding trade), and developing new popular services makes the productivity of work grow continuously, decade after decade, enabling everyone's incomes and standards of living to rise progressively.

World economic growth also requires international flexibility and agreement on rules of 'fair play'. For example, the rapid economic growth achieved by Japan from the 1960s until the 1980s caused considerable trade friction with the then more advanced countries as it changed the pattern of global specialisation-even leading the French Prime Minister Cresson to describe Japan as "France's number one enemy". Thus Japan's rapid growth depended on the richer countries' willingness to make adjustments to facilitate it, which Japan in turn is now required to show towards later developing countries.

However, as a measure of how much more adjustment in the structure of the world economy is going to be required, note that the combined populations of India and China are 20 times the population of Japan, and their average wages are just a small percentage of Japanese wages today. Consequently the adjustments in the pattern of global specialisation that will be required to accommodate the growth in these countries' shares of world trade will be proportionately many times larger than was required for Japan. The recent rapid growth of exports of clothing from both countries, and of food products, light manufactured goods and motorcycles from China, and bicycles and software from India, is just the beginning of this long process of adjustment. In principle the growth of exports resulting from such differences in labour costs will not end until average incomes in these countries reach broadly the same level as in the richer countries. (The current loss of competitiveness of certain industries in Korea Taiwan and other southeast Asian countries, as their average incomes rise relative to those in China, are examples of this process.). For humanitarian reasons, as well as from the wish to reduce friction between richer and poorer countries, we must hope that poorer countries' economic development continues successfully. But, as an inescapable corollary, to the extent that these countries' participation in the world economy grows through the 21st century, proportionately greater innovation of new industries will be required in the currently more advanced countries. If this is insufficient, unemployment will increase very substantially, and/or average incomes will fall proportionately because of inexorable competition from countries with lower average incomes.

Overall, as the human effort needed to produce the same output of goods and services becomes less and less through technical and managerial progress, and unless humans generate more total output and consume more goods and services, the total amount of work needed will fall. In this case, unless the remaining work is shared out through shortening average working hours (and reducing wages proportionately), more and more people will become unemployed. During the 20th century demand did not reach such a limit; instead, although employment in many older industries shrank drastically in the richer countries, the continuation of economic growth was stimulated by the creation of new industries.

Creation of New Industries

During the 20th century, as the number of people in economically more advanced countries who worked in such fields as agriculture, horse-drawn transport, steam-engines, mining, textiles, clothing and many other traditional activities declined, a wide range of new industries arose which re-employs those displaced. These included car manufacturing and associated activities (such as oil production, refining and distribution and road construction and maintenance), electricity generation and distribution, the film, radio, television and video industries, aircraft manufacturing and operation and associated activities (such as airport construction and operation and air traffic management), telecommunications, computers, tourism and an ever-growing range of leisure industries, including many sports activities.

During the 20th century also, government activities expanded from <10% of GNP to some 40%-though this trend has more-or-less stopped or even begun to reverse in most countries with the recent moves towards privatisation. This new trend has been stimulated by work in the field of 'Public Choice' economics, which has provided the theoretical explanation for the fact that, in general, government activities are economically very inefficient, as outlined for instance in.

It is a sine qua non for continuing economic growth in the 21st century that the rich countries continue this process of creating new industries which will employ people displaced from older industries as they progressively automate and migrate to lower-cost countries. During the 20th century this process created high-productivity employment for hundreds of millions of people around the world, and enabled many more people in developing countries to gain employment in exporting and importing businesses, thereby facilitating their economic growth. It is a key desire of companies in poorer countries today to be allowed to increase their exports to richer countries, but these are restricted by international treaties designed to protect relatively uncompetitive activities in the richer countries, in order to reduce local unemployment. For example the governments of the USA and the EU subsidise the production of many agricultural products, thereby reducing the market for imports from cheaper countries, and they also subsidise the export of agricultural surpluses, providing a second blow to poorer countries' price-competitive agricultural industries. The G7 countries also limit clothing and textile imports from poorer countries.

The development of new industries has another important aspect, namely the 'leading sector' effect: as investors anticipate the future profits that they expect to be earned in new industries, market prices of relevant companies' shares rise. This attracts more investment to these companies, helping them to grow faster, while the 'wealth effect', whereby shareholders spend their new (anticipated) wealth, spreads the benefits of expansion to other sectors of the economy.

This process was seen particularly clearly in the late 1990s in the USA, when share prices of many companies related to the major innovations of the Internet and World Wide Web grew by hundreds and even thousands of percent. As shareholders became wealthy, at least 'on paper', they increased their spending on a wide range of goods and services including houses, cars, restaurants, travel and leisure, thereby greatly stimulating the general economy. Unfortunately, in this particular case, much of the rise in share prices of 'new economy' companies was distorted in an economic 'bubble' in which investors had become unrealistically optimistic. Consequently the companies in question did not achieve the high level of profits that stockbrokers' analysts were predicting, and their share prices have since fallen steeply to date, destroying several trillion dollars of the 'wealth' that had been anticipated. (Controversy continues over the relative blame attributable to failures of business ethics, stock-brokers' conflicts of interest, auditors' standards, market regulation, media reporting, economic policy and investor caution.)

Today the need for new industries is particularly urgent because of the serious imbalances in the world economy. These include the decade-long recession that has led to the highest unemployment in Japan for 50 years, with continuing deflation and negative economic 'growth'; continuing double-digit unemployment in much of continental Europe-as well as in Russia, Southeast Asia, South America and many other countries; and a deepening recession combined with an unsustainably high trade deficit and private indebtedness in the USA. The fundamental reason for this deflationary condition of the world economy is the excess capacity in many older industries and insufficient investment in the establishment and growth of profitable new industries, which alone can create new employment for those no longer needed in mature industries. The record US trade deficit of more than $1 billion per day, first reached during the 'Clinton bubble', is a measure of many US industries' lack of economic competitiveness: toys, clothing, electrical goods, steel, televisions, personal computers and mobile telephones are just some of the industries in which fewer and fewer US-based manufacturers can match global competition. The only way in which the currently richer countries can maintain higher average incomes than currently less-developed countries is through working with higher productivity: people earning higher incomes cannot compete with people using the same technology and know-how but working at significantly lower incomes. The solution to enabling those in already rich countries to maintain or increase their standards of living while also enabling poorer countries to grow rapidly, is for companies in G7 countries to work at newer activities that poorer countries cannot yet perform. The need for this was explicitly recognised in a 2001 article in the Washington Post: "What this country needs is a really good $500 billion technology-something to reignite popular enthusiasm and the economy".

What, then, are the new industries that are expected to generate new fields of large-scale high-productivity employment? It is important to note first that commentators' inability to predict future industries is no evidence that they will not arise: almost no-one in 1902 could even imagine, let alone predict, the rise of passenger air travel, nor a fortiori its growth to its current world-changing scale. Economic commentators today predict growth in employment in many areas of the information industry (although it is important to recognise that the growth of the Internet is also eliminating work in many related fields); in bio-technology, including the use of genetic information in agriculture and medicine; and in activities aimed at environmental preservation.

Many new opportunities could also arise through restructuring the incentives created by the government-imposed pattern of taxation and subsidies. For example, in many countries employment is heavily taxed and large companies are subsidised, while the use of non-renewable resources and environmentally damaging activities are lightly taxed or even subsidised. Reversing these undesirable distortions could increase the quantity of employment in many different fields, including particularly recycling activities. An important clue to the identity of other fields in which new jobs will arise in rich countries can be found in the 'Engel coefficient', which is defined as the proportion of peoples' income spent on food (although alternative definitions based on expenditure on 'necessities' are also used). The average Engel coefficient in any country falls progressively as it develops economically; in G7 countries it is now typically <25%. Further economic growth in such rich countries depends less on providing for consumers' real 'needs' and more on satisfying their 'wants'. Broadly speaking, this explains the relatively rapid growth of leisure-related industries. Although many people feel that there are more 'important' things in which to invest than leisure industries, once average productivity reaches the level in the G7 countries, most basic needs of the society can be satisfied by a fraction of the workforce-for example agriculture typically employs <5% of the workforce. Thus there is no longer enough 'essential' work to employ more than a fraction of the population in richer countries.

One problem that arises in low-Engel-coefficient societies is that the demand for non-essential goods and services is relatively unstable, since by definition their consumption can readily be cut if necessary. This inherent instability is seen clearly in the demand for tourist air travel which periodically falls sharply as a result of heightened concern about the risk of terrorism. Another example of this instability is that as the number of two-, three-and four-car families increases, sales of used cars can grow rapidly at times of recession, leading to dramatic falls in the demand for new cars.

The truth of the 'human condition' at the start of the 21st century is that economic development has progressed so far in the G7 countries that, if the average standard of living is to continue to rise, there is an urgent need for the growth of major new industries, most of which will probably be leisure services broadly defined. The reason for this is that in order for a new industry to grow to large scale it must provide services that will be purchased by a large proportion of the middle-class population-most of whom already possess most of the goods they 'need'.

Arguably the most significant industrial development of the 20th century was the development of passenger air travel from zero in 1900 to 1.5 billion passengers per year in 2000. Among other effects, this development has helped the hotel and restaurant industries to reach their present scale, employing some 60 million people or 3% of the world's total labour-force, and some 6% in Europe. As a pointer to the future growth potential, a survey performed in 2001 showed that the majority of middle-aged and older Japanese do not wish to purchase any more goods; the main service they wish to buy is foreign travel-which has notably been booming even during the current recession.

Until 2001 the aviation industry was predicting 100% growth over the next 20 years, although airlines' increased costs for security and customers' fears of terrorism may reduce this. However, it should be noted that tourism is already having damaging environmental impacts as a result of ever-growing numbers of tourists visiting popular destinations. It is not clear that this activity can reasonably grow by a factor of 1000% as would be necessary by the time-perhaps 2100?-when most of the world population attains a middle-class lifestyle which includes foreign travel.

Some commentators, mostly in the richer countries, take the view that most of those living in the presently poorer countries will remain poor forever. However, living standards are rising in every country, and the desire for material comfort is strong everywhere that living standards are low. While attaining a 'middle-class lifestyle' in the same form as seen today in G7 countries for a world population of perhaps 10 billion people would cause many industries-energy, construction, cars, agriculture, waste disposal-to degrade the environment severely, it must be anticipated that technological progress will greatly ease currently foreseeable problems.

The application of even only presently foreseeable advances in already existing fields-such as genetic engineering and hydroponics in agriculture, energy efficiency and non-fossil (solar) energy, city planning, and Internet-based tele-commuting, to name but a few-holds such clear promise that simple extrapolations based on multiplying existing economic activity by increased population numbers without allowing for technological improvements are unrealistically pessimistic. As a result it may be that the main limits to the potential for terrestrial economic growth are political ones. It is clearly in the self-interest of the already-rich countries to try harder to help overcome these in order to reduce the friction that would be inevitable in a globalized world with continuing gross inequalities in living standards.

Whatever the longer term future, assuming that economic growth will continue for at least a few more decades, the popularity of leisure travel in low-Engel-coefficient societies raises the question of what other newer destinations people could travel to. Tourist destination development is proceeding rapidly around the world, but a new possibility which has received ever-increasing attention is passenger travel to space, or 'space tourism'. It is now clear that this idea is not only not fantasy, but it is a promising candidate to grow into a major new activity as economically valuable and socially significant as passenger air travel.

Economic Potential of Passenger Space Travel

On the 'demand side' of passenger space travel, market research performed in Japan, Canada, the USA, Germany and the UK, and summarised in has shown that there is enormous pent-up consumer demand. It is sometimes suggested that this demand is fictitious; for example a recent letter to Aviation Week & Space Technology stated: "People were already travelling in the early days of aviation-by trains boat and car. They had a reason for travelling and infrastructure to support them when they reached their destination. The aeroplane became another mode of transportation. The reasons for travelling do not exist for space. No one is visiting relatives, emigrating nor going to business meetings. And there is no infrastructure in space".

However, it is a mistake to have preconceived ideas about people's reasons for wishing to travel to space, which are obviously different from reasons for travelling on Earth. The market research referred to above shows consistently that a large proportion of the middle class population of the richer countries does want to go to space, and that their major reason for wanting to do so is to be able to look back at the Earth. The fact that all of the 400 people who have been to space to date say that it was the greatest experience of their lives probably has some connection with this immense popularity. While there is a great need for more market research, and it will remain uncertain how many people will actually travel to space until the service becomes widely available, there is no justification for denying facts shown by market research.

Furthermore, contrary to what the above letter states, there is infrastructure to support travellers-a partly assembled space station which was sufficient for the first customer, Dennis Tito, to describe the Russian section as "paradise". The second piece of infrastructure for space travellers, Mir Corp's 'Mini-Station', is due to become operational for an investment of $100 million. And as launch costs fall to a few hundred dollars/kg as passenger traffic grows, it will be possible to assemble even very large accommodation facilities in orbit at a cost acceptable to hotel companies.

On the 'supply side' of passenger space travel technical studies by the Japanese Rocket Society (JRS), Dietrich Koelle, Ivan Bekey, Bristol Spaceplanes, Buzz Aldrin and others have shown that the cost of developing the required vehicles and infrastructure would be a small fraction of the $25 billion that G7 taxpayers already pay every year for government space activities. The great potential of passenger space travel for 'space commercialisation' has also been acknowledged in reports published by Nasa; the American Institute of Aeronautics and Astronautics (AIAA) which concluded: "In light of its great potential public space travel should be viewed as the next large new area of commercial space activity"; and the Japan Federation of Economic Organisations, among other organisations.

One particularly interesting conclusion of the Nasa report namely that "generally available trips to orbit and week-long stays in low Earth orbit hotels now can be seen as certainly feasible" gives a further indication of how large the economic impact of space tourism may become. This is because in all market research to date most people say they would like to spend several days or a week or more in orbit, rather than only a few hours or a day. Thus in addition to economical launch vehicles the demand for space tourism will also drive the construction and operation of accommodation in orbit-that is space hotels.

The only detailed professional study of the potential development of passenger space travel published to date is that of the Japanese Rocket Society (JRS) briefly reviewed in. (A large number of other papers from the pioneering JRS study are available in the library of the six major JRS reports published as of 2002 are available only in Japanese.) According to the JRS scenario, the number of customers would reach 700,000 per year 17 years after starting the development of the ' Kankoh-maru' passenger vehicle, with a return flight price of some $20,000 per passenger.

The JRS cost estimates are in line with those of Koelle and Bekey. Extrapolating from this, when the number of guests reaches one million per year after perhaps 20 years, there will need to be accommodation for more than 10,000 people in orbit, and several thousand staff will work in orbit. Since no one has identified any other space activity that offers anything approaching this level of demand, we reach a conclusion that is still not widely appreciated-the hotel industry will probably become the largest employer in space.

From the economic point of view it is very significant that the development of orbital accommodation will lead to the participation of a wide range of associated industries, thereby greatly expanding the number of different industries involved in space activities including particularly such consumer-oriented activities as construction, interior design, hotel management, catering, fashion, entertainment and sports. This will have the effect of bringing the economic energy of the consumer economy to bear on space activities, which are cutoff from this source of economic growth, except for certain information services.

In addition to stimulating innovation in these many different fields, the growth of space tourism in this way could also exert a 'leading sector' effect, whereby an expansionary economic influence will diffuse through the economy as direct investment and optimism lead to increased shareholder wealth. Furthermore, the increase in employment and economic growth which the development of passenger space travel causes directly in more advanced economies will in turn reduce the pressure for protection against imports from less developed economies. Such a scenario is strikingly different from the effect of existing governments' non-science space activities which, sadly, contribute very little to the economy or employment, despite the very large financial resources they consume.

Low Economic Value of Space Agencies' Activities

The desirability of initiating passenger space travel might be less if space agencies were engaged in work that was of great economic value or urgency-but they are not. Some 20% of their budgets are typically used for scientific research, including astronomy and Earth observation, which can be assumed to have value per se. However, the remaining 80%, some $20 billion per year, is used for the development of technological systems and technologies for such purposes as "space infrastructure development". The economic value of the results of this expenditure can be considered in two parts, direct and indirect.

Direct Economic Value

The definition of economic value is the present value of future profits to which an activity gives rise. Since space agencies' investment mostly does not lead to commercially profitable activities, it has far less economic value than normal business investment. The difference between commercial activities and space agencies' activities is shown in Figure 1. In round figures when a company invests $1 billion it typically generates commercial sales revenues of some $1 billion per year, from which the cumulative profits over several years exceed the initial investment by a sufficient margin to satisfy investors and increase the assets of the company. (For example, $1 billion investment might generate profits of $3 billion over 10 years, from which $2 billion would be repaid to investors, and $1 billion would add to the company's assets.) By contrast, the expenditure of some $20 billion per year by government space agencies on non-science activities generates little or no increase in commercial space activities: employment in space activities is currently shrinking, rather than growing cumulatively, as would result from commercial investment on this scale.

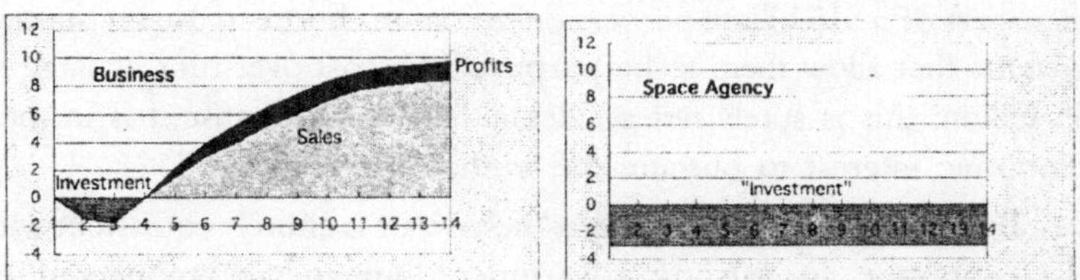

Figure 1. Contrast between Business and Space Agency Activities.

For example, the development and operation of expendable launch vehicle systems are heavily loss making; such launchers never repay their development costs, and depend in many cases on continuing government funding of periodic 'upgrades'. At the time of writing, the most recent of many articles describing the lack of demand for satellite launch services states that, of the three main launch vehicle manufacturers: "Arianespace, the only company that discloses its annual earnings, posted a loss in 2001 for the second straight year..." and predicts that because "the market could remain flat for the next 10-20 years..." one of the three companies may disappear in the anticipated 'shake-out'.

Following the conventional definition of economic value given above, the ' International Space Station' (ISS) project has very little economic value: almost no companies want to pay to use its facilities, and their total contribution will represent a small fraction of its running costs alone, let alone repaying taxpayers' investment of some $50 billion. The probability of researchers on board the station making a valuable scientific discovery must also be judged to be low: research in microgravity has been underway for more than 30 years, and there is little expectation of any major discoveries in the near term, particularly since the microgravity environment on board the station will be of low quality. This and the station's very high cost led many science research bodies, including the US National Science Foundation and the British

Science Research Council, not to support the project. In 2001, as the latest step in the ISS's ever-growing cost and ever-shrinking capabilities, Nasa's announcement of further 'cost growth' of $5 billion led to it becoming the subject of a special investigation by the US government's General Accounting Office. Upon the departure of its then administrator it was decided to appoint the deputy director of the Office of Management and Budget (OMB) as his replacement. (It is perhaps worth noting that accounting is not a mysterious activity. When the managers of a $15 billion per year organisation choose to use accounting systems that allow them to be 'surprised' by cost over-runs as large as $5 billion, this is surely not accidental-it is done because it is in their economic interest to obscure the truth.

In this, space agency managers' behaviour is entirely consistent with the economic analysis of government bureaucracy pioneered by Niskanen. Because of the incentives which a bureaucratic organisation creates for its staff, they are motivated primarily to increase their budget; they have no motivation "either to know or seek out the public interest or to act in the public interest". Until the 'crisis' of 2001, successive Nasa administrators' policy of having such inadequate accounting information was successful in preserving its budget; and it seems very unlikely that Nasa or its management will suffer any significant cost-certainly nothing approaching that experienced in commercial companies when their accounts are revealed to be untrustworthy, such as the 'carnage' among 'new economy' companies in the USA in 2001-2002.)

Indirect Economic Value

Advocates of larger budgets for government space agencies frequently argue that government spending on space is much more beneficial for the economy than other forms of economic activity, thanks to the useful inventions arising from the development of space-related technology. The original source of this idea was a study performed during the 1970s by Chase Econometrics, which claimed to find such an effect. In a recent citation members of the US Congressional Research Service in 1998 wrote: "Studies by Chase Econometrics Inc., and the Midwest Research Institute in the late 1980s determined that every Nasa R&D dollar produced $5-$9 in economic activity".

However, it is rarely reported that when Chase Econometrics tried to reproduce their work in 1980 they concluded that: "productivity changes from Nasa R&D spending proved not to be statistically different from zero". Hertzfeld studied the issue in detail and concluded: "due to theoretical and data problems with the macroeconomic model and data sets available, this approach to finding aggregate economic returns to R&D expenditure is difficult at best, and probably impossible". Other studies of particular technologies developed at Nasa which have subsequently been used in new products are said to have shown reasonable rates of return. However, such studies do not enable any conclusions to be drawn concerning the relative value of alternative innovations that would have arisen if the same funding had been applied in other fields, such as marine engineering, electrical engineering etc.

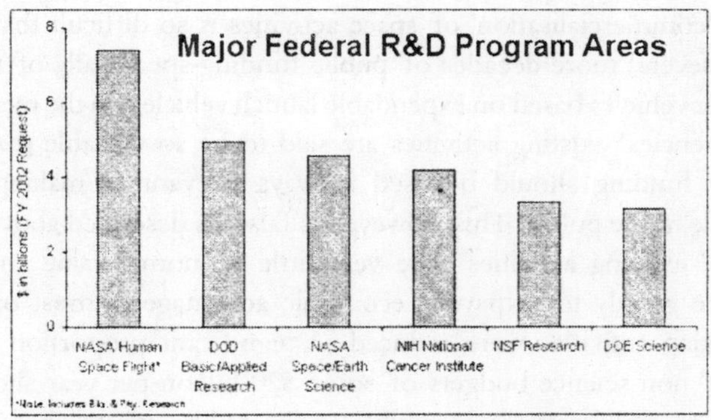

Table 1: Major U.S. Federal R&D Program Areas

In this context the bar chart presented to the US Congressional Science Committee by Sean O'Keefe, when Deputy Director of the OMB during 2001, is of interest. This shows that Nasa's budget of $15 billion per year is twice the combined research budgets of the US National Science Foundation (NSF) and the US National Cancer Institute (NCI). Since scientific research funded by these organisations has contributed to many of the Novel prizes and scientific advances which US researchers generate, the lack of Novel prizes or major technological advances arising from Nasa's work-let alone twice the annual output of the NSF and NCI combined-is striking.

Seen in this light, the claim that US government spending on Nasa projects (including the $5 billion cost-growth during 2001) is particularly valuable for the economy is not credible. It appears rather to be a convenient myth that serves the economic interests of the government-funded space industry. Much more credible is the 'common sense' view that Nasa's expenditure of more than $100 billion during administrator Goldin's 1992 2001 tenure, during which employment in the space industry grew not at all and passenger space travel was starved of research funding (as discussed below), was a serious misuse of economic resources which could have been used much more productively on other activities.

Economically Valuable Space Activities

Commercially profitable space activities today include communications, broadcasting and, on a much smaller scale, Earth observation, but little of the space agencies' $25 billion per year expenditure is justified by these activities. The agencies maintain that further 'commercialisation' of space activities is so difficult that it will require several more decades of public funding-specifically of the ISS and other vehicles based on expendable launch vehicles. In the meantime, space agencies' existing activities are said to be so valuable that none of their funding should be used in ways relevant to making space accessible to the public. This, however, is false: as described above space agencies' existing activities have very little economic value and so it would be greatly to taxpayers' economic advantage if most of these loss-making activities were reduced. A significant proportion of the agencies' non-science budgets of some $20 billion per year should be devoted to making space accessible to the public, which shows every prospect of becoming the most economically valuable activity in space.

In this context it is also worth noting space agencies' advocacy of a crewed mission to Mars as the centrepiece of future space activities. Such an activity could have scientific value, and some social value if it had wide and spontaneous popular support. However, it would have very little economic value, and if carried out before the development of low-cost launch vehicles, it would burden taxpayers with a cost of hundreds of billions of dollars while further delaying the commercial development of space. Space agencies' preference for such a project also fits Niskanen's analysis closely. It would be economically far more valuable to develop passenger space travel first; the low cost of access to space that this would bring about would greatly reduce the cost of all future activities such as Mars exploration.

Space Agencies' Anti-space Tourism Policy

In view of the low economic value of space agencies' current activities, it is very unsatisfactory that they are making no attempt to realise or even evaluate passenger space travel. In this the agencies do not simply show a lack of enthusiasm-they appear to have deliberately delayed progress towards this economically valuable objective, and even to have concealed valuable information from the public.

For example, the largest government space agency, Nasa, is required by US federal law to "encourage, to the maximum extent possible, the fullest commercial use of space". In its 1998 report, 'General Public Space Travel and Tourism', Nasa confirmed that space tourism is a realistic objective; that most people will be able to take a trip to space; that suborbital space travel (similar to that experienced by the first American to travel to space, Alan Shepard) is easily feasible using long-available technology; and that passenger space travel is likely to grow into a major commercial use of space. The report also included a long list of recommendations as to how to encourage this commercial use of space. However none of the recommendations in this report have been implemented, and no funding at all was allocated to advance the possibility-out of the $56 billion that Nasa has spent between that report's publication and time of writing. This behaviour is clearly contrary to Nasa's obligation to "encourage, to the maximum extent possible, the fullest commercial use of space".

It is worth noting that Nasa's 'space tourism report' can be judged the most economically valuable report Nasa has ever published, since it describes what is likely to become the largest commercial activity in space, and steps to realise it. It is therefore of particular interest that the then Nasa administrator Goldin refused to allow the report to be made available via Nasa's website for over 3 years. The author spoke to both Goldin in 1999 and then deputy associate administrator Graver in 2000 at public meetings at which they both stated (in recorded sessions) that NP-1998-03-11-MSFC would be put upon the Nasa website. However, this simple step did not take place until 2002.

Early in 2001 Nasa administrator Goldin attempted unsuccessfully to prevent the US citizen Dennis Tito visiting the international space station; his high-profile campaign was widely reported in the media. Yet the 80% popular support shown for Dennis Tito in US opinion polls provides a good indication of the great popularity of passenger travel and the misguidedness of Nasa's stance on this matter. Subsequent events during 2001 included the announcement that Goldin would not continue as Nasa administrator; testimony requested by the Subcommittee on Space and Aeronautics of the Congressional Science Committee from Nasa deputy associate administrator W. Michael Hawes on 26 June concerning Nasa's work relating to space tourism; and the appearance on Nasa's internet website of its space tourism report after over 3 years delay. Also during 2001 newly appointed Nasa Chief of Staff Courtney Stand drafted a plan for the agency under which it was proposed that Nasa would "provide commercial projects with engineering support for private-sector development of commercial manned spaceflight vehicles for commercial space tourism". (It is perhaps worth noting that the main supporter of space tourism in the US government today is the associate administrator for Commercial Space Transportation in the FAA. As the first head of the then Office of Commercial Space Transportation within the Department of Transportation Stand could be expected to take a more commercial approach.)

The selection of Nasa during 2001 as the fourth-worst-managed activity within the US government, and the recently initiated probe into its extraordinary mismanagement of the ISS project provide further testimony to the very poor value-for-money that US taxpayers receive in return for $15 billion per year-over and above Nasa's deliberate delaying of the development of passenger space travel services. The growing political disenchantment with this behaviour is reflected in the recent comment that "space spending is moving from the back burner to completely off the stove".

Other Countries' Activities

Other countries' government space agencies also have responsibility for commercialisation of space activities, but they take a similar stance towards passenger space travel. For example the European Space Agency (Esa) joined Nasa's unsuccessful attempt to prevent Dennis Tito visiting the international space station, and has likewise provided almost no funding whatsoever for research on the economic potential of passenger space travel. The senior staff of Esa and their political paymasters do not want to know about the commercial potential of passenger space travel, any more than their counterparts in Nasa and the US Congress, exactly as Niskanen's work describes.

Uniquely among G7 countries' space agencies, the British National Space Centre (BNSC) invests in neither expendable launch vehicles (such as the European Ariane) nor the international space station, since it is required to focus on space science research and activities with potential to be commercialised. However, in 2000 it was criticised by the UK Parliamentary Trade and Industry Committee for investing some 1 billion Sterling over the past decade in remote sensing systems that have generated far less commercial revenue than planned, and for actively discouraging any British government investment in research aimed at realising passenger space travel. The BNSC staff responsible for this stance, Director-General Colin Hicks, Deputy Director-General David Leadbeater and Director of Policy and Finance Alan Cooper, ignored the Committee's suggestion to perform some analysis of its feasibility. They have still provided no justification for their decade-long prevention of funding of work towards passenger space travel-which is clearly contrary to the BNSC's stated objective "to help industry maximise profitable space-based business opportunities".

Space agencies' negative behaviour towards the largest commercial opportunity in space can be termed a 'Conspiracy of Silence'. The economic reasons for their acting so strongly against the public interest in this matter are discussed in, and some of the 'cultural' reasons why the heads of space agencies unanimously refuse to permit any work to facilitate passenger space travel are discussed in the appendix to. Because of government space agencies' organisational structure making them responsible for commercialisation presents a conflict of interest with their own economic interest in survival and expansion, since it would mean handing over some of their operations to private companies.

They resolve this conflict, predictably, in their own interests by suppressing the most promising commercial application, which is ipso facto also the most threatening to their own interests. Nasa, Esa and other countries' national space agencies also exert a strong influence on the news media, being a near-monopoly source of information about space activities. This has helped to delay, though not to prevent, the growth of interest in passenger space travel in the mass media.

By contrast, Russian companies have now already profitably carried two space tourists to orbit, and are currently planning an orbiting 'mini-station' for tourism accommodation at a cost of $100 million.

This is particularly noteworthy since, at the time of writing, Nasa's mobile exhibition 'Starship 2040' is publicising the idea of a small module being feasible for space tourism in 2040. 'Starship' is smaller than the first US space station 'Skylab' that operated 70 years before this date. Together with the suppression of the 1998 Nasa space tourism report until July 2001, this can only be seen as deliberate 'disinformation' designed to mislead the US public, media, government and others about the potential for space tourism. In view of the potential for passenger space travel described above, it is clearly greatly against the public interest that space agencies are knowingly resisting progress in these ways in favour of continuing their existing activities despite their low economic value.

Future Scale of Space Tourism Industry

As discussed above, meeting the needs of the new Millenniums, or at least of the early 21st century, requires the development of major new industries in the more advanced countries. Failure in this would lead to a further rise in the already high levels of unemployment worldwide, with corresponding undesirable social effects. In view of this need for new industries to facilitate continuing global economic growth, it is interesting to consider how large a scale passenger space travel might eventually reach and how much it might ultimately contribute to world economic growth.

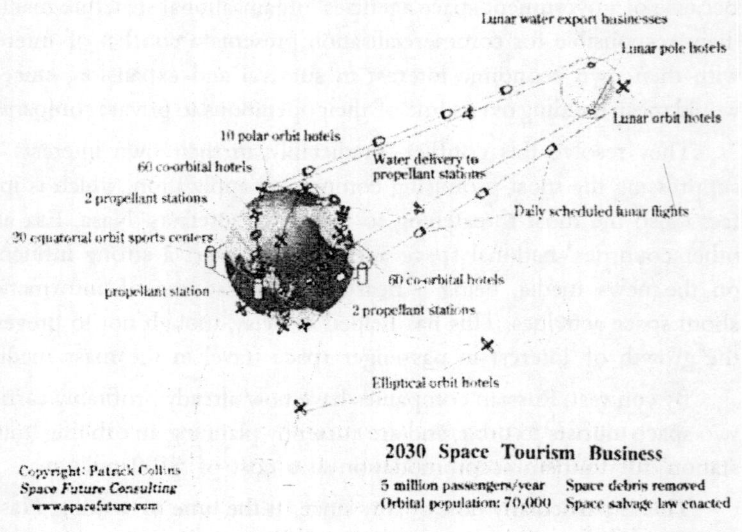

Figure 2: Feasible Space Tourism Scenario

As described above, the unique potential of passenger space travel was acknowledged by Nasa, the AIAA and the Keidanren as long ago as 1998. Since none of these organisations has made any further attempt to investigate or assess the scale of this opportunity during the four years since these reports were published (during which time government space agencies have spent a further $100 billion on economically unprofitable activities), the author outlines a simple estimate in this section.

Although some critics have claimed that space tourism will be no more than a pastime of the very rich, the basic scenario of the Japanese Rocket Society is aimed firmly at serving the middle-class market, and leads to some 700,000 passengers paying a little more than $20,000 each for return flights to orbit in the 17th year. Further growth to reach, say, 5 million passengers in the 30th year as discussed in would require an annual growth rate of some 16% which is not unrealistic by comparison with growth rates seen in other popular services. This would give a scenario like that shown in Figure 2.

Several comments are worth making about this figure.

(1) On this scenario, some 40 million people would have visited space by 2030, that is perhaps 2% of the middle class of that time-yet market research has shown that most middle class people (that is, more than 50%) would like to make a 'space trip'. Consequently this scenario certainly does not seem over-optimistic in relation to the potential market.

(2) The cost to taxpayers to realise this scenario would be far less than the $750 billion that they would have to pay through 2030 for space agency activities on their existing budgets, since most of the investment would come from the private sector. The economic value of the scenario, based on the difference in expected profits, would be about $1 trillion higher.

(3) Several million people would be directly and indirectly employed in related activities, and tens of thousands of people would work part-time in space as hotel staff.

(4) Such a scenario makes some people uneasy as they think that leisure industries are not 'important', and that people should be doing more 'serious' work, like making machines or buildings. But, as described above, the G7 countries have made such

> progress that producing necessities does not keep many people busy: a smaller and smaller proportion of the population can produce all that is needed, and a growing proportion work to provide services that are 'wants' rather than true 'needs'. The growth of service industries in turn creates demand for manufactured products-as the demand for tourist air travel creates a massive market for the aerospace manufacturing industry. Thus the growth of passenger space travel as shown would stimulate a genuine 'renaissance' of the space industry, after the post-cold-war period of stagnation and shrinkage.

In addition to its economic value as a popular consumer service, making space travel available to the general public would have great social value. Thanks to its well-known inspiring and educational value it would seem highly desirable in comparison with many other 'unnecessary' activities that are proliferating in rich countries, such as the use of recreational but often addictive drugs, gambling and pornography, to mention a few.

For some years there has also been talk of a "crisis in aerospace" because of the sustained decline in interest among young people in working in the industry. The author's proposal that the development of passenger space travel would also resolve this problem by putting work in space engineering at the forefront of a popular new industry was published as a 2001 editorial in Aviation Week & Space Technology.

For simplicity, if it is assumed that the progressive fall in service price thanks to increasing scale of operation is balanced by growth in demand for more expensive services, average expenditure of $20,000 per passenger would give a turnover of some $100 billion in 2030. How much further passenger space travel services might grow depends on many factors; however it does not seem likely to be limited by a lack of demand in the foreseeable future.

In addition to the great popularity of the activity itself, there is enormous scope for provision of even more interesting experiences in space with the development of progressively more advanced hotels, orbiting sports centres, lunar hotels and other facilities, as discussed in the references in. As an example, growth of 8% per year after 2030 would lead to a turnover of $1 trillion per year in 2060, that is some 50 million passengers per year (less than two weeks' of air travel passengers today). As a different way of looking at the potential, a rough estimate of the potential cumulative market.

Cumulative revenue of $40 trillion is equivalent to some 2 billion people travelling to space once each. Although this may seem a large number, we note again that aviation has already reached 1.5 billion passengers-i.e. equivalent to one quarter of the world population every year. Criticism of this suggestion by staff from government space agencies, by those indirectly funded by space agencies or by others in such terms as that it is "unconvincing" or "pure guesswork" could of course be readily answered if agencies were to devote even as little as 1/10 000 of their annual budgets to study the possibility.

It is also interesting to consider how a correct prediction made in 1902 about the future scale of passenger air travel during the following century might have been received, at a time when the main form of transport was still horse-carriage, and no one had even flown in an aeroplane. Talk of "millions of passengers per day" and "one billion passengers per year" would surely have been dismissed not as "guesswork" but as sheer madness. Yet, by contrast to the non-existence of aviation in 1902, crewed space travel has been under way in 2002 for more than 40 years already, making the projection of future passenger space travel services-based on known technology and market research data-far less uncertain.

The low cost of access to space that would be brought about by such large-scale space tourism would also lead to other forms of economic development in space which are not possible at present high launch costs. Many writers of both fiction and non-fiction have described futures in which human activities spread far beyond Earth-a genuine 'Space Age'. The fundamental reasons why this has not happened yet are because the cost of access to space is too high, and there is very little demand for the services utilising space that are currently being offered. By bringing costs down by providing services for which there is known to be a very large consumer demand, space tourism uniquely offers the promise of realising these long-term possibilities. Even if the possibility of realising this scenario was estimated to be only 1%, space agencies should still be investing tens of millions of dollars/year to investigate it. The fact that they devote nothing to this work is proof that they are not trying to maximise the growth of commercial space activities, despite their legal responsibility to do so.

'Opening the space frontier' is a phrase used in the literature published by government space agencies-but despite spending $25 billion per year they offer taxpayers no such prospect. The research-oriented activities funded by government space agencies are of little value for commercialisation, which is the key to enabling space activities to contribute to economic growth. The fact that the development of consumer-oriented commercial services in space is likely to be far more effective than government 'space development' activities at bringing about economic development in space should not be surprising-and it should be particularly obvious to economic policy makers.

Imperative for Economic Policy

Space activities generally receive little or no attention from economic policy makers for a number of reasons: they are very small-scale by comparison with commercial industries; they are largely government-funded; and they show little prospect of significant growth-at least according to government space agencies' forecasts. In truth, economists should know better than to rely on the views of government monopoly organisations concerning either costs or future prospects, since they have a well-understood tendency to have excessively high costs, to avoid risks, and to resist innovation, in pursuit of their own economic interests. However, although these problems of government organisations are well-known within both business and the economics profession, it is easy for government organisations that use large budgets for public relations to appear impressive and authoritative to non-specialist members of the public, including many journalists and politicians. And it is notable that both journalists and politicians-and indeed most of the general public-tend to accept the statements of space agencies as definitive even in matters of cost.

Sadly, government space agencies have avoided proposing that space activities could have economic value commensurate with their costs. On the contrary, the way in which they are structured and funded gives them a strong economic interest in exaggerating the difficulty of space activities, playing down future prospects, avoiding risks, and minimising the public's expectations by such means as ignoring proposals for passenger space travel, in line with Niskanen's description. Before being appointed Nasa Administrator, O'Keefe himself drew attention to the unsatisfactory form of many of Nasa's stated objectives, such as to "chart our destiny in the solar system" which do not allow the measurement of success or failure. In this way, by reducing the likelihood that they will receive criticism for having 'failed' in their work, space agencies thereby maximise the likelihood of continuing to receive funding.

To date, government space agencies have spent some $1 trillion of taxpayers' money. But whereas commercial investment on that scale would have created businesses earning revenues of some $1 trillion per year, commercial space activities today are roughly one 50th of this. Even allowing for the fact that 10-20% of this funding is for scientific research, and perhaps $1/2 trillion spent in the early decades was explicitly for political purposes, the return on investment is still < 10% of what commercial activities would achieve. If space agencies were genuinely motivated to achieve economic benefit for taxpayers, then in view of this extremely poor economic performance they would be urgently investigating potentially promising new commercial opportunities. Since passenger space travel is recognised to have the potential to grow into a major new service industry similar to passenger air travel space agencies' unanimous refusal to investigate it, despite being required by law to promote commercial space activities, shows that space agency leaders do not want to know about the potential of passenger space travel, and moreover that they do not want the public to know about it either.

In view of space agencies' economic interest in maintaining government funding of their existing activities, it seems likely that they will continue to refuse to do anything to help the development of passenger space travel until they are compelled to do so. Unfortunately the interests of the politicians who control their budgets are very similar to those of the agencies themselves, as Niskanen explains. Consequently reform will require intervention from outside existing arrangements, which will take time.

From the economic point of view, a particularly damaging effect of the present situation is that, until such change occurs, it will remain very difficult for private companies to raise funding to develop passenger space travel services. Major aerospace companies are 'captives' of space agencies, in the sense that they cannot do any independent work that might jeopardise their chances of continuing to receive large, low-risk contracts from them, while small companies lack the credibility to raise the funding they need in financial markets, since financiers tend to accept the 'conventional wisdom' about space which comes from government space agencies. This problem has been documented in such cases as Beal Aerospace Inc. Stopping their project to develop a low-cost satellite launch vehicle in 2001 because of competition from Nasa, and difficulties caused for other companies trying to raise funding for similar projects by public comments from space agencies.

Macroeconomic Viewpoint

From the macroeconomic point of view, in the absence of detailed analyses demonstrating errors in the Nasa report and similar published work, it is clearly desirable that passenger space travel services should be developed as soon as possible. This is because in 2002 the major blocs of the global economy are sinking into recession simultaneously, and the severe overcapacity in many older industries, combined with a serious lack of profitable new industries creates a real risk of a prolonged depression.

Historians and economic policy makers must not forget that the slide towards the second world war gathered pace through the depression of the 1930s when unemployment reached 20% in many countries. If current high levels of unemployment rise even higher in the coming years, they may lead to dangerous impatience in many regions of the world. It is already clear that in some of the poorest countries religious extremism can seem attractive by comparison with a life of impoverished unemployment, from which escape is hampered by G7 countries' protectionist trade barriers against their cheap exports. These trade barriers are motivated by the high unemployment in richer countries caused by the lack of new industries (as discussed above).

It would be economically beneficial to taxpayers if economic policy makers insist that our accumulated space engineering capabilities be used for activities with greater economic value than government space agencies' current unprofitable ones. As they operate today, instead of contributing to economic growth, government space activities are a hindrance to it-by using $20 billion per year of taxpayers' funds on activities which have an annual rate of return close to minus 100%; by indirectly preventing companies from developing lower-cost launch vehicles; and by deliberately hindering the growth of the activity which they have themselves confirmed is the most economically promising use of space-passenger space travel.

As described above, if present budgets continued and passenger space travel services were not developed as proposed in Figure 2 above, the net loss to taxpayers from continuing the present pattern of government space activities for several more decades would be around $1 trillion. This would be a terrible miscalculation of economic resources-particularly at a time of inadequate economic growth-and the quicker it is remedied by prioritising the development of passenger space travel the more the space industry will contribute to world economic growth, and thereby to 'Meeting the Needs of the New Millennium'. In addition to this economic cost, there would also be an incalculable human cost: in unnecessarily prolonging the poverty of hundreds of millions of people in late-developing countries; in postponing the development of an exciting new goal for the young in the currently richer countries; and in aggravating the risk of global conflicts through high unemployment. If government space agencies were genuinely trying to "encourage, to the maximum extent possible, the fullest commercial use of space" they would obviously investigate this potentially major new business opportunity in depth. But instead, they are currently suppressing discussion of this possibility by refusing to provide even the smallest funding to study it, despite having endorsed it in print. Economic policy makers should act to correct this serious policy failure as soon as possible.

Another cost of this policy of deliberate neglect is that it ensures that there will inevitably be a further delay before passenger space travel grows to a large scale. Although it seems possible that passenger space travel could grow to reach a scale of $1 trillion per year later in the 21st century, turnover during the next 10 years will clearly be limited, and even with vigorous growth it seems unlikely to be measured in more than tens of billions of dollars by the 2020s.

How best to stimulate the development of passenger space travel services is a separate question, which has been discussed elsewhere. Some preliminary actions can be simply described: following the first recommendation in senior staff of space agencies should speak formally, positively and often about the economic importance and social value of developing a vigorous, commercial passenger space travel industry; they should also establish well-resourced offices tasked with encouraging the development of passenger space travel; and they should collaborate closely with the aviation industry in realising this goal. The latter action will require significant restructuring since government space activities have little relevant contact with aviation. Yet the vast experience of the airline industry is essential to realising passenger space travel.

To the extent that space agencies do not participate effectively in implementing these and other economically beneficial changes to their existing activities, taxpayers will benefit economically if space agencies' budgets are cut-both directly by making large savings in subsidies to high-cost activities with little economic value, and indirectly by reducing misinformation about the potential for space commercialisation in general and passenger space travel in particular.

The chapter has described the potential economic benefits from developing passenger space travel services, which could contribute greatly to the continuation of peaceful world economic growth. By contrast, the vision of the future offered by government space agencies, based on continuing government domination of space activities centred on a crewed mission to Mars, is tragically narrow-minded and would merely preserve space agencies' near-monopoly status rather than contribute to economic growth. In view of the potential economic importance of passenger space travel in creating a major new field for economic expansion it is most unfortunate that little progress is being made today in developing this promising new consumer service industry, mainly because governments spend some $20 billion per year on a range of unprofitable 'space development' activities and nothing at all on work that would help to realise passenger travel. Claims by space agency leaders that they are fulfilling their legal responsibility to encourage space commercialisation are disingenuous at best.

The sooner that policies are implemented to accelerate the development of passenger space travel, the sooner the space industry will be able to claim honestly that it is contributing to meeting the needs of the 21st century-rather than holding back world economic growth by suppressing a new field with great business potential. For government space agencies and the politicians responsible for their budgets to continue to remain silent concerning their potential contribution in this area at a time of growing economic difficulty worldwide would be a shamefully wasted opportunity.

It is highly desirable that economic policy makers should be informed of the opportunity for economic growth that is being wasted by government space agencies. They will then be in a position to implement policies to bring about the attractive future shown in Figure 2, thereby creating a wealth of new business opportunities for the innovative leaders who are so sadly lacking in space agencies.

Demand for Space Tourism in America and Japan

In considering the feasibility of space tourism, assessing the potential market is very important in providing information on the potential scale of the demand at different service prices. North America is the largest single consumer market in the world, and consequently data on the potential demand for space tourism services in the USA and Canada is of great interest.

In 1993, the first market research on demand for space tourism was carried out in Japan, supported by the National Aerospace Laboratory (NAL). That survey of 3030 Japanese people across all age groups revealed a surprisingly strong popular wish to visit space: more than 70% of those under 60 years old, and more than 80% of those under 40 years old stated that they would like to visit space at least once in their lifetime. Furthermore, some 70% of these said that they were prepared to pay up to three monthly salary for such a trip. Despite the fact that the authors of the Japanese survey urged other countries to do similar research, no US survey was performed in the following two years. Consequently, NAL took steps to have a comparable survey carried out in the USA and Canada during August and September 1995. Although estimates have been published before, this is the first actual market research of its type to be conducted in America. The results illustrate that interest in travelling to space is also very high among North Americans, Overall, 60% of the people surveyed were interested in travelling to space for a vacation.

These results have significant implications for the future of space activities in that the resulting estimates of the potential size of the civilian space travel market far exceed estimates for any other commercial space market. As a consequence, many of the current vehicle designs for future space transportation systems may need significant design adjustments

Market Research Procedure

The market research was carried out by means of a telephone poll of 1020 households selected quasi-randomly across the USA and Canada.

For purposes of comparison between this study and the study conducted in Japan in 1993, the telephone questionnaire was modelled as closely on the written questionnaire used in Japan as possible, considering translation and cultural differences. It was expected that consumers opinions would be influenced somewhat by the different surveying procedure, and this point is considered further in the discussion on the international comparison of data below. Like the earlier surveys, there are a number of uncertainties that must be kept in mind concerning the interpretation of the results of this study. These points and others are discussed at some length in an earlier paper.

The Sample

The sample taken was designed to represent all those individuals in both the US and Canada who have access to a telephone and are between the ages of 20 and 50. At the time the sample was taken, this represented a potential market of approximately 170 million people based on almost universal telephone ownership in North America. The sample of 1020 respondents was divided up among the geographic regions of the two countries based on the population distribution of the states and provinces. The respondents were sampled by randomly selecting telephone numbers from the white page phone listings of each region. A constant digit was then added to the selected phone number. By using this method, all individuals with access to a telephone, including those not listed in the telephone book, became a part of the sample. In total, almost 5500 calls were placed to complete the survey. 80% percent of the numbers dialled were registered phone numbers, and 45% of those were answered by a person. The response rate for being interviewed was high in terms of standard telephone marketing research, with 52% of the calls connected to a potential respondent completed. It is important to note here that the respondents were not informed of the subject of the interview until after they agreed to participate in the survey. In this way, no bias was made towards interviewing only those who were interested in completing surveys relating to space travel or the like.

Sampling and Non-sampling Error

Due to various constraints, the authors believe a small amount of sampling error exists in the survey data. First of all, error was introduced in the sample by interviewing the first person who answered the telephone on each call. Although, in many cases, the person who answered chose to pass the call on to another, in the majority of cases the initial respondent completed the survey. An example of the error that can be introduced by doing this is that, in western households, women are statistically more likely to answer the phone than their male counterparts. In order to produce a sample that better represents the population, one needs to select a respondent randomly from all the individuals who reside in each household. This can be accomplished, for example, by asking to interview the person in the house with the next birthday. This procedure or others like it, however, considerably complicate the survey procedure and increase the time needed to take the sample. A comparison of the sample taken in this study with national statistics of gender and age shows very little difference in composition, and therefore this type of sampling error is considered small. Further details concerning the representativeness of the sample are discussed later in the paper.

The largest source of sampling error in a telephone survey can usually be attributed to non-response. This arises because many people are not at home when called (54% of the numbers dialled), and many individuals (48% of those contacted) choose not to participate in the survey. This survey was administered during selected periods of time during the week: Monday-Friday from 5 pm to 9 pm, and on Saturday from 11 am to 7 pm. These set time-frames were chosen to reduce non-response due to refusals, and to increase the likelihood that more people in each household would be at home to answer the phone. It is recognized however, that calling during specific time periods can exclude certain portions of the population who may be doing shift-work, or certain age-groups who may not typically be at home during these time-periods. Calling on Saturdays and also on the Labour Day holiday may have helped to reduce this error. Possible ways to determine if biasing is present include making call-backs to numbers where there was no answer, and interviewing individuals who refuse to do the survey on their first option by coaxing them with some type of reward. These measures however, were considered unnecessary in this case because of the nature of the survey. All in all, it is very unlikely that significant error has been introduced into the data with the sampling method used.

Non-sampling error for this study is considered to be very small since the interviewing sessions were conducted in a highly controlled manner. The use of computer programs to dictate the survey text so that each participant received exactly the same information, as well as to collect, process, and analyse the data, decreased the possibility of error being introduced in these processes to a minimum.

The Survey

The survey consisted of 17 questions and took approximately four minutes to complete. Respondents who were not interested in travelling to space had a much shorter survey to answer that took only half the time. The first section of the survey collected basic personal information on the respondent, as well as information concerning interests and travelling preferences. The second half of the survey began with the following space tourism concept statement: ýÿConsider for the moment that it is possible to travel to space as a potential vacation alternative. Imagine that people are able to go to there using a means of transportation similar to a planed The respondent was then asked would you be interested in travelling to space-yes or noway If the respondent answered no, they were queried as to why. If they responded yes, the survey continued with more specific questions concerning a space trip. Several open-ended questions in the survey stimulated many interesting opinions and comments from the respondents, which suggests that many people have given considerable thought to the idea of travelling to space for themselves. In the future, a more detailed analysis of the results of this survey will be published, and those comments will be given further attention. For the present, the following paragraphs briefly describe the studious main findings.

Survey Results

Table 1 shows the overall distribution of the survey participants by age and gender, and compares them to the US population as a whole. (Adding the figure in the variant column to the corresponding age group yields the percentage of that group in the overall US population, census data-1990. It has been assumed that the Canadian population distribution is similar.) The distribution by age matches the overall population very closely; none of the five age groups considered is over- or under-represented by more than 2.2%, confirming the representativeness of the sample in this respect. The distribution by gender, however, is significantly different, with women over-represented and men under-represented by 6.3%. In the following, wherever necessary, the figures are adjusted to compensate for this.

Gender	Male	Female	Total	Male Var	Female Var	Total Var
20's	11.4%	13.8%	25.2%	0.6%	-2.1%	-1.5%
30's	10.5%	12.5%	23.0%	1.7%	-0.2%	1.5%
40's	7.4%	11.6%	18.9%	1.7%	-2.2%	-0.4%
50's	5.7%	8.2%	13.9%	0.5%	-1.6%	-1.1%
Over60	7.2%	11.8%	18.9%	1.8%	-0.3%	1.5%
Totals	42.1%	57.9%	100.0%			

Table 1: Breakdown of surveyed respondents with comparison to the US population

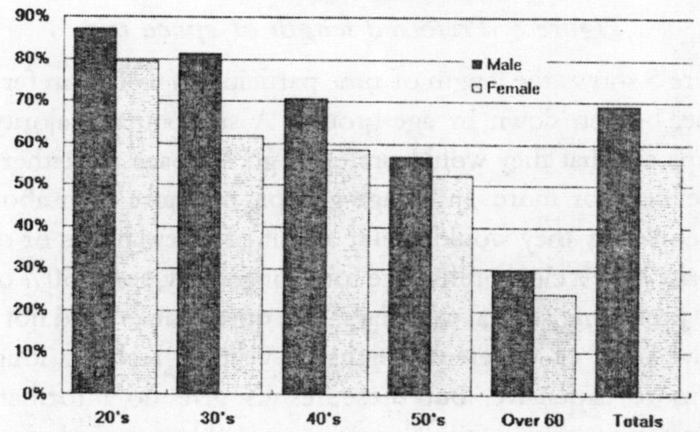

Figure 4: Percentage of respondents interested in travelling to space

Figure 4 shows the basic level of interest in travelling to space, broken down by age and gender. As an overall average, more than 60% of the population say they are interested, with a higher proportion of younger people being interested, as one might expect. The overall average figure is comprised of more than 75% of those under 40 years old; 60% of those between 40 and 60; and more than 25% of those between 60 and 80.

It is notable that in every age group men were more interested than women, the average difference being about 10%. This is rather different from the results of the survey in Japan, where no significant difference was found. This may be due to the fact that many US astronauts are military staff, whereas all the Japanese who have visited space are civilians.

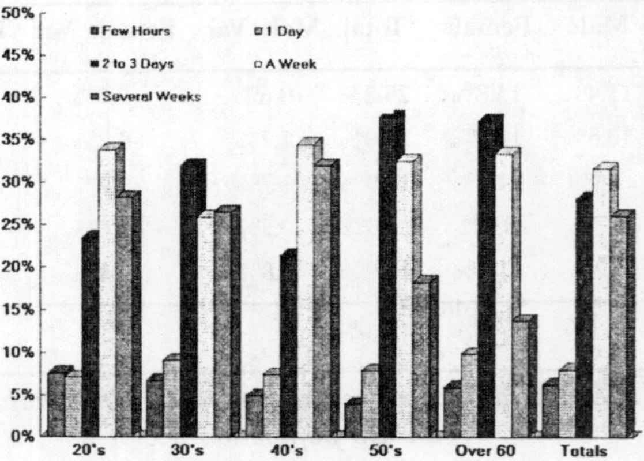

Figure 5. Preferred length of space trip

Figure 5 shows the length of time participants would prefer a space trip to be, broken down by age groups. A substantial majority of all age-groups say that they would prefer to go to space for either several days, one week or more. In all age-groups, no more than about 15% of the people say they would prefer a visit of a few hours or one day; the majority have a clear preference for a longer stay, some 30% of those under 50 preferring several weekdays. The questionnaire did not discuss the relative price of different lengths of visit. In reality, a longer stay will be more expensive, but these results give no information on participants price-sensitivity. It seems reasonable to conclude that, in the absence of orbital accommodation enabling people to stay for a few days, the demand for space tourism will not reach its full potential.

Figure 6 displays the amount that respondents interested in travelling to space would be prepared to pay for a trip, expressed in months of salary. The first point to note is that there is little difference between the various age groups on this variable. At the upper end of the range, it is interesting that 2.7% of those wishing to visit space (representing almost 3 million people) say that they would pay three hearsay salary. Clearly for these people travelling to space is a very strong desire.

10.6% (representing 11 million people) say they would pay one year's salary, which is still a very substantial expense. 18.2% of participants (representing 19 million people) say they would pay 6 months salary, and 45.6% (representing 48 million people) say they would pay 3 months salary.

In further analysis of the data, average income statistics for different age-groups will be used to derive a demand curve and study market segmentation for the North American market. For the present we simply note that the overall average income for North Americans is approximately $2,000 per month, or $12,000 for six months salary, and $24,000 for a year. In addition, two thirds of those wishing to visit space said that they would like to do so several times, not once only. Consequently, even allowing for a substantial gap between consumerism intentions and their actions, space travel could clearly become a $multi-billion per year market in America alone. 10% of the above estimate is still more than $60 billion in funds that people say they are willing to spend on a space trip.

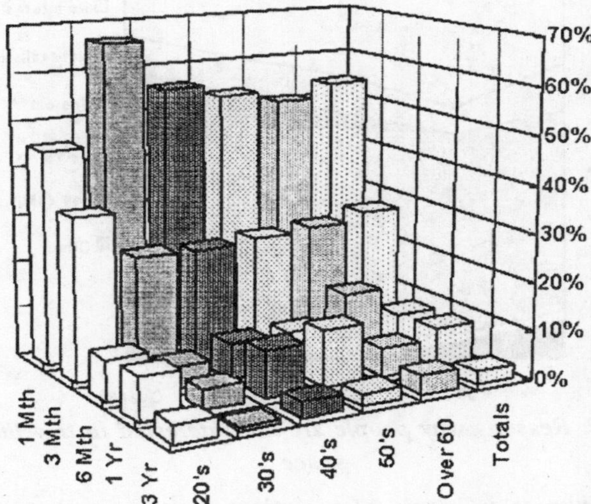

Figure 6. How much people feel is the proper proportion of their income for a space trip

Figure 7 shows a breakdown of the reasons given by those who did not wish to visit space. Roughly 1/3 of each age group said that they are simply not interested in the idea. It seems likely that these people would not go, even if the service was available. However, some 5-10% said that they consider the idea unrealistic, and presumably some of these would wish to go once the service was really available. Roughly 1/3 were concerned primarily about safety, which emphasises the overriding need for reliable space transportation. Some of these would presumably reconsider once the service was something like that of toadies airline travel. A substantial fraction of these respondents however, said that they were afraid of flying, and so it must be assumed that they would remain unwilling under any circumstances. Finally, most of the people who considered themselves too old to go, were still interested in travelling to space if it had been available when they were young. Overall, it seems that the average of 60% interested in visiting space could grow to 70% or more in the event that a regular service became available.

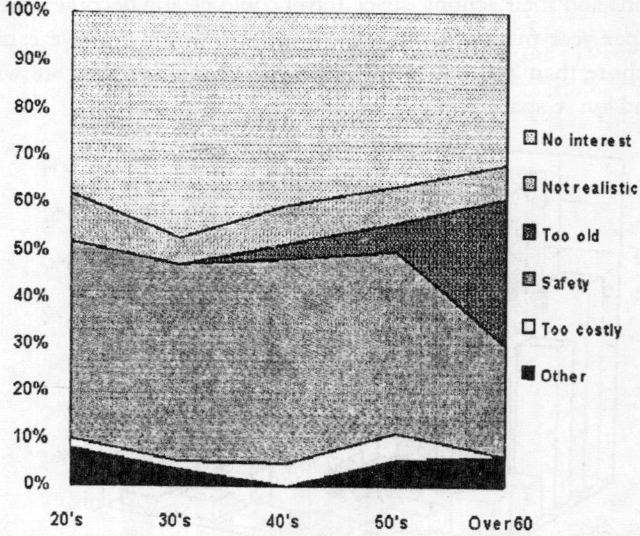

Figure 7: Reasons why people are not interested in travelling to space

A weakness in terms of complete consistency between all respondents is suspected by the authors in terms of the personal interpretation of the space tourism concept statement. Since the respondent was free to envision what the space trip and vacation would entail, it was felt that in some cases the respondent thought that they might be travelling to faraway places or planets on their trip. Whenever questions arose as to where they might be travelling on a space trip, it was suggested by the interviewers that these trips would be mainly in orbit around the Earth.

Although some misinterpretation may be present, it is felt that most respondents had a clear picture as to what would be involved; a vacation orbiting the Earth or slightly beyond. Discussions with the interviewees during and after the study attempted to elicit information concerning this issue. If bias is present due to the lack of clarity involved, it could move the results in either direction, but probably not by a substantial amount.

International Comparison

One of the more interesting aspects of this study is that it enables a comparison of data to be made between different national markets. It appears from these results and others that the desire to travel to space is consistent with the popular idea that people of all cultures are intrigued by, and eager to experience living in space for themselves. Here we briefly compare the results of the two similar studies carried out in Japan and Germany.

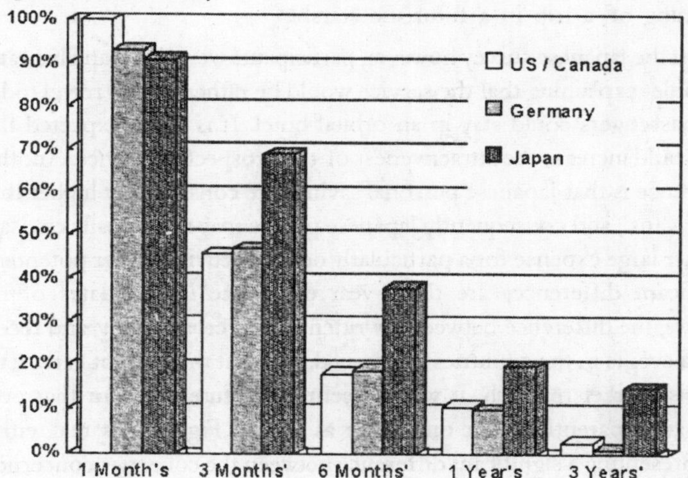

Figure 8: Comparison of the amount people would pay in several countries

A survey using a similar format was recently carried out on 200 people using the two airports in Berlin, of which the results will be published in detail in the near future. The data are particularly interesting in being the first such market data to be collected in Europe. Because airport users are a well-characterised economic group, the results allow us to draw conclusions about the middle and upper income group of the German population, and also reasonably firm conclusions about western Europeans as a whole. In combination with the American and Japanese data, Figure 8 shows the comparison of the amounts that people said they would pay in these four countries. More detailed analysis is required to draw precise comparisons, but the similarity between the North American and German data is striking. The figures for Japan are noticeably higher.

In comparing the American results with the earlier data on the Japanese market, we must make allowance for differences in the circumstances of the two surveys that might lead to differences in the results. A significant difference between the two survey procedures was that in the telephone survey participants were given minimal information about what form the service would take. It was clear from comments made by some respondents that they were envisaging something rather similar to a flight in an existing launch vehicle, and at the other extreme, dreaming of a trip in a futuristic starship.

In the Japanese survey however, participants were given an illustrated pamphlet explaining that the service would be rather like air travel today, and passengers could stay in an orbital hotel. It is to be expected that this would increase the attractiveness of the prospective service. Another difference is that Japanese personal savings are considerably higher than Americans', and consequently Japanese people may more easily envisage a rather large expense for a particularly desired activity. Other potentially significant differences are the 2-year difference in the dates of the surveys, the difference between a written and a verbal survey, and recent media events in the countries concerned. Thus, at the present early stage of this market research, it would seem premature to claim that even such an apparently major difference as that in Figure 5 is real, either as representing a significant difference between the countries concerned, or in terms of the data being in error.

More striking than this possible difference is surely the fact that people from such different countries, approached in such different ways, answer the basic question of whether they wish to visit space with such a high similarity. A large majority of young people, a majority of the middle-aged, and a substantial minority of people in their 60s and 70s say that they wish to visit space, and many are prepared to pay several months salary to do so. We can surely conclude that personally travelling to space is an almost universally popular ambition.

5

Tourism Product Development

Tourism product development is mainly undertaken to facilitate product diversification, development or improvement of tourism products with the help of knowledgeable and qualified staff. It aims at enhancing visitor experience by building consensus and strategic alliances with business stakeholders in order to bring about socioeconomic growth. Tourism product development seeks to support in the maintenance, development and enhancement of the tourism product.

A large number of companies offer training programs and advice on tourism product development. The services include sustainable tourism product planning and development, presentations, seminars, campaigns and strategies for destination marketing organizations, individual operators and agencies. These companies make use of a community and stakeholder-based approach to assist businesses and destinations to plan for successful tourism in the long-term from cost-effective, environmental and communally sustainable perspectives. These companies provide an extensive range of specialized services designed to help individual tourism operators, associations and product clubs, educational institutions and government agencies effectively attain their short and long-term goals. Some of these companies are designed to assist government and quasi-government agencies in the development of the tourism industry, principally by coordinating and aiding timely action between public and private sector interests.

Tourism product development aims at long-term sustainable development by the execution of a number of strategies. These strategies bring into focus a generic idea to increase competitiveness, build an inclusive industry by promoting closer integration of people and develop and maintain the environment. Tourism product development is designed to increase the income in the sector. Tourism product development involves implementation of a comprehensive plan of action that will guide towards dealing with estimated increase in business over the short, medium and long-terms. Tourism product development helps in improving product quality by complying with the standards set by international benchmarks. It helps in product improvement by tourism training. It helps in product diversification by acting as a channel, facilitator and controller for development through sports and community based development with stress on culture, heritage and ecotourism.

New Product Development

New product development is one of the most important components of product policy and product management. Product lines and products are appraise and are positioned effectively. Brand decisions are taken wisely. For a higher level of growth, a firm has to look beyond its existing products. A progressive firm has to consider new product development as a cardinal element of its product policy.

Innovation is the essence of all growth. This is especially true in marketing. In an age of technological advancements, change is a natural outcome — change in food habits, change in expectations and requirements. Any business has to be vigilant to these changes taking place in its environment. People always seek better products, greater convenience, newer fashion and more value for money.

A business firm has to respond to these dynamic requirements of its clientele and these responses take the shape of new products and new services. Through such a response, the firm reaps a good deal of benefits. New products become necessary from the profit angle too. Products that are already established often have their limitations in enhancing the profit level of the firm. Profits from products decline as they reach the maturity stage of their life cycle. Thus, it is necessary for business firms to bring in new products to replace old, declining and losing products. New products become part and parcel of the growth requirements of the firm and in many cases, new profits come to the firm only through new products. New products can be broadly classified into two groups: new products arising out of technological innovations and new products arising out of marketing oriented modifications. The first group involves innovations leading to intrinsically new products with a new functional utility behind them. The second group involves mere marketing oriented innovations in existing products; it gives rise to new versions of the existing products.

New Product Development

In business and engineering, new product development (NPD) is the term used to describe the complete process of bringing a new product or service to market. There are two parallel paths involved in the NPD process: one involves the idea generation, product design, and detail engineering; the other involves market research and marketing analysis. Companies typically see new product development as the first stage in generating and commercializing new products within the overall strategic process of product life cycle management used to maintain or grow their market share.

Types of New Products

There are several general categories of new products. Some are new to the market, some are new to the company, some are completely novel and create totally new markets. When viewed against a different criteria, some new product concepts are merely minor modifications of existing products while some are completely innovative to the company.

* Changes to Augmented Product.
* Core product revision.
* Line extensions.
* New product lines.
* Repositionings.
* Completely new.

These different characterizations are displayed in the following diagram.

Product Newness based on Company and Market

The process

There are several stages in the new product development process...not always followed in order:

1. Idea Generation (The "fuzzy front end" of the NPD process).
2. Ideas for new products can be obtained from customers

(employing user innovation), the company's R&D department, competitors, focus groups, employees, salespeople, corporate spies, trade shows, or through a policy of Open Innovation. Ethnographic discovery methods (searching for user patterns and habits) may also be used to get an insight into new product lines or product features.

3. Formal idea generation techniques can be used, such as attribute listing, forced relationships, brainstorming, morphological analysis and problem analysis.
4. Idea Screening .
5. The object is to eliminate unsound concepts prior to devoting resources to them.
6. The screeners must ask at least three questions.
7. Will the customer in the target market benefit from the product?
8. Is it technically feasible to manufacture the product?
9. Will the product be profitable when manufactured and delivered to the customer at the target price?
10. Concept Development and Testing.
11. Develop the marketing and engineering details.
12. Who is the target market and who is the decision maker in the purchasing process?
13. What product features must the product incorporate?
14. What benefits will the product provide?
15. How will consumers react to the product?
16. How will the product be produced most cost effectively?
17. Prove feasibility through virtual computer aided rendering, and rapid prototyping.
18. What will it cost to produce it?
19. Test the concept by asking a sample of prospective customers what they think of the idea
20. Business Analysis.
21. Estimate likely selling price based upon competition and customer feedback.
22. Estimate sales volume based upon size of market.
23. Estimate profitability and breakeven point.

24. Beta Testing and Market Testing.
25. Produce a physical prototype or mock-up.
26. Test the product (and its packaging) in typical usage situations.
27. Conduct focus group customer interviews or introduce at trade show.
28. Make adjustments where necessary.
29. Produce an initial run of the product and sell it in a test market area to determine customer acceptance.
30. Technical Implementation.
31. New program initiation.
32. Resource estimation.
33. Requirement publication.
34. Engineering operations planning.
35. Department scheduling.
36. Supplier collaboration.
37. Logistics plan.
38. Resource plan publication.
39. Program review and monitoring.
40. Contingencies-what-if planning.
41. Commercialization (often considered post-NPD).
42. Launch the product.
43. Produce and place advertisements and other promotions.
44. Fill the distribution pipeline with product.
45. Critical path analysis is most useful at this stage.

These steps may be iterated as needed. Some steps may be eliminated. To reduce the time that the NPD process takes, many companies are completing several steps at the same time. Most industry leaders see new product development as a *pro-active* process where resources are allocated to identify market changes and seize upon new product opportunities before they occur (in contrast to a *reactive strategy* in which nothing is done until problems occur or the competitor introduces an innovation). Many industry leaders see new product development as an ongoing process (referred to as *continuous development*) in which the entire organization is always looking for opportunities. For the more innovative products indicated on the diagram above, great amounts of uncertainty and change may exist, which makes it difficult or impossible to plan the complete project before starting it. In this case, a more flexible approach may be advisable.

Because the NPD process typically requires both engineering and marketing expertise, cross-functional teams are a common way of organizing projects. The team is responsible for all aspects of the project, from initial idea generation to final commercialization, and they usually report to senior management. In those industries where products are technically complex, development research is typically expensive, and product life cycles are relatively short, strategic alliances among several organizations helps to spread the costs, provide access to a wider skill set, and speeds the overall process.

Also, notice that because engineering and marketing expertise are usually both critical to the process, choosing an appropriate blend of the two is important. Observe that this article is slanted more toward the marketing side. For more of an engineering slant, see the Ulrich and Eppinger reference below.

People respond to new products in different ways. The adoption of a new technology can be analysed using a variety of diffusion theories such as the Diffusion of innovations theory it include economical support of social serctor

Protecting New Products

When developing a new product many legal questions arise, including: How do I protect the innovation from imitators?; Can the innovation be legally protected?; For how long?; How much will this cost?. The answers are complicated by the fact that several legal concepts may apply to any given innovation, product, process, or creative work. These include patents, trademarks, service marks, tradenames, copyrights, and trade secrets.

It is necessary to know which are applicable and when each is appropriate. This varies somewhat from jurisdiction to jurisdiction. The advice of a lawyer that specializes in these matters and is knowledgeable with your corporate philosophy regarding IP protection is essential. Generally, copyrights are fairly easy to obtain but are applicable only in certain instances. Patents on the other hand, tend to involve complex claims and approval processes, tend to be expensive to obtain, and even more expensive to defend and preserve.

Fuzzy Front End

The Fuzzy Front End is the messy "getting started" period of new product development processes. It is in the front end where the organization formulates a concept of the product to be developed and decides whether or not to invest resources in the further development of an idea. It is the phase between first consideration of an opportunity and when it is judged ready to enter the structured development process. It includes all activities from the search for new opportunities through the formation of a germ of an idea to the development of a precise concept. The Fuzzy Front End ends when an organization approves and begins formal development of the concept.

Although the Fuzzy Front End may not be an expensive part of product development, it can consume 50% of development time, and it is where major commitments are typically made involving time, money, and the product's nature, thus setting the course for the entire project and final end product. Consequently, this phase should be considered as an essential part of development rather than something that happens "before development," and its cycle time should be included in the total development cycle time. Koen et al. (2001) distinguish five different front-end elements (not necessarily in a particular order):

1. Opportunity Identification.
2. Opportunity Analysis.
3. Idea Genesis.
4. Idea Selection.
5. Concept and Technology Development.

The first element is the opportunity identification. In this element, large or incremental business and technological chances are identified in a more or less structured way. Using the guidelines established here, resources will eventually be allocated to new projects.... which then lead to a structured NPPD strategy. The second element is the opportunity analysis. It is done to translate the identified opportunities into implications for the business and technology specific context of the company. Here extensive efforts may be made to align ideas to target customer groups and do market studies and/or technical trials and research. The third element is the idea genesis, which is described as evolutionary and iterative process progressing from birth to maturation of the opportunity into a tangible idea. The process of the idea genesis can be made internally or come from outside inputs, e.g. a supplier offering a new material/technology, or from a customer with an unusual request. The fourth element is the idea selection. Its purpose is to choose whether to pursue an idea by analysing its potential business value. The fifth element is the concept and technology development. During this part of the front-end, the business case is developed based on estimates of the total available market, customer needs, investment requirements, competition analysis and project uncertainty. Some organizations consider this to be the first stage of the NPPD process.

The Fuzzy Front End is also described in literature as "Front End of Innovation", "Phase 0", "Stage 0" or "Pre-Project-Activities".

Enterprise Risk Management

Enterprise risk management (ERM) is the process of planning, organizing, and controlling the activities of an organization in order to minimize the effects of risk. Enterprise risk management includes not just risks associated with accidental losses, but also financial, strategic, operational and other related types of risks.

In recent years, many external risk factors have lead to a heightened interest in ERM packages. Industry and government regulatory bodies, as well as investors, have begun to scrutinize companies' risk-management policies and procedures. In an increasing number of industries, boards of directors are required to review and report on the adequacy of risk-management processes in the organizations they administer.

In a service driven economy, businesses cannot afford to let risks remain unidentified. Currency fluctuations, wide distribution channels and an unprecedented dependence on technology are just a few of the new risks businesses must assess. Many organizations are choosing to implement an Enterprise Risk Management process to ensure that a uniform approach is adopted towards risk identification, analysis and treatment. The Sarbanes-Oxley Act of 2002 became the driving force behind Enterprise Risk Management. Financial institutions are good examples of companies that have benefited from effective ERM.

There are a few basic strategies that can be adopted in the process of Enterprise Risk Management. Experts in ERM recommend a five-year financial plan whereby a business can identify, prioritize and map all aspects of the most critical risks. Businesses must subject themselves to regular financial audits in accordance with government accounting standards. ERM calls for stricter corporate governance that provides greater transparency to stakeholders.

More empowerment and responsibilities are given to Internal Audit Departments. A greater emphasis is laid on the code of ethics. ERM improves the way a company handles the more predictable risks that businesses face. It allows a company to avoid bad investments, and conversely, make investments that might intuitively seem too risky. Companies that have adopted risk management methodologies report fewer failed ventures and less damage from unforeseen events.

An Alternative Method for Developing New Tourism Products

The principal motivation behind such a paper came to us when we started searching for Indian tourism related marketing literature. We found, after going through national as well as international journals that there is hardly any report of the multivariate method conjoint analysis being used developing new products in Indian tourism sector. In terms of a methodology conjoint analysis provides excellent forecasts and its use has ever been increasing right from its inception in the early 70's. It has also received widespread acceptance and use in various industries and sectors with the usage rate increasing tenfold in the 1980s. But Indian tourism sector, it seems, still uses managerial expectations and apprehensions to develop new products. Our argument in this respect is simple and straightforward.

A new product must satisfy the needs and wants of the consumer and not the needs and expectations of the management team. In India, it also presents a verysorry state of affairs concerning the incompatibility between the developments in the academia and the industry.

Apart from wide use of conjoint analysis in multifarious fields it has also undergone much refinements so as to make it more powerful in solving complex marketing decision situations over these years. In the current paper we attempt to demonstrate the power of conjoint analysis and identify areas in the Indian tourism sector where it can be effectively administered for better predictable efficacy. We also discuss the simplicity and flexibility of this method along with certain special uses to show the reader that this method goes beyond just identifying new products and attempt to simplify managerial decisions relating to other marketing concepts and objects.

Background

Tourism undoubtedly emerges as one of the most remarkable economic and social phenomena of the last century. Apparently it seems that it is all set keep this position for the next century as well. Every year a bigger portion of the world population takes part in tourism activity and for the majority of countries tourism has developed as one of the most dynamic and fastest growing sectors of economy. On a global scale the number of tourists is constantly increasing. Especially in the past 50 years the growth of tourism has been phenomenal in terms of its expansion. Between 1950 and 1999 the number of international arrivals has shown an evolution from a mere 25 million international arrivals to the current 664 million, corresponding to an average annual growth rate of about 7 per cent. In addition to its strong overall expansion,. the development of modern day tourism is also characterized by its ongoing geographical spread. Numerous countries have been successful, not only in attracting significant numbers of tourists, but also in turning tourism into a source of wealth. A notable diversification in tourism destinations has taken place, with those of Asia, North Africa and Latin America and the Caribbean being the emerging destinations joining in.

With these developments taking place around lets understand India's interests as well as the needs of the hour. India has the potential to release foreign exchange earnings from current $3 billion to over $10 billion and attract 10 million tourists by 2008. This is possible even with the existing infrastructure, may be a marginal investment in certain specific segments, rational management of hospitality industry and adjusts in the mindset of various players in the field. But India's share in world tourist arrivals and receipts is dismally insignificant.

In the post liberalized scenario Indian private sector is assumed to play a greater role in the development of tourism sector compared to government efforts. Therefore, it is a concerted effort by all players in the private sector that can properly position India as a better tourism destination option by uniquely designing products and promotions that distinctly focuses on specific market segments with definite needs. Traditionally India's tourism is promoted on account of its diversity and vast variety offering in terms of its flora, fauna, cultural heritage etc.

Now the problem lies in properly designing products that suit to different needs of international tourists. Reports indicate that though recreation and leisure holidays remain as the principal segment of tourism purpose but other small areas are registering a better growth such as visiting friends and relatives, religious purposes/pilgrimages, health treatment etc. In the last ten years, especially the share of this category has been rising. This pattern reflects the trend towards market diversification and the division of holidays, with people travelling for shorter periods of time and for different reasons. This growth has basically detracted from the share of total trips made for leisure, recreation and holiday purposes, the share ascribed to travel for business and professional purposes having remained relatively stable.

Against this backdrop, we strongly feel, there is a need to understand the changing preferences of the international tourist and identify suitable products/packages that yields better choice and in turn can increase revenues. Therefore the importance of appropriate marketing research further gets emphasized as compared to the past practices of going by management instuitions. Need has come to promote specific products/packages rather than promoting the whole of India as a tourism destination. Hence, we propose a flexible but enormously powerful multivariate method *Conjoint Analysis* and show how this can identify ideal new tourism products that can better address the future needs.

What is Conjoint Analysis?

As a research method, conjoint analysis portrays consumers' decisions more realistically as tradeoffs among multi-attribute products or services. The authors, in this paper, revisit this technique in developing new tourism products and show the flexibility and prowess of this methodology that helps evaluate any set of objects or concepts related to tourism marketing. The authors also point out the importance of conjoint models that help in predicting optimum combinations of new tourism products, estimating customer judgments to predict market shares among objects with differing sets of features, isolate groups of potential customers and identify opportunities for feature combinations not currently available among tourism product offers. With the increase in use of information technology and personal computer based programs, the authors finally conclude the ease in estimating the entire process, i.e., from generating combinations of predictor variables to creating choice simulators.

Conjoint Analysis is a "what-if" experiment in which buyers are presented with different possibilities and asked what they would buy.

Despite its name, conjoint analysis is not like other multivariate methods such as factor analysis, cluster analysis etc. Rather it is a type of thinking experiment that is designed to show how various elements of products or services (elements such as price, brand name and features) predict consumer preferences for certain hypothetical products or services. Conjoint analysis is a multivariate technique used specifically to understand how respondents develop preferences for products or services. It is based on the simple premise that consumers evaluate the value or utility of a product or service (real or hypothetical) by combining the separate amounts of utility provided by each attribute.

The Conjoint Model

Essentially in conjoint analysis the analyst tries to understand the "preference structure" of a respondent. It is actually a family of techniques and methods, all theoretically based on the models of information integration and functional measurement. In terms of the basic dependence model conjoint analysis can be expressed as Y1 = X1 + X2 + X3 + … + XN *(nonmetric, metric) (metric)* From the above it is clearly evident that the flexibility of conjoint analysis primarily arises from its ability to accommodate either a metric or a nonmetric dependent variable and use of categorical predictor variables. Moreover, it makes quite general assumptions about the relationship between dependent and independent variables. We have presented the operationalization of this in the later part of our paper. But this clearly shows the suitability of conjoint model in the field of tourism, as very often an analyst is likely to come across categorical variables while identifying ideal new product designs.

The basic method of conjoint analysis asks consumers to imagine products or services that vary along some dimensions of interest and to score these products or services in some way. The scoring is usually done by ranking or rating as per the preference of consumers. These scores are then used to decompose for the purpose of estimating the values of each attribute level in the experiment. The interesting difference here from other methods is that the respondent need not tell the researcher about the attraction or evaluation of specific attributes of a given product or service. Because the researcher constructs the hypothetical products or services in a specific manner, the importance of each attribute and each value of each attribute can be computed from the respondents' overall rating.

Therefore to be successful in a conjoint experiment the analyst must be able to properly and in clear terms describe the product or service in terms of both its attribute and all relevant values of each attribute. The respondents may be asked to rate the hypothetical products (may be using a 10-point scale) or rank all of them that are presented to them by the analyst. Conjoint method is also sometimes referred as a "trade-off analysis" because in making a judgment on a hypothetical product, respondents must consider both positive and negative characteristics of the product to form a preference. Thus the respondents must weigh all the attributes simultaneously in making their judgments.

By drawing a contrast between specific treatments (combinations or stimuli or hypothetical products/services) the analyst attempts to understand the overall preference for each treatment. This overall preference that represents the "total worth" of a treatment is thought of as based on the "part-worths" for each level of each attribute. Here the general form of the conjoint model presented as:

Total worth for product $_{ij...n}$ = Part-worth of level for factor *1* +

Part-worth of levels for factor *2* + ... +

Part-worth of leveln for factorm.

Where the product/service has *m* attributes (referred as factors), each having two or more levels (a mandatory requirement). Thus the hypothetical product consists of leveli of factor 1, levels of factor 2, ... upto level$_n$ for factor$_m$.

In general most of the dependence methods assume a linear relationship. However, conjoint analysis is not limited to types of relationships between the dependent and independent variables. It can make separate predictions for the effects of each level of the independent variables and does not assume they are related at all. Thus conjoint method can easily handle non-linear and even curvilinear relationships.

Extensions and Special Topics in Conjoint Analysis

One of the most common uses of conjoint analysis is to group respondents with similar part-worths to identify specific marketing segments. Often it may become necessary for the researcher to identify these groups and understand their relative magnitude to ascertain the attractiveness in the tourism sector. Through conjoint analysis an analyst can also do a marginal profitability analysis of the hypothetical products and services. If the cost if each feature is known, the cost of each proposed product can be combined with the expected market share and sales volume to predict its viability.

Conjoint analysis can also give birth to choice simulators. First the conjoint models for each respondent (or group) is estimated and validated. Second selection is made of a set of stimuli (treatments) that may resemble the competitive scenarios. Then simulation is done for the choices of all respondents (or groups) for the specified sets of stimuli and predictions are obtained for each stimulus by aggregating their choices. Conjoint analysis with large number of attributes seems to be very difficult to handle. But one variant of the main analysis method known as Adaptive Conjoint Analysis (ACA) developed by Sawtooth Software handle these with great ease. One more extension is developed utilizing the conjoint principle known as Choice Based Conjoint model. Traditional conjoint analysis assumes that the judgment task based on ranking or rating captures the respondent choices. But some researchers have argued that this may be less realistic way of reflecting the actual market setting. Past research has shown that choice is often a two-stage process. Therefore it would be more prudent to ask the respondent to identify a choice set from among the options laid down rather than rating them. This helps the analyst to observe the threshold above which the respondent makes his/her choice.

Assumptions and Cautionary Issues in Conjoint Analysis

Even though we presented the conjoint model in an attractive manner but it involves certain care to be observed by the researcher. One of the key issues to be addressed in the conjoint experiment is of realism though most of it deals with hypothetical concepts. Respondents must be able to visualize in real terms what kind of hypothetical tourism products are being presented by the researcher. In designing the experiment the analyst must specify differing attributes as the respondents to arrive at a choice ultimately trade these off. These attributes should also be relevant to ones own marketing program. Using appropriate levels is another key issue that should be realistic and believable. The success of the conjoint experiment also depends on the selection of proper study design, selection of respondents, specifying the main effects model, specifying the data collection method and above all professional execution of the experiment. Conclusion We did not attempt to explain the procedure of conjoint analysis; rather the scope of this paper is to show the power of this model in addressing the new product development issues in the Indian tourism sector. Due to cost considerations, conjoint analysis usually should be reserved for studies of product improvements or new product developments. The ability of conjoint analysis to model market response is especially valuable in its application to Indian tourism sector. Therefore the reader should note that the conjoint method should not be used for the primary purposes of measuring the importance of product attributes or market segmentation as cheaper methods provide adequate data for these purposes. Conjoint analysis places more emphasis on the ability of the researcher/manager to theorize about the behaviour of choice than it does on analytical technique. Though this technique has strong theoretical foundations, its applications have increased dramatically without corresponding theoretical development. Today it is simple to use conjoint analysis especially after the easy availability of many personal computer based software programs. Some of the popular computer programs for conjoint analysis are MONANOVA (Monotonic Analysis of Variance), LIMAP and SPSS etc.

What is Tourism Product Development?

Tourism product development involves coordinating effort behind viable, sustainable projects that will help to develop North East England as a successful tourism destination.

It includes:

1. Developing tourism related products focusing on quality, sustainability and industry involvement to gain maximum economic benefit.
2. Ensuring a product matches and exceeds customer expectations.
3. Enhancing public product through provision of signage and interpretation.
4. Promoting local distinctiveness.
5. Creating new niche areas to entice and target new visitors to the region.
6. Looking at existing products in the region and improving their current offer to ensure visitors have a wonderful experience and make repeat visits.

7. Improving the quality of the existing tourism accommodation product– to ensure visitors have a wide choice of quality accommodation in the region to choose from.
8. The way in which marketing, investment (including capital) and business development are aligned around product priorities to have a greater impact.
9. A coordinated response to evidence from research.

What Exactly is a 'Tourism Product'?

The term "product" is something of a misnomer since leisure and tourism are service industries and the bulk of leisure and tourism activity is concerned with the customer's experience.

Examples of tourism products are:

* Short breaks.
* Leisure centres.
* Nature reserves.
* Museums.
* Attractions.
* Holidays.
* Art galleries.
* Events.
* A 30 min horse riding session.
* Local food/craft product.

Some products are tangible: you can see and touch them. However many tourism products cannot be seen and are therefore intangible. You can't see a short break, but you can experience it. It is this aspect of intangibility that makes tourism products so difficult to describe. It could be argued that hotels, leisure centres, tourist attractions etc. are simply facilities in which the intangible products are experienced, e.g. a short break could well involve staying at a hotel.

In essence a tourism product can be defined as a visitor service, activity, attraction or an experience (in itself, a collection of services, activities and attractions). A product is 'something' you decide to take to market to satisfy a want or need. Therefore a product is identified through prioritisation and decision making, guided by a process.

Niche Tourism Product Development

A "niche" is a specific segment usually with a well-defined tourism product that can be tailored to meet the particular interests of a set of visitors that share similar interests/aspirations/lifestyles etc.

Examples of some of the existing regional niche tourism product development areas in North East England are:

* Cruise Tourism.
* Gardens.
* Luxury Group Travel.
* Mountain Biking.

Developing Tourism Products and Services

Tourism is a vital and increasingly important part of the regional and local economy. Successfully developing the tourism products available to visitors and locals increases the diversity and appeal of North East England as a destination, attracting more visitors and higher spending customers.

Tourism product development involves looking systematically at our region, areas, offering, markets and niches to determine which are the right tourism businesses, markets and products to develop: those with the potential not only to thrive economically, but to improve the overall offer and experience of the region.

It also aims to help identify the 'wrong' sort of developments: those that are likely to fail, impact negatively on the local environment, or degrade or devalue the overall area and regional offering.

This guide explains the North East England product development process and is intended for tourism development staff and businesses working on larger scale projects. However the principles can be applied to any project of any size. In all cases, Business Link can provide tailored help and advice for specific projects or businesses.

Commercial Implications of Market Research on Space Tourism

In the post-Cold War era, the justification for the space industry to continue to receive the large government budgets on which it has depended to date is being questioned. In particular, the value of government investment in the development of new launch vehicles when there is oversupply in relation to the worldwide launch rate of just a few tens of launches per year is questioned. Yet in the absence of a new generation of fully reusable launch vehicles with much lower launch costs than today, the space industry has little possibility to grow into a commercially profitable and self-sustaining industry. Justifying such investment will require the development of new launch markets which have the potential to grow to traffic rates many times greater than the present limited demand for satellite launches.

One possible source of demand for future launch services, and so of future revenues and profits to finance the development of erasable launch vehicles, is tourism-the making of short visits to low Earth orbit by fare-paying customers. In the modern world tourism represents one of the largest, most international industries, and it is growing fast, particularly in the more economically advanced countries. Furthermore, space travel has a high level of popularity among the general public. The desire of many people, particularly the young, to explore the unknown world of space and face new challenges seems likely to create growing demand for popular space travel. Thus it seems possible that the commercial demand for space tourism could be very high, and that the widespread desire of humankind to have the experience of going to space for themselves could become a driving force for the space industry in the future.

However, the attractiveness of "space tourism", or "orbital tourism" (at least in the early stages), as a potential target market for commercial companies will depend critically on the actual scale of future demand for space tourism services at different prices. To date very little data has been collected on this subject in any country. During the summer of 1993 a market research questionnaire on the potential demand for orbital tourism was completed by more than 3000 people from all age groups in Japan. The questionnaire was distributed face-to-face mainly in large companies, universities, schools, obtaining a response rate of well over 90%. Details of this survey, and initial results have been published in, but the idea of space tourism was very popular. Nearly 80% of those under 50 said that they would like to travel to space, and 45% of those over 60, with no significant difference between the 1465 men's and 1565 women's answers. Some 70% of those who wished to travel to space said that they would pay three months' salary or more, and the great majority said that they would like to stay in orbit for a few days. In the following we discuss some further details of the results. In considering whether a new service such as passenger flights to Earth orbit could become a profitable business, companies must estimate both the costs that they would incur in providing the new service, and the revenues that they could earn. The costs depend on how low engineers can reduce the manufacturing and operating costs of reusable launch vehicles, and the revenues depend on the size of the potential market for the service, that is on how popular the service could become. Consequently in order to assess the feasibility of this business we need to do both engineering and market research. Currently the Japanese Rocket Society is studying the engineering and other aspects of space tourism in its Space Tourism Study Program. The authors of this paper have been carrying out preliminary market research.

Limitations of Market Research

In principle, if firm data were available concerning the future demand for space tourism at different price levels, it would be possible to plan a business to provide such a service, provided that the vehicle costs could be reduced sufficiently. In practice, however, any conclusions that can be drawn from market research data on this subject can be only tentative, for a number of reasons. First, the reliability of all market research concerning future products and services is inherently limited. There have been many cases of new products' sales being very different from the results of market research, both greater or less. This is due fundamentally to the impossibility of predicting the future, and more particularly to peoples' inability to foresee their own future behaviour accurately.

Second, this uncertainty is particularly strong in the case of a new and futuristic service such as space tourism about which peoples' expectations are particularly likely to be mistaken. Thus the reliability of market research results must be more uncertain than usual. This is not to say that the results must be inaccurate, but rather that it is not possible to know how accurate they are.

Third, it is uncertain how representative the market research data that have been collected are of the Japanese population as a whole. The authors tried to ensure a wide distribution to people outside the space industry. As discussed in, by distributing the questionnaire on a face-to-face basis, the response rate was nearly 100%, which avoids the common bias of receiving answers only from those who are interested in the subject.

There are nevertheless some biases in the results. For example, 64% of Japanese households are salaried, and their income is some 5% above the average, while 36% are self-employed and their income is some 10% below the average, but only 2% of the participants in our survey were from the self-employed population. However the proportion of self-employed participants who said that they would like to go to space was not very different from the self-employed, 77% versus 81%. Consequently, while recognising this limitation in the survey, it was not felt necessary to correct the data as a result.

Fourth, it is uncertain how representative our data are of the populations of the advanced industrial countries as a whole. Although similar market research has not been carried out in these countries, the market for space tourism seems sure to be international. Consequently, in order to understand the true potential market we need to consider at least North America, Western Europe and Australasia as well as Japan, the total population of which countries is some 6 times that of Japan.

There may be significant differences in demand between these countries due to the cultural differences between them, which are significant. But there are also important common strands in modern popular culture. Science fiction and particularly space fiction, international organisations such as the Young Astronauts Club, and the worldwide popularity of big-budget space-related films such as "2001" or "Star Wars" suggest that people in many countries enjoy these ideas. Thus, although it is possible that Japanese people are more interested in space travel than other countries, it seems likely that such an interest is also widespread in America and Europe.

However, there are also significant differences between Japanese consumer behaviour and that of Americans and Europeans. One difference is the much higher savings ratio in Japan (which is related to the low interest rates, the high rate of investment, and the low level of unemployment in Japan). Because of their high savings, typically amounting to one year's income held in financial assets, Japanese are able to spend relatively large amounts on things that have particular value for them, such as education, weddings, foreign travel. Another difference is the relatively equal income distribution in Japan compared to America or Europe. From this we might guess that demand for space tourism services may be higher in the latter countries while the price is so high that only the rich can afford it, but may be relatively greater in Japan if the price is low enough to become affordable by a large proportion of the population.

Fifth, since the number of people who said that they would pay one year's income or more to go to space was considerably fewer than those who said that they would pay less, the figures must be considered statistically less reliable. That is, a small number of unrepresentative answers could bias the results significantly. Likewise, the 3-4 % of non-student participants in each age-group over the age of 20 who said that they would pay 3 years' or 5 years' salary for a trip to orbit may be unrepresentative, so that the proportion of people with similar opinions may be significantly less than this. Even so, and even if these people are wrong in the sense that in the event of such a service becoming available many of them would not actually pay such a high price, we must still recognise that for a significant number of people the idea of going to space is clearly a powerful dream. However, although there may well be significant demand for space tourism even at very high prices of more than 10 million, this will probably be mainly from uncommonly rich people, rather than from people with average incomes paying a multiple of their annual salary. Consequently, in analysing the results we have included these multi-year answers with those who said that they would pay one year's salary. Despite these limitations of our market research data, it is nevertheless interesting to use the results as a basis for estimating the future demand for space tourism services. Indeed we have no choice but to do this if we are to develop a successful commercial service. We must also remember a fundamental difference between scientific research and business. Businesses do not require proof before they invest in a project, but reasonable probability. Investment entails risk because the future is uncertain. Businesses that wait for proof risk being beaten by bolder competitors.

Demand Curve

Initial results of our survey are described in. For the present analysis, in order to derive a demand curve for space tourism, we excluded teenagers, as lacking experience about financial matters, and those over 70 years old, as being unlikely to travel to space. By making the assumption that the participants in the survey are representative of the Japanese population as a whole, we can estimate the proportion in each age group who say they would pay each price, in terms of months of salary. National income statistics allow us to estimate the monetary value of the monthly salaries for different age groups. By using national population data broken down by age we can then estimate the total number of people in Japan who would go to space at different prices.

In order to estimate the number of people who would travel to space each year, we need to develop a traffic growth model, and we plan to do this in the next phase of our analysis. For the present, in order to obtain a single figure representative of a future space tourism business, we simply divide the total demand by 25, that is we assume that 4% of those who wish to would go to space each year. Figure 1 shows the results of this simpler case with an exponential curve fitted. At first sight the demand shown in Figure 1 seems very high. For example, at prices of \5 million and \2.5 million the demand figures of 100,000 and 500,000 passengers per year are some 10-20 times higher than the estimate published by Citron in 1985 of 5,000-10,000 passengers per year at a price of $50,000, and 20,000-50,000 passengers per year at $25,000. However, in order to compare these figures accurately we need to make some adjustments. First we should adjust the earlier figure for inflation from 1985 to 1993, which reduces the difference to some 5-12 times for the lower price. If we further adjust the figures to use a "purchasing power parity" exchange-rate between the yen and dollar, which is arguably more appropriate for comparing consumer prices between Japan and the USA, the difference falls to perhaps 3-7 times.

However, Citron also proposed that demand at a price of $25,000 might grow as high as several million passengers per year. Thus, though demand in Figure 1 is greater at higher prices, the demand at lower prices is less, since it shows demand in excess of 1 million passengers per year only at prices below 1.4 million ($14,000). But the results are also incompatible in a number of ways.

The earlier estimates were for world demand, whereas the market research data was from Japan alone. The earlier data relate to just a trip in a launch vehicle, whereas a large proportion of the market research data represents people who wish to stay a few days in orbit. Finally the earlier estimates included projections of growth over the next 30 years, whereas the market research data has no explicit time-scale.

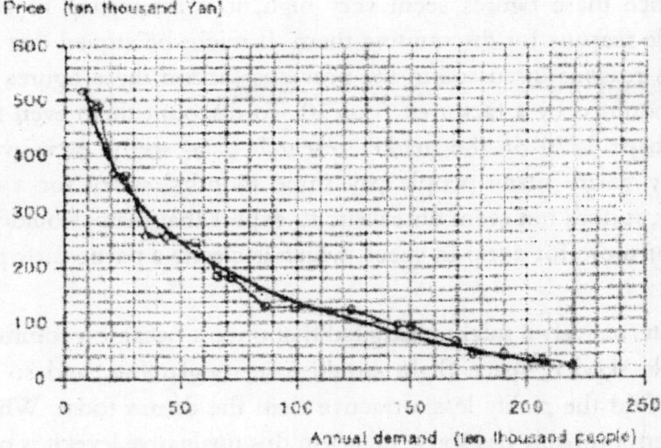

Figure 1. Potential demand curve for space tourism services.

Based on the data in Figure 1, Figure 2 shows the annual revenue that would be earned at each price level, with quartic (solid) and quadratic (dotted) curves fitted. Annual revenues reach a peak of some \1.35 trillion ($13.5 B), though there is some uncertainty about the price at which the maximum revenue would be earned. In the smoothed curves it lies between \1.2 million and \2.4 million. The correct figure will in practice depend on the different services that are offered, as discussed in the following section, but which are not distinguished in Figures 1 and 2.

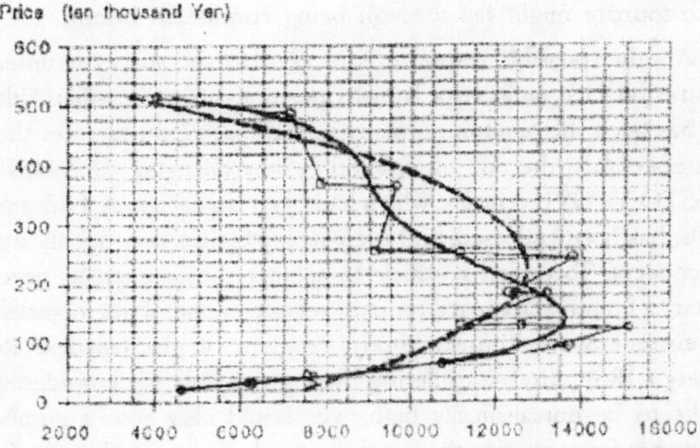

Figure 2. Potential revenue curve for space tourism services.

Since these figures seem very high, it is interesting to consider possible reasons for discounting them. It might be argued that for the various reasons discussed in the previous section these figures should be discounted by a factor of 5 or 10. To discount them even further, to perhaps 1/20 of the market research data, seems excessive: In a country where many people pay three months' salary for a foreign holiday, it does not seem unrealistic to expect that many would pay the same or more for a trip to space, which is clearly a particularly popular dream.

Alternatively it might be argued that once it became a commercially available service, space flight would lose its glamour, and so people would find the reality less attractive than the dream today. While this argument probably has some value, on this qualitative level it is possible also to argue the opposite: that in the coming years, a visit to orbit to see the Earth from space and to experience living in weightlessness could become the defining experience of the new post-cold-war era, in which advanced technology will be used for peaceful more than for military purposes, as foreign air travel might be said to have become in the late 20th century. In addition, the marketing industry, which grows ever more influential with the spread of the mass media, would surely be pleased to be offered the challenge of keeping the idea of space travel exciting. In view of its existing popularity, and of the almost limitless range of interesting future entertainments that can be developed in orbital facilities and beyond, it does not seem a serious danger that space tourism might fail through being considered boring.

Another possible response is to say that the survey is unrealistic because low-cost, airline-type launch operations are not feasible. Although this has been the opinion of many in the space industry over the past quarter-century, the tide of opinion is now changing. Hudson's work on SSTO VTOVL vehicles, which had been largely ignored through the 1980s, has been endorsed, and even senior figures now openly support the concept. To design a vehicle to achieve the cost targets necessary to start a commercial space tourism service is one of the objectives of the current Space Tourism Study Program of the Japanese Rocket Society (JRS). After considering these arguments for considering the results to be unrealistically high, we should also note a number of arguments for correcting the figures upwards. These are first, the figures used for average salaries are those for Japanese manufacturing industry in 1990, which are significantly lower than national average incomes in 1993 at the time of the survey. Second, we have not included bonuses, which typically represent some 25-40% of annual income in Japan. Third, since we are considering the demand for a service to be available some years in the future, we should allow for economic growth in estimating salaries. If incomes grow at 3.5% per year, this would represent growth of 50% over 12 years, and 100% over 20 years. Fourth, it is a well-recognised feature of consumer expenditure in advanced countries, that once a certain income level is reached, spending on leisure activities increases proportionately faster than on other expenses, taking a larger share of income. Future spending on space travel would fall into this category. If we were to make allowance for all these factors, it is therefore arguable that we should increase the price at each demand level by as much as 100%.

As discussed above, it seems reasonable to assume that world demand for space tourism services might be 6 times greater than demand in Japan alone, although to be sure about this will require further surveys. Consequently, if we took the demand shown in Figures 1 and 2 as provisional estimates of world demand for space tourism, we would be effectively discounting our questionnaire results by some 90%. Thus it seems a reasonably conservative interpretation of our data to assume that world demand for orbital tourism services could reach a level of more than \1.2 trillion ($12 billion) per year at a service price of between \2.4 million ($24,000) and \1.2 million ($12,000). It therefore seems reasonable to conclude that the commercial revenue earned by space tourism services would be several times larger than the entire launch industry today, and has the potential to grow to many times its size. Consequently, in considering the design of a reusable launch vehicle from a commercial point of view, developing a vehicle for the tourist market seems to be an attractive target.

Pattern of Development

The JRS Space Tourism Study Program assumes that the first phase of space tourism will comprise short trips to orbit lasting a few hours. However, it seems likely that once space tourism begins, like other commercial activities the variety of space tourism services will grow progressively and, in particular, orbital accommodation will become available. At first no more than a simple "hostel" comprising a few accommodation units, these orbital vehicles will later become large and sophisticated "hotels", offering a range of entertainments that exploit the unique features of the orbital environment, as discussed in. It is therefore interesting to consider the possible pattern of development of such services.

Although Figures 1 and 2 do not make any distinction between demand for different services, in our questionnaire participants were asked to state a preference between a day-trip to orbit, a trip lasting 2-3 days, a week-long stay in orbit, and a stay of 2 weeks or longer, without reference to price. The replies showed a strong preference for stays of a few days or longer, as described in. From a commercial point of view the important questions are: "How much more would guests pay for a longer stay in orbit?"; "How much higher will the cost of providing such services be?"; and "How much greater would demand be for these services?" Participants in the survey were not asked how much they would pay for different lengths of stay in orbit, but were asked to state their preference for a single visit length, independent of price. Consequently our data does not allow us to determine confidently the relative demand for trips of different lengths. Nevertheless, in the absence of more precise data, it seems reasonable to use the increasing popularity of different trip lengths at the same price as a proxy for the growth of demand that would occur as better services were offered.

Following this approach, Figure 3 shows the relative annual demand for the different stay lengths offered, on the same assumption as above, namely that annual demand is 4% of total demand. The revenue figure is not identical to that in Figures 1 and 2 above because we use a single average national income figure, which is not broken down according to age, but it is reasonably comparable.

As orbital accommodation services grew, the share of space tourism revenue accruing to launch vehicle operators would fall, as a larger proportion is paid for accommodation. Thus a significant proportion of the revenues shown in Figure 2 would accrue to operators of orbital accommodation rather than to launch companies. It is notable that the demand for stays of 2-3 days and 1 week show the same pattern of dependence on price, with a revenue peak at a price below \2 million. This is different from the demand for day-trips, which shows a different pattern, with demand being relatively inelastic and growing only relatively slowly as the price falls. However, this is of course affected by the increasing attractiveness of the alternative offerings at the same price. It is an important gap in the present data that, because the demand for longer stays in orbit is, not surprisingly, greater than the demand for day-trips at the same price, we can deduce little from our data about what the demand for day-trips would be at a time when this was the only service available-other than it would be greater than the figures in our results, which represent only those who would prefer a day-trip to a longer stay at the same price.

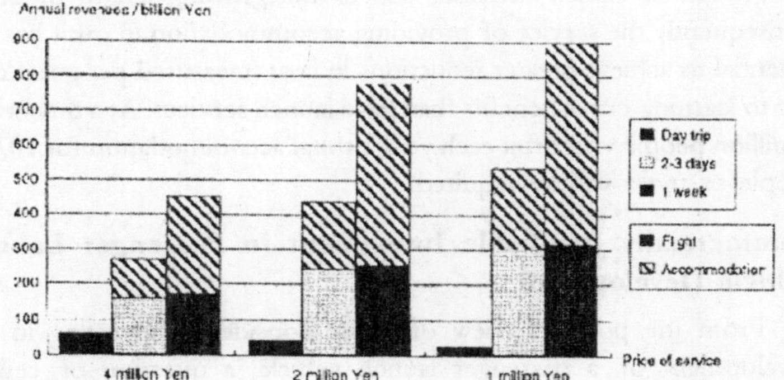

Figure 3. Growth of revenues from launch and accommodation.

Thus, as space tourism services develop, as in other forms of tourism the overall price that passengers pay will comprise two separate components, that for flight to orbit and that for accommodation in orbit, and the price of each will fall progressively as demand increases. Stays in orbit will become available at a given price only once flight to orbit has fallen sufficiently below that price. Longer stays will become available later, when the price of shorter stays will be less than that of the longer stays.

If we make a simple assumption that the unit cost of launch services will fall according to a learning-curve of 90%, the cost of a flight to orbit will fall by about 30% as demand grows approximately 10 times from the day-trip phase to 2-3 days in orbit, and by about 37% as demand more than doubles again by the 1-week stay phase. Thus if the price of the service remained constant, as assumed in the questionnaire, the cost of accommodation would be successively 43% and 60% of the cost of flight to orbit. This is comparable to the rough estimate published in that the cost of a few days' stay in orbital accommodation will be approximately 50% of the cost of a flight to orbit. In the future we will analyse this in more detail, breaking down the data collected in our survey according to age and other factors. It will be interesting to compare the results with "bottom-up" economic analysis of orbital accommodation using inputs from the hotel and real estate industries.

It is noteworthy that the growth in demand for orbital accommodation, measured by number of guest-days will be faster than the growth in launch demand, due to the growing length of stays. Consequently the service of providing accommodation in orbit has the potential to achieve greater reductions in cost (measured per guest-day) due to learning-curve benefits than have launch services. At a time when 1 million people visit orbit each year, orbital accommodation for 10,000 people or more will be required.

Commercially Justifiable Investment in Passenger Launch Vehicle Development

From the point of view of those considering investing in the development of a passenger launch vehicle, a question of central importance is "How high an investment cost can we expect to recover from profits from sales of vehicles?" In order to answer this we should make bottom-up estimates of vehicle operation and maintenance costs, propellant costs, staff costs and indirect costs. By comparing these with estimates of traffic rates at different prices, it would be possible to estimate justifiable vehicle price against passenger fare. By making further assumptions about vehicle production and sales, it would be possible to derive a figure for the maximum development cost that would be commercially recoverable. This is one of the intended outputs of the JRS passenger launch vehicle design study.

For the present paper we take a simpler approach. We assume a certain profit margin on the price that passengers pay. By doing this we can estimate the profit per year obtainable according to the vehicle utilisation. From the overall traffic we can estimate the number of vehicles needed, from which the maximum supportable investment can be calculated by making conventional financial assumptions.

However, we must also take into account the fact that the flight price will fall progressively below the overall service price, which we do by assuming a 90% learning curve, as above. For Figure 4 we use the initial assumptions of the JRS passenger launch vehicle study, that each vehicle carries 50 passengers, and flies to orbit 300 times per year. In addition we assume a 2% profit margin on the price of the passenger flight (which is less than the overall service price).

On this analysis, the most profitable flight price is about \1,200,000, corresponding to a service price of some \1,700,000. Development of a vehicle designed to fly passengers at such a price could be financed commercially at a development cost of up to some \150 billion ($1.5B), 25% more than a vehicle with passenger flight costs of twice this level. To provide the service would require 50 such vehicles, compared to only half this number of a vehicle with twice the passenger cost. The results of such a simple, preliminary analysis can only be considered tentative. However, the underlying concept of Figure 4 is fundamental to the future of the launch business.

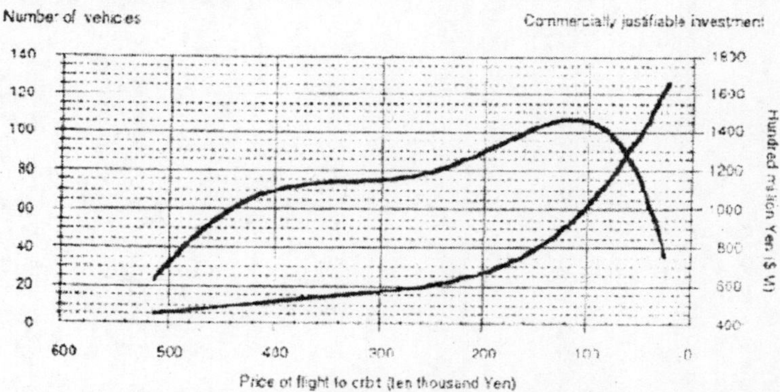

Figure 4. Commercially justifiable launch vehicle investment versus price of flight.

If further research on both the demand for space tourism and on the cost of supplying the services that people want supports our results, it is clear that carrying passengers to orbit and back has the potential to become a mainstay of the space launch business. No other payload which has so far been proposed in the space industry literature offers such a potential. The only other candidate for which launch demand could be of a similar or greater magnitude is the project to deliver solar-generated microwave power from space to Earth. This will become feasible only after a number of technologies have been developed beyond their present stage, in addition to the development of low-cost launch vehicles. By contrast, space tourism can start as soon as an appropriate vehicle is developed.

Further Results

Another interesting and potentially valuable subject not mentioned in the above discussion, which can also be analysed using the survey data, is market segmentation. As in terrestrial tourism, there seems to be a relatively inelastic demand for a high-priced service, and a separate, more price-elastic demand for low-price, mass-market "pack tours". From our results the possibility of a number of other more detailed categories of customer are apparent-graduation travel, young family holidays, "full moon" travel. These suggest directions for developing a range of distinctive space tourism offerings, which we will investigate further.

6

Global Tourism Growth

Globalization Process: Challenge for Tourism Countries with SME Structures

Tourism is one of the world economy's growth sectors. Despite crisis-induced slumps the long term growth trend appears to be stable.

Tourism is a beneficiary of the irreversible process of globalization and indeed is an accelerating factor for this process. The trend to a division of labour on a worldwide basis has been particularly favourable to tourism, resulting in increased productivity and prosperity in a great many countries. We owe these welcome developments to the introduction of a market economy and democracy in many of the emerging and transitional economies, a process that has been encouraged by the OECD.

Tourism is today one of the most internationalised sectors of the world economy. The world tourism market has been extended a lot, adding considerably to the potential for further growth and at the same time bringing about greater competition between tourism countries.

This raises the question whether or not tourism will be able to survive and prosper in such a competitive world economy in countries where the structure in this sector is based mainly on small-to-medium-sized enterprises (SMEs), and if so how.

It is for this reason that the overriding objective of the conference in Gwangju, Korea, is to devise new concepts that can help to make tourism countries in which small businesses dominate more competitive. These efforts require a good analytical understanding of tourism market structures.

Demand-driven Phenomenon: Importance of Visitors' Spending

Tourism is a creation of the modern industrial economy and the leisure society to which it has given rise. It is a sector that can only be defined in terms of demand. The key unit of measurement is the visitor. Whether travelling for business or pleasure the visitor spends money and creates demand for tourism products and services. In each case the decision to travel precedes the act or acts of consumption. There is no tourism industry as such. The supply side structures of tourism are volatile. They only make their appearance once the potential visitor has made the decision to travel and become an actual visitor, consuming a variety of goods and services. Visitors from the home country as well as from abroad pay money for individual goods and services, for reasons and motives that vary considerably. These products and services are produced by many different sectors of the economy and by companies both small and large. In this context it makes a great difference whether or not the goods and services consumed are selected by the individual tourists themselves, or on the contrary are put together by professional tour operators.

Macroeconomic Approach: Typical Tourism Related Industries

Thanks to a concept initiated and developed in the 1980s by the OECD Tourism Committee, the so-called Tourism Satellite Account (TSA), it is possible today to track the spending of visitors and see which specific sectors of the national economy benefit from this spending and to what extent. This makes it possible to measure the extent to which tourism contributes to value added and employment in a given country or region. This complex and time-consuming approach has also made it possible at the macro-level, with the help of a theoretical-statistical construct, to achieve a better understanding of the heterogeneity of production in tourism. Industries which obtain the lion's share of their earnings from the spending of visitors can now be identified as "characteristic branches of tourism, or collectively as the "tourism industry". In addition to identifying these specific tourism-dependent sectors of the economy we can now determine the extent to which the spending of tourists also benefits other industries which are connected or non specific to tourism.

The core sectors of the tourism industry are the passenger transport segments, the hotel and catering segments and the leisure, culture and sports segments. It is clear, however, that economic sectors that do not have any formal relationship with tourism, such as the retail trade, the construction industry, or the banking and insurance sector, also benefit a lot from the spending of visitors.

Microeconomic Approach: Tourism Systems and Service Chains

Visitors of course do not see tourism as a statistical construct. For them the journey to and from, and the time spent in the destination, all add up to a single experience. Given this holistic perception of the potential customer we need to adopt a system-oriented view of tourism market structures. The increased value of tourism as an experience has forced suppliers to develop packaged services, and to do everything they can to create a more magical atmosphere, in short to orchestrate and dramatise the whole tourism experience. It is increasingly worthwhile therefore to view the production of tourism goods and services in the context of service chains or networks, made up of a variety of companies and sectors. It follows therefore that tourism product systems must be of a complex nature.

Dual Industrial Structure: The Rise of a New International Travel Industry

The field of tourism has developed a dual economic structure over the years. Whereas in the target countries or destinations SMEs continue to offer such tourism services as accommodation, catering and leisure time activities, an international travel and tourism industry has gradually emerged in the source countries as part of the globalization process.

This new tourism industry is based on many innovations. In civil aviation charter flights were invented as a way of dealing with seasonal peaks in demand. Hotel chains that sprouted from family firms, including the Hilton and Marriott empires, grew out of a desire to satisfy the needs of business travellers, initially those travelling from the USA. The rent-a-car sector, which is today a giant industry, allows visitors to have the same mobility abroad as they do at home. Credit cards have made international money transfers much easier while at the same time reducing the risks involved in foreign exchange operations.

The international travel and tourism industry consists mainly of big companies that organise tours to various destinations on an industrial basis. They offer standardised products, and develop global strategies that enable them to make the best use of the local potential anywhere on the planet. The available statistics seem to indicate that the number of big tourism companies is relatively small, in all of the more developed tourism countries. Even so, this handful of majors generally accounts for more than half of total turnover in this sector. Sixty to ninety per cent of all companies in the hotel sector, a leading branch of tourism, and also in the travel agency sector, are micro companies, i.e. firms that employ between one and nine persons.

Thanks to standardisation the bigger tourism companies are in a position to offer their clients more attractive services at very competitive prices. They are able to develop new tourism markets and offer new products. This helps them to increase the "customer value" and to reduce their production costs. Many visitors do not want standardised products however. They prefer to tailor the holiday experience to their own specific needs and tastes. They insist on personalised services. Thanks to the multi-optional supply of products and services they are able to offer, destinations are in a position to adapt relatively quickly to the ever changing requirements of the individual tourist.

Dominant Market Structure: Imperfect Competition

Truly perfect competition should be the rule in a world tourism market which has been extensively liberalised, with prices being dictated by the market. But the fact that the availability and distribution of resources varies greatly from one place to another creates a situation of monopolistic competition in tourism markets. The different natural, cultural and civilisation-related attractions that exist in each country make it possible to differentiate destinations on a geographical basis. Each tourism country, region and place is thus unique and unmistakably individual.

Global Tourism Growth: A Challenge for SMEs

Tourism companies profit from this uniqueness of destinations. Thanks to the customer's increased willingness to pay for these special attractions, tourism companies can set prices that are higher than the market costs. "Value based pricing" allows a wide range of pricing policy measures. Differentiation is the market strategy of destinations. It brings individual SMEs a rent in the form of "brand value". Differentiation strategies work because of the need for variety. This "love of variety" also helps to explain the exchange of tourists between the countries of the industrialised world. The monopoly rent of the

SMEs in destinations is returned to the visitors in the form of an increased variety of products and services. Competition in tourism is therefore primarily competition between destinations, and only secondarily competition between individual service providers. Visitors begin by choosing a destination. Only then do they choose the combination of products and services they wish to consume. It is the availability of attractions and the relative importance of each that to a great extent determine a destination's tourism potential.

SME Problem in Developed Countries: Cluster Advantages and Size Problems

Tourism-dependent SMEs benefit greatly from the host destination, which are in almost all cases unique, difficult-to-imitate competitive systems. They can also be described as "clusters". Most tourism destinations have emerged after a long process of specialisation. Companies compete within very narrow confines. They have the benefit of competitive experience, they take advantage of existing test markets, and they can count on reliable suppliers. However these competitive advantages are no longer enough to resolve all the problems of tourism-dependent SMEs. In the industrialised world, where productivity in this labour intensive industry is lower than in less developed countries, SMEs in tourism suffer from the cost disease. They have to increase their prices to compensate for their relative lack of productivity, which in turn harms their ability to compete in the world market. Furthermore the size disadvantage of SMEs reduces their profitability. Bigger companies are able to produce at less cost thanks to economies of scale. Their products and services are more attractive thanks to reduced costs and offer more customer benefits. The bigger firms attract more visitors and produce at lower cost.

Integration and Cooperation: A Necessity for Destination Oriented SMEs

Generally speaking, SMEs in destinations never produce with the most efficient structures. This is one of the drawbacks that result from monopolistic competition, despite its various advantages. Most producers reduce the quantity and set their prices higher than the costs. It is for this reason that individual tourism is expensive in destinations, with a structure dominated by small businesses. It is also a fact that each service in the chain of services has to be paid for separately, and the cumulative final price is high. There are few service packages on offer within destinations. The fragmented small business sector that dominates tourism in the destinations often finds it difficult to remain competitive in the international market, as in the factor markets. Subject as they are to fluctuations in demand the capacity of these small firms is often under-utilised and their earning power is limited. They do not have sufficient cash flow.

Global Tourism Growth: A Challenge for SMEs

The way forward for tourism-dependent SMEs is to take far greater advantage of the potential for internal growth. Additional rooms in hotels, more seats in restaurants, these are some of the ways small firms can reduce their average costs. SMEs that make the effort can gravitate towards the optimal size. External growth is also urgently needed however, to overcome the disadvantages that go with insufficient size. At the vertical level of the destination production and marketing need to be increasingly based on partnerships, which would enable SMEs to better position themselves in the markets.

Horizontal cooperation is also necessary to increase production and lower costs. Cooperation should only be considered however if it is cheaper than producing in house or buying in the market. The OECD's Centre for Entrepreneurship, SMEs and Local Development is reviewing the organisation and functioning of global value chains for various industries as a way for SMEs to participate more fully in global growth and become more productive.

In the case of tourism, one of the five industries covered in this project, the hotel sector, a leading sector of the tourism industry, consists on the one hand of internationally active hotel chains that are continuing to expand, and on the other of small local hotels. In the worldwide competition to attract visitors with the greatest purchasing power, independent family-run hotels in the SME category are increasingly forced to cooperate at the level of marketing or themselves to become part of a hotel chain of some kind.

State Incentives for Tourism Dependant SMEs

Another question that needs to be asked is whether or not the further development, and indeed the economic survival of tourism-dependent SMEs require any specific state incentives. Tourism policy is basically concerned with the creation of more favourable framework conditions for destinations. It does not specifically address the problems of SMEs. Support for infrastructures or for marketing efforts does not take company size into consideration. Opportunities are always seized however, in the context of tourism policy, to help overcome the disadvantages that go with insufficient size. Few measures exist that are specifically aimed at tourism-dependent SMEs. Such measures include state assistance to promote urgently needed efforts in the area of cooperation, as a way of reducing high transaction and organisation costs. It can make sense in this context to promote cooperation projects in order to update existing products and services through innovation. A number of governments do in fact promote innovation and cooperation today.

The differentiation strategy of destinations does not only bring advantages to SMEs however. The development of umbrella brands is difficult and expensive. These promotion efforts have to be borne by the SMEs themselves. Furthermore, brands have to be maintained in quality through constant investment in product improvements and quality assurance systems. For these reasons virtually all governments promote market communication, or destination marketing by their national tourism office. Finally, it should not be forgotten that the multi optional nature of the products and services on offer in destinations is expensive, since a great variety of infrastructures, goods and services has to be provided. This is why many governments also support tourism-dependent infrastructures. This includes rejuvenation of the accommodation sector and the creation of new companies. There is a real need for policy action in the tourism sector. However, the granting of credits can result in certain market distortions at the expense of SMEs.

The Evolution of Space Tourism from Novelty to Opportunity

At a space business forum in June 2008, Dr. George C. Nield, Associate Administrator for Commercial Space Transportation at the Federal Aviation Administration (FAA), addressed the future of commercial space travel: 'There is tangible work underway by a number of companies aiming for space, partly because of their dreams, but primarily because they are confident it can be done by the private sector and it can be done at a profit.'

Indeed, private companies and entrepreneurs are currently aiming to make this dream a reality. While the current economic downturn will likely slow industry progress, space tourism, currently in its infancy, is poised to become a significant part of the hospitality industry.

Unlike the space race of the 1950s and 1960s between the United States and the former Soviet Union, the current rivalry is not defined on a national level, but by a collection of first-mover entrepreneurs that are working to define the industry and position it for long-term profitability. The race includes and depends on technology firms focused on developing the safest, most reliable, and most economical spacecraft, as well as service firms, or space lines, that will ultimately market and provide space travel experiences to willing "Novanauts."

In this race to send private citizens into space, the first team to cross the finish line will not necessarily win international bragging rights, but can expect to benefit from establishing a name within the space travel industry. Companies that hope to have any chance at success must first establish credibility and demonstrate reliability and safety to a population that may be skeptical of the prospect of commercial space travel. Specialty firms have announced intentions to develop the technology and/or market commercial space travel to the masses, with some currently collecting deposits for future suborbital flights and, in one instance, lunar missions.Billionaire Charles Simonyi joined a team of astronauts for his second paid visit to the International Space Station on March 25, 2009. While this experience may currently be available to the world's wealthiest individuals, opportunities for the average earthling to experience space travel are on the horizon.

"Space-like" experiences such as the Zero G Jet are currently available, while true space flight opportunities are in development. This article will explore the latest advancements in space tourism and will consider opportunities for this fledging industry. The impact of the current global economic conditions on the evolution of space travel is also considered. We further investigate who the current major players are, review the existing space tourism studies published by industry experts, and provide our expectations for the future of this industry.

Commercial Space Travel: Types of Experiences, Major Players, and Offerings

No longer an exclusive endeavour of the government, space travel is being pursued for commercial gains – enabled by the FAA's Commercial Space Launch Amendments Act of 2004[2] (CSLAA) and further influenced by the $10 million Ansari X Prize. Within the past decade, private citizens have paid large sums to be among the first to experience a variety of space and space-like experiences, including parabolic flights simulating weightlessness, suborbital flights, and higher-altitude weeklong orbital flights to the International Space Station. The prices associated with these experiences have ranged from roundly $5,000 per person for a parabolic flight to roundly $20 million for a trip to the International Space Station. The following figure provides definitions for space-like and space flight experiences. Private investors, companies, and the industry as a whole are currently working towards making space travel possible from a variety of "Spaceports," which would be located around the globe. Locations noted during our research include, but are not limited to, the United States (California, Florida, New Mexico, Texas, and Oklahoma), Kazakhstan, French Guiana, Russia, Sweden, Australia, Singapore, and the United Arab Emirates.

As more spaceports are developed, commercial space travel providers anticipate providing point-to-point global travel. Other projects under way include the development of orbital space facilities that would serve as "space hotels." Ultimately the goal of the industry is to provide a profitable means of offering suborbital, orbital, and possibly lunar-and-beyond expeditions. The development pace of the more complex service offerings (orbital point-to-point flights, space hotels, lunar expeditions, etc.) will be greatly influenced by the initial success of the commercial space tourism industry's first movers, offering suborbital experiences.

Parabolic Flights and Beyond

Established in 1993, Zero G was the first company to market a simulated space experience, offering tickets for parabolic flights based in major tourist destinations in the United States. Zero G offers passengers the sensation of weightlessness without travelling to space. The company's specially fitted jumbo jets perform parabolic manoeuvres to recreate the sensation of Martian and lunar gravity, as well as total weightlessness.

The Las Vegas-based company has flown over 100 flights and currently offers tickets for roundly $5,000 per person, as well as charter flights for groups. In January 2008, Zero G was acquired by Space Adventures, Ltd.

To date, Space Adventures is the only private company to have sent citizens into space – including the "first space tourist," Dennis Tito. Space Adventures sent Tito into orbit for nearly eight days in 2001 via the Russian Soyuz shuttle for a reported $20 million. According to a 2007 article from FOX news, Space Adventures has sold almost $200 million in tourist space flights since 2001[4]. The company is looking to expand its offerings and is currently taking reservations aboard the "first private expedition to the moon" for $100 million per seat.

Others forging their way into commercial space travel include Sir Richard Branson's Virgin Galactic. Virgin Galactic has teamed with X-Prize winner, Scaled Composites, to shuttle private citizens on suborbital flights beginning in 2010. Tickets are currently priced at $200,000, and the company has collected a reported US$30 million as of January 2008. Other companies collecting money for reservations for suborbital flights include Rocketplane for $250,000 per person and XCOR for roundly $95,000. Another player that has received media attention is Bigelow Aerospace. Currently the sole manufacturer for several of NASA's key expandable space station modules, the company is developing a family of modules to serve as the first commercial space habitats. Bigelow plans to launch the first "orbital resort" in the near future but currently has no target timeframe for the launch.

A similar initiative is being pursued by Galactic Suite, a Spanish Company with plans to package pre-space training on a remote island, with space travel to the orbital resort by 2012. A 2007 press release indicated a roundly €3 million per person price for this experience. With the space tourism industry in its infancy, each prospective operator and space technology development firm is working to set the standards for safety, comfort, and the overall Novanaut experience. One thing can be concluded from our research of existing space tourism companies: Multiple organizations and individuals believe that there is a future for us in space travel. The following figures provide details on a selection of players in the space travel industry as of the time of our research.

Understanding the Market Potential

As Space Tourism has yet to establish itself as a viable industry, there is little tangible evidence to conclude that a substantial market exists. However, an in-depth market study was conducted to forecast potential demand and revenues for space tourism activities through 2021 by Futron, a U.S.-based firm specializing in technology management consulting. In 2006, Futron revisited an extensive market study they conducted in 2002, adjusting for the year, ticket prices, and updated population wealth statistics.

The original study was based on a pool representative of those able to purchase such a luxury experience – surveying 450 wealthy individuals to determine their interest in space tourism and willingness to take part in such flights at a number of price points. Such luxury travellers are estimated as 3% of the total international tourist arrivals worldwide, yet account for 25% of total international travel expenditures – totalling US$180 billion in 2006. Considering the world population of people wealthy enough to afford space flights, as well as their fitness and interest levels, Futron used a 40-year maturity model to forecast demand and potential annual revenue from suborbital services in 2021 to reach 13,000 passengers and an estimated US$676 million – taking into account declining ticket prices due to economies of scale and applying the Fisher-Pry S-Curve to the potential demand pool. The original study also estimated orbital flights to generate $300 million per year, generating a $1-billion industry by 2021.

While Futron's updated forecasts for 2006 are down from 2002's estimate of 15,000, the study concludes "despite a delayed introduction of commercial passenger suborbital flights, and an increase in initial ticket prices over earlier expectations, demand for suborbital space tourism remains strong." In addition, one should note that the FAA's Office of Commercial Space Transportation has set no specific health or fitness requirements for passengers, suggesting a wider range of acceptability. In addition, the updated study does not take into account any changes in "the public's perception of, or level of interest in, suborbital space tourism," which is likely to have changed since the Ansari X Prize was awarded and companies like Virgin Galactic announced their plans. Although the Futron study cannot provide us with certainties for the future of commercial space travel, the report does give us a sense of potential revenues and scale of the primary demographic. As of the summer of 2008, over 250 people had put deposits down or paid the full price for Virgin Galactic's suborbital flight tickets, while another 600 had signed up to buy tickets once flights begin. As with any new innovation, these individuals will lead the way for the industry's expansion, eventually creating economies of scale, lowering ticket prices, and increasing accessibility to a wider demographic.

Impact of the Current Economy and Future Trends for the Space Tourism Industry

Is there enough demand to warrant long-term success of the

commercial space travel industry? Only time will tell. With the current economic recession, technological advances and the launch of regularly scheduled suborbital (and beyond) flights are likely to be delayed.

However, when we consider the forecasts from the Futron study and the inclinations of a large population towards adventure tourism and activities generally perceived as higher risk, or extreme (i.e., skydiving, scuba diving, rock climbing, etc.), the authors foresee the progression of commercial space travel as a viable industry in the long term. While information is limited on the payoff and functionality of each company's plan and proposed operating models, long-term success will rely on basic critical factors such as safety, reliability, service differentiation, and value. As spaceports are built and ticket prices lowered as a result of economies of scale, we predict point-to-point space travel to spur demand and a sustainable source of business. As demonstrated by the cruise industry, combining a destination with the travel experience may justify this mode of travel for some and support repeat purchases, avoiding the possibility of becoming a once-in-a-lifetime experience. In this case, destinations may include "hotels" in space or locations across the globe that can be reached quickly and conveniently.

We also predict that existing and new luxury brands will partner with space technology developers to offer upscale service and accommodations for affluent travellers in the first space hotels and hotels located proximate to space training and launching sites. We expect to see tourism centres (hotel accommodations, entertainment, and restaurants) to be developed adjacent to spaceport locations to house guests during space training. These supportive developments will be especially necessary in remote Spaceport locations.

As the first space flights are expected to be affordable to only the wealthiest individuals, who are accustomed to the finest accommodations, we expect that these hotels will be in the luxury segment.

For some, the dream of space travel could be a reality within the next decade. The innovators in the space tourism industry will do much to define the future experiences of prospective Novanauts, setting the standards for safety, creating realistic expectations of the in-flight experience, and developing packages and experiences that will represent the most value for the target market.

The start of the second space race is currently under way, with possibilities that are truly out of this world!

7

Tourism Attracts Retires

Tourism is also an important aspect of community economic development. Unfortunately, the economic potential of travel by the public often is not taken seriously. Public decision makers fail to realize the true extent and complexity of tourism, although every U.S. community has a tourism industry of some kind. Almost every business providing goods or services at retail is a part of the industry. Tourism produces profits, jobs, taxes, and rents, similar to most other economic activities. Furthermore, it is compatible with most other economic activities, and almost everyone is a tourist at one time or another.

Tourism Is Economic Development

Long considered "fluff," or a mere nuisance to local residents, tourism today is big business. The U.S. Travel Data Centre (1990b) has published impressive statistics related to tourism. Travellers spent $350 billion in the United States during 1989, an increase of 7 percent from 1988. This was equal to 6.7 percent of the gross national product. Spending by travellers in the United States generated 5.8 million jobs in 1989, paid nearly $74 billion in wages and salaries, and produced $43 billion in federal, state, and local tax revenue. If considered as a single industry, the tourism sector is the third largest retail industry in terms of business receipts. Those larger are automotive dealerships and food stores. Not only are statistics concerning tourism in the United States impressive, but the industry is still growing. Vacation travel in 1989 increased 7 percent over the previous year, making it the sixth straight year of increase in vacation travel.

Alabama has benefited substantially from these changes. In 1990 tourists spent an estimated $3.1 billion in Alabama, a 7.6 percent increase over 1989 and an increase of 26 percent over the past 2 years. These expenditures support more than 53,000 full-time jobs and in 1990 created more than 5,000 new jobs in the state. Alabama directly collected $67.7 million in state taxes and communities collected $70.9 million in local taxes.

The tourism and travel future for Alabama appears bright. In 1989 the southeast region of the United States received the greatest amount of travel with almost 350 million person-trips, which was 30 percent of all domestic travel. The southeast also enjoyed the greatest amount of growth as a tourist destination in 1989.

Tourism is Compatible with Attracting Retirees

Among the economic goals of local communities should be the development of a balanced economic base and the identification of the comparative advantages of the community from its resource and economic base. To achieve this end, many communities have identified both tourism and retiree attraction as one means of achieving economic development goals. Consider the small prosperous town of Hendersonville, North Carolina (population 8,000). Well known for its success in attracting affluent retirees, Hendersonville employed a four-pronged economic development strategy focusing on agriculture, industry, tourism, and retirees. Among significant tangible results is an increase in bank deposits from $16 million in 1961 to $465 million in 1990. Retirees are estimated to account for 60 percent of these deposits.

Officials of Hendersonville recognize that many individuals who have retired in their community first visited as tourists. Even though tourism and retiree attraction are often identified as economic development strategies for a community, few seem to recognize the important link between the two. The community is not going to be able to attract retirees unless they are first able to attract them as tourists.

Recognizing that individuals approaching retirement are likely to embark on travel in an attempt to find the most desirable retirement location opens new and affluent tourism markets to the community.

Current Travel Trends

Travel is now an important segment of American life styles, and the rate of growth in travel during the 1990s should exceed that during the 1980s.

Several trends may have an impact upon tourism related to the mature Americans market. The mature citizen market segment of most interest to communities desiring to attract retirees is the 45 to 64 age group. Those 65 and older are most likely to be currently retired and settled in the community in which they wish to enjoy their retirement years. The mature adults group of interest can best be examined by dividing them into two segments: those beginning to make tentative retirement plans, but who are still examining many possibilities (the 45 to 54 age group), and those very near retirement and likely to make final retirement plans relatively quickly (the 55 to 64 age group).

The 45 to 54 age group. Between now and the year 2000, the greatest population growth will be in the 45 to 54 age group. It should experience a 63 percent increase. Most should remain in good health for the next decade. Currently, more than 60 percent of this group indicate that their health is good or excellent.

This particular group took 15 percent of all trips in 1987. They are active business travellers and frequent users of air travel, rental cars, and hotels. On the average they are more likely than other groups to take day trips, travel by camper or recreational vehicles, and travel outside the United States.

The 55 to 64 age group. Householders aged 55 to 64 have the highest median net worth of any age group. The value of their assets is 21 percent greater than the average. Most members of this group are in good health and physically able to engage in a variety of leisure activities.

Fourteen percent of all trips taken in 1987 were made by persons of age 55 to 64. They are less likely to spend discretionary income on purchases of material possessions than on items that offer social reinforcement and enjoyable experiences, such as leisure activities and travel. This group is more value-sensitive than price-sensitive. If they believe a product or service is worth the cost, price becomes less important and only a matter of what they can afford.

Tourism Marketing Implications

To be successful in attracting both tourists and retirees, a marketing plan is necessary. Few communities can be all things to all people. Priorities must be established, audiences targeted, and a marketing strategy developed. Based on current population and travel trends, several marketing strategies warrant consideration. Concentrate On Nearby Large Metropolitan Areas. Although Americans are taking more vacation trips, they are spending less time on each trip. In 1985 the average stay was 5.7 nights per trip. By 1989 this had slipped to 4.7 nights. There is a definite trend toward more weekend vacation travel. In 1980 there were 311 million weekend vacation person-trips. This increased to 427 million by 1989. Such data support a marketing effort targeting large metropolitan areas within a day's drive of your community.

Do Not Ignore Other Large Metropolitan Areas. This does not suggest that local leaders ignore markets several days' distance from their communities. While the length of stay per trip is decreasing, individuals of more than 45 years of age take fewer weekend trips and travel farther. Obviously, this is a group to target when attracting potential retirees. Therefore, tourism marketing areas should extend to other regional metropolitan areas.

Concentrate On Specific Segments Of The Mature Market. An aggressive approach in marketing to the 55 to 64 age group is necessary, because they will be finalizing retirement plans. Off-season travel should be popular with them. Most have fewer time restrictions, so travel enticements should focus on opportunities for personal growth in specific interest areas rather than on age.

In most cases, there is ample time to reach the 45 to 54 age group, but they must be contacted early so the idea of retiring in a given community will have time to mature. With above-average financial resources, reduced expenses, and more leisure time, this age group tends to travel more often. Travel that offers opportunities for personal growth is also attractive to this group.

Develop Group Tour Packages. Communities should aggressively market themselves to the escorted group traveller, or tour group. A recent study indicated that while about 10.3 million American adults participated in group tours in 1989, more than 15 million plan to take an escorted tour within the next 2 years. This represents 11 percent of the entire adult travelling public. Current tour group participants tend to be females of more than 60 years of age, retired or homemakers, with less than $25,000 household incomes. However, examination of those planning to join a tour group within the next 2 years indicated that future tour group travellers were likely to be younger, just as likely to be male as female, better educated, and most likely to be in either the $25,000 to $49,000 or $50,000 to $74,000 income ranges. Since people in the 55 to 64 age group will be looking for convenience and ease, special group tours designed to provide these qualities and social companionship should be attractive.

Care must be taken to remember that these are broad-based generalizations. While they may be valid for the entire population, each community should carefully examine its particular strengths and weaknesses to determine which generalizations apply locally.

The Retirement Industry

Economic development has occurred mostly in urban areas as a result of manufacturing growth. Rural areas and smaller communities have difficulty competing for the relocation of manufacturing plants and have typically depended on agriculture for economic development. Such communities are discovering that they have the infrastructure to support tourism and another newly developing industry—the "retirement industry." Older migrants in the United States are relocating to areas with amenities to provide them with a comfortable life style for their retirement. They have steady incomes that are not vulnerable to normal down cycles in the national economy. Their income is used mostly for discretionary spending, which usually occurs locally and leads to economic development and job creation in the community of relocation.

Persons of age 50 and above in the United States have:

* 77 percent of the nation's personal financial assets.
* 80 percent of the money in savings accounts.
* 68 percent of all money market accounts.
* Nearly 50 percent of all corporate stocks.

Persons of age 50 and above in the United States:

* Earn 42 percent of total after-tax income.
* Buy 48 percent of all domestic new cars.
* Own their houses in 80 percent of the cases, and 80 percent of those are mortgage free.
* Have accounts with brokerage firms in 27 percent of the cases.

Major assets of the mature market include:

* Financial assets that are 80 percent larger than average.
* Savings accounts that are 90 percent larger than average.

* Checking accounts that are 50 percent more than average.
* U.S. savings bonds that are 50 percent more than average.
* Other securities that are 50 percent more than average.
* Houses worth 20 percent more than the U.S. average.

The large sums of financial assets involved in the interstate redistribution of income because of elderly migration is directly influencing state economies. Older migrants have generated a "new" industry with the major growth segments being real estate, finance, recreation, health care, insurance, and retail.

A 1986 study by the Federal Reserve Bank of Kansas City found that rural counties where incomes are based on retirees have out-paced all others in per capita income growth. Also, counties designated as retirement sites witnessed the largest increase in personal income and employment among all non-metropolitan counties.

The "retirement industry" boosts the local economy and increases the tax base. Large investments in infrastructure or tax abatements are not required by government. Retirees do not pollute or destroy the environment. They increase the number of volunteers and contributors benefiting many organizations. Obviously then, retirement is a good industry to recruit for economic development.

As a result of understanding the net benefits of the retirement industry, more towns, counties, and states are beginning to recruit retirees. Some governmental units are getting involved with project financing and efforts to develop retirement housing that will attract retirees and create jobs. Examples are common in housing and community development in Florida, Arizona, and Arkansas.

Retirement income can lead to job growth in the same way that industrial payrolls generate jobs. Retirees spend their income in the local economy, creating a demand for goods and services. When the demand:supply ratio becomes more favorable for investment and employment, capital and labour follow, stimulating economic growth. Retirement income benefits local economies by increasing the demand for local goods and services, creating a source of investment funds, and generating a deposit base for financing community development projects.

Local communities are benefiting from the wave of incoming retiree dollars. That trend is expected to continue and will transform the economic structure of many more communities in the future. Nondurable goods and services will be major aspects of these local economies with food, travel, recreation, entertainment, and health care dominating.

The number of older migrants will continue to increase and they will have multiple income sources, better education, better health, earlier retirements, and longer lives. They will continue to be a favorable source for economic development.

Developing Marketing Resources

Once you have established your perfect tourism business, the challenge to sell your product to attract visitors begins.

Advertising, printed material, the internet, public relations and media exposure are the communication resources you could use to showcase your product to potential customers. International visitors and trade are exposed to a wealth of information, and you want your business to stand out from the crowd.

Where to Begin

Your marketing and communications need to emphasise your point of difference. What are the benefits that customers will experience with your product that they wouldn't in any other? What is your point of difference?

Your collateral should focus on your unique selling points and highlight any advantages you have over your competitors. The quality of your material should also be of a high standard to attract the international visitor. Remember to include any industry accreditations such as Remember that first impressions always count.

Brand

Establishing your brand is one of the most important aspects of promoting your product. It will help consumers identify with your product.

Your brand must reflect what it is you do. Your brand will usually consist of your product name and your logo; sometimes it might also include a tagline (slogan). Your brand should be consistent across all the marketing material associated with your product.

Intellectual Property

When you are setting up a business, it is very important to think about the intellectual property of your business. This is about more than just the company name. It is about the goodwill of your company and the reputation that you have or intend to build up.

If you do not protect your brand, you open yourself up for others to start companies which then benefit from your hard work.

Check the Intellectual Property Office of New Zealand. This has a searchable trademarks and patents area so you can see if anyone else has already tried to trademark your brand.

What is the best Way to Promote your Product?

There is a range of marketing tools you can use to promote your product-and a mix of a few will probably be the best fit for your business. Most visitors will use a number of different sources to plan their travels, so diversifying your marketing spend is important. It's also important to look for the communication tools that your target market is most likely to use.

Do your visitors plan ahead and do research before they arrive? If so, it could be that getting your website up and running and linking with the right regional and international sites is your top marketing priority. On the other hand, if your target market is likely to make spontaneous decisions, getting your brochures into your closest i-SITE Visitor Centre, and local retailers and accommodation providers could be the best way to encourage business.

Tourism New Zealand's target market tends to use websites, guidebooks such as Lonely Planet, Rough Guide and Frommers and travel agents prior to arriving in New Zealand to help them plan their trip.

Images

For all of your marketing, you'll need excellent, high-quality images, and it is recommended that you use a professional photographer. Generally your images should be presented on a branded CD Rom, and also be available to be sent by email. The standards for print quality images are:

- Jpeg format.
- 300 dpi (high resolution).

Your images should capture your Unique Selling Points, what makes your experience different from other tourism activities. It's also a good idea to show people enjoying the activity or place that features in your product.

Printed Material

Brochures

Brochures are a good first marketing step. While you don't need to spend a lot on them, it's important they are consistent with your brand, include high-quality images and are professionally produced.

Your brochure needs to carry enough information to motivate customers to choose your business, and give them the details they need to book it. Try and make the traveller's purchasing decision as easy as possible. Keep your information relevant, clear and concise, and don't forget to list all contact details including opening hours and clear details of where you are located. If you haven't worked with a printer before, shop around and get some quotes. Some printers will also handle the design of your brochure. You'll need to brief them on your target market, specify where the brochure is to be distributed, and provide them with your wording and images ready for print. Be careful not to oversell your product with your words. When choosing how your brochure will look, do some research at your local i-SITE Visitor Centre, and talk to staff about which brochures work best. You'll want to choose a size that is easy to display (usually DLE), and ensure your name is prominent, along with accreditations.

Make sure your Qualmark accreditation is displayed clearly on the front cover as this identifies you as a quality product and demonstrates that you have been independently assessed as a quality tourism business.

Getting the Simple Things Right

- If you plan to distribute your brochure through visitor centres or brochure racks, make sure your name isn't covered by the stand/rack. This means the top quarter of the brochure cover becomes very important.
- Make sure you have a map clearly showing which region your business is in.
- Remember not everyone will be familiar with your area (or even New Zealand) so step-by-step details of how to find your business could be useful. Test your location map with a non-local before including it in your brochure.

- Don't get thousands printed as details are likely to change.
- Include the area code, and +64 for New Zealand on your phone and fax details in the international format if you plan to distribute your brochure offshore, i.e. (+64 3) 123 4567.
- Give customers an idea of how far in advance they will need to book.
- Don't forget to include your Unique Selling Points.
- Remember that "a good picture tells a thousand words".
- Ensure your photographs are compelling and relevant. For example, show people enjoying your experience.
- Use short sentences, and remember some of your clients might have English as a second language.

Make sure that the information in your brochure is consistent with your website.

Before you go to your printer also work out the:

- size of your brochure.
- number of colours (full colour is usually more expensive, but also more effective).
- quantity to print.
- deadline.

Also make sure you arrange to sign off each step of the process, and even consider an independent proof-reader, so you don't run the risk of any embarrassing types.

If this is your first brochure, or your business has just started, it might be wise to do only a small quantity in your first print, particularly if you are including prices for your product.

Your prices need to be valid for the circulation life of your brochure. You have responsibilities under the Consumer Guarantees Act 1993 to provide accurate product information to potential customers, so don't make claims you can't live up to.

Online Marketing

International travellers, travel professionals and travel trade are increasingly using the web to do their travel research, demanding current information that is innovative and motivational. The internet is a global platform for communication which allows cheap, fast and cost-effective marketing worldwide. Having a presence on the internet is not only beneficial, it is essential.

To assist in your online marketing efforts, Tourism New Zealand has invaluable online resources which are easily accessible and free. These online resources act independently of one another, but all combine as an effective marketing tool, suitable for anyone involved in the New Zealand tourism industry.

Tourism New Zealand's Consumer Website

Tourism New Zealand's consumer receives more than 300,000 user sessions per year. By registering for free on the site you will be connecting with thousands of potential visitors.

- influence where visitors choose to take holidays.
- aid holiday planning.
- assist decision making.

We do this by connecting consumers directly with tourism businesses through the operator listings. These roles have been enhanced by the new travel planner tool.

Travel Planner

The travel planner increases the profile of individual operator listings even further by allowing (consumers) to collect each individual operator listing they wish to experience.

The travel planner allows users to collect activities, transport, accommodation and event listings from across the website, displaying a calendar and map. It also gives them the ability to share their collection with friends and family.

Listing your Business or Event

By listing a business or event you have the opportunity to become part of Tourism New Zealand's global marketing campaign, providing potential visitors with your business details and linking them to your website. Listings take about ten days to be approved, and there is no cost involved. Listed operators are required to log in and check their details once every 12 months. Creating a listing is free, but an email and contact phone number which are answered regularly are essential. description of service, contact details, a map, photo, Qualmark© rating and Tourism Award (if applicable).

Tourism New Zealand's Travel Trade Website

The trade-specific database is the ultimate resource for all travel professionals based overseas and involved with promoting, planning or booking travel to New Zealand. This tool allows travel professionals to gain a more accurate view of products provided in New Zealand, with detailed information specifying interests, facilities offered, language support, and months of operation, special requirements, latest updates and newest products.

Trade Listings

Trade listings provide the advantage of being regularly used and extremely beneficial to international and domestic travel trade, thus giving operator listings further exposure. Trade listings can be created at the same site as consumer listings,

E-Marketing

As your business grows you can build a database of your customers. Consider giving your customers a feedback form to fill in as they leave. This will give you valuable feedback and contact details. You could also email your visitors a 'thank you for visiting' message. This is a good way of reminding them how fantastic their experience with you was, so they will recommend you to friends and family.

Once you have a reasonable list, consider doing some pro-active email marketing. Since these people have already visited you once, they are a good target for a second visit.

Only email people who have agreed to receive further company information from you as unsolicited email is likely to be viewed as unwanted spam. Include media contacts, Regional Tourism Organisations and local i-Sites on your mailing list so you can keep them up-to-date with your product. It's a good idea to develop a simple template you can use for a newsletter or update. Keep the look and tone consistent with your other marketing material.

Technically, the following are some good guidelines for email marketing:

- Keep email contacts private by entering them in the BCC (blind carbon copy) line.
- Put a pertinent subject in the subject line-don't leave it blank.
- Always give an option to withdraw from your email list.

- Focus on something new or different or include a special offer only for email recipients.
- Don't email too frequently.
- Ensure the file size is small and the design isn't too busy so it will download quickly.
- Keep the content short and punchy and remember to get someone else to proof read it before sending.

Advertising

Another outlet for your marketing messages is advertising opportunities. These include:

- newspapers.
- magazines.
- visitor guides and directories.
- radio.
- television.
- cinema.

Print advertising is generally the cheapest form, and a good first step. One major drawback of advertising is that it can be less personal than other forms, but if you choose your advertising outlet carefully, it can be a very effective way of reaching a large number of consumers.

Operators who are new to the game should be vigilant when approached by people asking for them to advertise on their website or in their guide. The best thing to do in this situation is approach your local Regional Tourism Organisation and ask for their advice. They will know which ones are reputable and which ones are not. The main types of tourism advertising you could consider are:

* Visitor guides-which will reach the customer in New Zealand and your region.
* Travel trade publications-which will reach channels of distribution such as inbound tour operators and wholesalers.
* Consumer publications-which will reach the customer, i.e. 'Tourist Times'.

Assess all offers and approaches for advertising you receive. You must be confident that the advertising opportunity will effectively reach your target market.

The following checklist can provide a guide on whether the advertising is going to work for you:

- Who does the advertising medium target?
- What is the reach of the advertising (circulation/readership)?
- Is the medium well supported by other products from your region?
- What editorial contact about your region, city or town is included?
- Is the quality of the publication or medium appropriate for your product?

Your advertisement should be eye catching and well produced and contain relevant information. You should include your 'Unique Selling Points', a fantastic picture and a description of what your product offers. For example, an activity operator would include trip details, duration of trip, hours of operation and booking details. You should always include all contact details, an 0800 number if you have it, and your website address.

Public Relations and Working with the Media

Print media coverage can be a fantastic marketing option for your business. One of the major advantages is that this coverage is seen by readers as being more objective than advertising. It also tends to provide more information and background than other forms of advertising.

The obvious disadvantage is that you have little control over what is written, which makes it even more important to have a well-developed media strategy and know how to deal with media.

As your business develops consider what media angles you might have, for example any quirky stories, new products, or personalities involved in your business, which you think would make a good story.

Also, start compiling a list of media. If you are targeting domestic visitors, find out details of media in your region and other target areas-your RTO may be able to help. You can also find media guides at most public libraries. Most metropolitan daily newspapers have travel pages as do some Sunday papers and lifestyle magazines.

If your focus is international, Tourism New Zealand's international media programme could be an option. See Working Internationally for more information.

The Media Release

If you are hoping to get media coverage of your product or service, a fundamental tool is an effective media release-and anyone can write one. The rule of a media release is to get your most important information in the first few paragraphs-only a few journalists will continue reading to the very end of your piece. This means identifying what your news angle is. Will it be interesting to a wider audience?

Make sure you have an eye-catching headline, the vital information in the first paragraph, and quotes from your organisation in the second or third paragraph. At the end of the media release ensure you list a range of contact options for your media spokesperson-and make sure all your staff know who the spokesperson is. In general, your press release should not be more than one A4 page. Use at least 12-point font to make it easy to read when it comes off a fax. Once you have sent the release (by fax or email usually) you can follow up to check that it has been received, and gauge any interest.

Working with the Media

If there is media interested in covering your business, you should make it as easy as possible for them to write the best story.

Basics could include:

- Have a media kit ready-including a sheet of background facts and figures, another copy of your media release, other story angles, your image CD containing high-resolution images, and your business card.
- If you are being interviewed, do some preparation to ensure you know what kind of audience the media goes to. Think about the points you would like to speak about before the interview-some media will even supply you with questions ahead of time so you can prepare.
- Help the media to identify other characters or advocates who could help fill out your story.

Preparation is the key. You are the expert on your business, and generally media are not looking to trap you into saying something you don't want to. Instead, by providing some snappy quotes and giving them good information, you are actually more likely to achieve positive media coverage.

Some hints when talking to media:

- Before you speak to them think about what their story is, so you can prepare relevant information.
- Prepare some key messages, and try to speak to those.
- Keep it simple; don't talk in jargon.
- Be helpful.
- Try to convey your excitement and enthusiasm about your business.

Evolution of the Tourism Industry on Guam

An Interpretive Essay

When one considers the evolution of tourism on Guam, it is useful to reflect on events that have happened since the advent of tourism in the early 1970s. Another perspective of this historical development is to consider the application of "A Tourism System Model" as documented by the company Mill and Morrison in 1992.

A typical tourism system consists of four distinct stages. First there is the creation of a demand. People such as Juan Tripe, a Pan American Airlines visionary; David Tuncap, former operations manager for Pan American Airlines; Herbert Fukuda and Earl Kloppenburg of Turtle Tours; Robert and Margaret Jones, Guam tourism proponents; Rex Willis of the Guam Tourism Commission; and Bert Unpingco, Guam's "Mr. Tourism" are some of the pioneers who helped cultivate this demand. This demand was created after an initial 109 passengers aboard Pan Am Flight 801 departing from Haneda, Japan travelled to a newly discovered, exotic, tropical destination called Guam in 1967. The second stage of this system is that of developing a means of transporting people to their desired destination.

The previous forty years showed a tremendous succession of international airlines like Pan American, Continental Micronesia, Northwest, Braniff, American, Trans World Airways, South Pacific Island Airways, Hawaiian Air and others who sought to capitalize on the interests of those who wished to travel annually to Guam, currently 1.3 million people. The island today serves as an air transportation hub for passage to and from Asia and the Western world. A third stage consists of providing a supply of attractions, lodging and accommodations for the traveller.

From the humble beginnings of a Pan American Hotel built in Sumay in the 1930s and the Cliff Hotel in Agana Heights established in 1959, there are now more than twenty-eight hotel properties in operation such as the Hilton Resort & Spa, Sheraton Laguna Guam, Pacific Islands Club, Guam Marriott Resort, Fiesta Resort, Guam Reef Hotel, Outrigger Resort, Guam Hotel Okura, and Nikko Resort Hotel Guam. Guam has also increased its attractions from a basic sightseeing, war relic, and *omiyage* (souvenir or present) destination to one that offers world class shopping and entertainment. In addition to ecotourism attractions such as marine sports and outdoor adventures, there have been an increasing number of shopping and leisure activities that have developed in response to visitor demand. The island's hospitality industry has also gradually moved from an eight-hour daytime operation to a round the clock operation.

The fourth and final stage of this tourism system is the communications, signage and marketing designed for visitor satisfaction. There has been a tremendous surge of promotions and advertising of the Guam experience and Guam companies on a worldwide basis. Visitor signage has also been greatly enhanced throughout the island and has encouraged more freedom in travelling throughout the island's villages than in the past. It is this overall system that contributed to the development of Guam as a favorable resort destination and produced a rate of twenty-five of every 100 visitors returning for multiple visits.

Tourism Today

A tourist is generally described as someone who has travelled more than fifty miles from home and has spent the night in another location. The Guam Visitors Bureau reported a total of 1.217 million arrivals in 2006, an increase of 0.6 percent from 2005 and a growth rate of 6.17 percent.

About 81 percent of visitor arrivals are from Japan with the remaining visitors coming from Korea, Taiwan, Hong Kong and other Asian countries. A typical visitor to Guam spends approximately $1,650 for a three night, four-day stay on the island. Of this total expense, $1,100 is for a package tour and the estimated balance of $500 is spent on entertainment, meals and other activities. Guam's lodging and accommodations consists of 7,250 hotel rooms as of April 2007.

The Guam Hotel and Restaurant Association reported 4,785 employees working in twenty-six hotels during April 2007. A March

2007 Current Employment Report issued by The Guam Department of Labour showed 5,440 workers employed in hotels and other lodging places and a total of 10,480 persons employed in the island's service industries.

Average hourly wages reported by the Guam Department of Labour for hotel employees was $6.86 for a 36-hour work week. Global Insight, Inc. In its Tourism Satellite Account Study reported an average salary of $19,468 ($9.36/hr.) for those in tourism employment.

Tourism Role

The Guam Economic Development and Commerce Authority presented details in 2006 which showed that military contributions to Guam's economy in the early 1960s amounted to sixty-five percent of the total economy, while tourism contributed thirty percent of the total and the remaining five percent was attributed to other sources.

This was at a time when there was a very strong armed forces presence on the island. However, GEDCA reported that during the 1970s contributions from the Armed Forces to Guam's economy had declined to approximately twenty percent. This decline was attributed to President Regan's executive order A1C that converted federal activities to privatized ventures. The U.S. Naval Station Guam was dramatically affected by the loss of an estimated 6,000 civil service skilled trade jobs that were transferred to other parts of the nation. This change also signalled the growth of a private economy fuelled by tourism, in terms of both visitor arrivals and high levels of spending.

The year 2007 showed yet another reversal in the geopolitical environment with the announcement of an impending withdrawal of military bases in foreign countries and a re-alignment of some defence resources in Japan to Guam. It is reported the U.S. Marines will relocate 8,000 soldiers to Guam with an estimated 14,000 dependents from Okinawa, Japan.

Plans are currently being made to bring 22,000 more military members and their families to Guam by 2014 which will undoubtedly bring the total population of Guam to more than 200,000. This increase in military presence has caused serious concern regarding the ability of the social and physical infrastructure to sustain a population of this size without significantly overtaxing its resources.

8

Toward the Evolution of the Tourism's Conceptual System

Introduction

The tourism is one of the main economic activities in the world. It generates an important investment and it can contribute to the economic growth and the social progress of the developing countries not only for its economic spill but also when favouring and encouraging the performance of activities that assist the demand of the tourists like lodging, feeding, transport, amusement, the knowledge of traditions, attractions and of the culture, among other, with the consequent generation of direct and indirect job positions; In addition it attracts national and foreign investment and it impels the regional infrastructure by means of the urbanization and construction of new and improved communication means (terrestrial, sea, air).

A great amount of foreign currencies enters the countries because of this activity, derived from the international exchanges, but also, the internal tourism that the national population practices inside its own territory, contributes to balance the national economy by means of the redistribution of the income.

At the same time, for the amount of services that it requires, the tourism is a factor of employment creation of in different activities. For instance in Mexico the Tourism contributes with more than 7.7% of the national Internal Raw Product (PIB) and contributes with more than 9% in direct and indirect job positions, reason why it is one of the strategic sectors in the national economic development.

Evolution of the Tourism's Conceptual System

The study of the tourist phenomenon at the present time requires a revaluation of the models that have been used for this aim, with the purpose of generating a holistic vision in its analysis. Science contemplates a series of specific knowledge that explain the concrete phenomena of real life, through it, scientists understand their study object, as long as the method allows to carry out valuations with certainty of the wisdom and agree to the theoretical structure to prepare.

Science in its historical evolution has suffered transformations, passing from the traditional reductionism to the totalizing approaches, with the firm conviction of achieving transcendence in the acquired knowledge.

The study of the social science, different from the so called hard sciences, has softening elements appreciated in the systems of human activity, reason why it cannot be approached from exact sciences' characteristic scientific perspectives.

The scientifically acceptable tourism has recaptured defined theoretical structures starting from their main manifestations (economic, social, and psychological) that are shown as weak to remark their theoretical synopsis when valuing the phenomenon from the whole that embraces. The scientific thought of Tourism, should be understood from totalizing methodologies view, able to overcome the antagonism of the singular vision of a science in particular. The prime scientific outcome, from which the tourist study can start, is constituted by its constant evolution, basic elements of the living systems that show the alignment of phenomena to the conditions of the environment, as well as its structural components.

In order to approach the epistemological problematic of the tourism, one can use the Systemic Emergent Paradigm as a methodology that provides a dialectical synthesis in the study of the composition of relating qualitative and quantitative combined elements to their different manifestations by means of constituting the aspects that compose it from a holistic optics, able to refer the phenomenon in all its possible manifestations.

Therefore it is convenient to try to approach the study of the tourist phenomenon from the perspective of the Systemic, with the intention of being able to propose a model of tourist system that shows the involved elements and their possible interactions. This way, it is sought to analyse the theoretical currents about the Science of Systems and the Tourism with the purpose of generating a reference mark to lead us toward a model of categorization of the tourism from the systemic considerations.

Science and Systems Sciences

The rational knowledge is derived of mankind's necessity to give answer to the events that surround them, and so it is that the philosophical method arises, along with the metaphysics and the Greek scholastic, giving a controllable order to the thought that separates the ideology from the application.

The systemic thought emerges of the Aristotelian teleology of "the whole it is more than the sum on its parts", agreed in the Hegelian and Marxist dialectics that constitute the advance of the holistic vision.

Evolution of the Tourism's Conceptual System

Overcome by the emergence of the Descartes reductionism whose proposal breaks into fragments the whole problem in as many simple and separate elements as it is possible, generating the resolute method of Galileo where the complex phenomena are reduced to parts and elementary processes.

Bertalanffy (1995), introduced the idea of the organisms like systems, showing by fact that the laws of the systems behave as analogies, that is to say that formally identical laws are applied to completely different phenomena.

The General Systems Theory or Theory of the Organized Complexity, treats phenomena that cannot be simplified, that to say that cannot be reduced, it embraces the living and not alive systems through isomorphic principles, leaving intact the internal interactions, studying the system like a whole and embracing its complexity. In general, inside the system conceptualization, the authors that have defined it agree that it is a group of coordinated parts and in interaction to reach a group of objectives.

The systems approach is used to solve complex problems of the organisations from a global perspective, it carries out an analysis of the entirety of the components as well as its interrelations, and it tends toward the application of a holistic perspective, it tries to reach the dialectical synthesis between the quantitative and qualitative methods, considering them as complementary and it is not only limited to the knowledge of the system but rather it promulgates its improvement.

Darwin's theory of evolution, postulates the living beings as a result of a slow evolution where the diverse species have derived from each other by natural selection. The evolution leads to the spontaneous appearance of systems of a grater and grater complexity where not alone the complexity increases in the system but also its effectiveness.

Epistemoligical Problems of Tourism

The advance of the scientific research of Tourism shows leisure (playful activity, vacation or free time), as main element of its theoretical consideration. Leisure according to Bullon (1990), leads to free time or work break that according to Mune (1986), represents the social wealth that constitutes the time in which the productive forces recover their vitality, through a playful self-regenerating of all that is human. The use of leisure time is a psychological activity since it depends on what each individual intends. The recreation on the other hand is any kind of use that the mankind makes of its free time, whenever this use is carried out in a pleasant attitude. This way the tourism is a peculiar form of recreation, but not its only presentation. Reason why trying to study the tourism through the use of the recreation and the free time, requires subordinating the recreation, human innate element to a specific use of the free time, which turns into an exhausting task that would not lead to its theoretical conformation.

Evolution of the Tourism's Conceptual System

The concept of Tourism has been approached from the practical definition deduced from the shortened interpretations emitted by the OMT (1991) that refers to the displacement of people outside of their residence place for different reasons, fact that scorns the tourist dynamics including it in the tourist's emblem as the only element of their conformation.

The tourism has been glimpsed from the tourist's vision whose elements that validate the tourist concept, are contemplated by 1) the activities to develop 2) the existence of a displacement 3) the permanency in the visit place for at least 24 hours where a night stay should exist to be considered as the use a tourist service 3) the interaction of the tourists with the hosting community. The debate on what is or not a tourist, derives from the previous elements, since only people that complete such condition are considered as tourists, therefore one should not considered 'a tourist' as the person that moves inside their habitual environment, consume tourist products, develop tourist activities and interact with the hosting community, however they are considered inside a tourist segment, they carry out tourist expense and act as tourists, but according to the previous considerations they should be classified as non tourist, due to the absence of one of the elements that gives them that categorization which is the displacement outside of his residence place.

The economic and social slopes have marked the rule to be able to locate the tourist issue as part of their theoretical happening, the first one with the economic science, in the offer-demand model where the tourism is an activity that generates revenues, job positions and expense with a multiplier and transformer effect on the regional development.

The social approach promulgates the social psychology that tries to refer it from the intercultural contacts, the sociological theory that shows tourism like a social phenomenon,, and the tourist anthropology that includes tourism inside its ethnic-cultural dynamism. These approaches present tourism like a playful activity that has as main function, the one of fomenting the human understanding among people of different cultures.

The epistemological problem of the tourist knowledge resides, more than in the same object, in the paradigm that studies it. The tourism has shown obstacles and continuous epistemological errors within the evolution of its theoretical knowledge, exposed in the theoretical lack pointed out by Bullon (1985), and revealed by the lack of general principles to harmonize its theoretical structure.

The tourist researcher should depart from its own knowledge, linking their experiences with the phenomenon, their rational understanding, and to be able to combine it with the knowledge of the scientific theory, to be able to propose a dialectical that leads to new and transcendent knowledge. This implies not to copy ordinary arguments, but making a dialectical rupture with the traditional foundations.

Systems Theory and Tourism

The best way to approach tourism is through the General Theory of Systems, in accordance with Leiper, who proposes the recommendation of a systems approach as a means for the research that deal with relative general matters related to the interdisciplinary issue.

The design of the tourist dynamics began to be develop from a particular systemic approach, cybernetics, based on it, the classic approaches are shown like the Molina tourist system, that is explained as an open system, established by the integration of a group of parts or subsystems that are related to reach a common objective, related in turn with their environment. For Boullon (1985), the tourist system is composed of three perspectives: to) an offer demand model that centres its interest in the operation of the commercial tourism b) a social anthropological approach that is in charge of the leisure and free time manifestations and c) inside the industrial tourism model that is interested in the massive production the commercialization and the profit. This tourist division denotes the disintegration of what should be a single system, what makes allusion to this model's inability to be able to integrate the elements and the relationships of the tourist system.

However, so much the system of Molina as well as Boullon's respond to the mechanical and organic models that locate tourism inside the relationships of exchange of information with the environment where the change is primarily endogenous even ending up changing the structure of the system. Alfonso Jiménez (2004), takes Leiper's model as a reference to dismember his contribution framing the tourist subsystems, inside an entropic process, feedback by the haemostasis established by the exterior environment, qualitative data (motivational of trip) and quantitative (statistical) and the environment of the impacts in the local populations based on the analysis of the origin region and the destination region, which stuck the development of the systemic advance of tourism when carrying out new interpretations of already established models.

The tourist system of Osorio (2005), is a soft complex system, composed by a net of numerous relationships that have a self-organisation and evolution capacity, subject to determining external changes of its transformation, among which there is the dynamic element that determines the form of making tourism, the static element referred to the destination, the consequential element that refers the impacts of the two previous elements, these elements form the subsystems that provide evidence of the relationships that happen in the tourist system.

However, in the model, soft complex systems are not defined nor complex systems taken as a reference that are defined based on the mathematical structuring of their variables and take fractal geometry as a reference; specifically the behaviour of the mathematical variables and their stationary capacity, in a bifurcation point known as saturation of the system.

The above-mentioned constitutes the contributions carried out inside the research on tourism with systemic linking, although it is certain that they represent relevant advances to the study of the tourist issue, the study of the tourism in Mexico has not been developed due to the epistemological incongruity applied of the knowledge of the Systems Science and the use of the new systemic methodologies that would allow to establish a more direct approach to try to define it.

Tourist System Evolution

The tourist system presents a constant evolution expressed in the factors of the international tourism development such as: a) the increase of the personal income, b) larger leisure times c) the revolution transportation d) technological changes e) and the freedom of travelling. The previous factors allow contemplating tourism like an economic political group that surpasses, the continental, national and regional issue being constituted in the tourism of masses that has shown an evolutionary, interesting tendency, generated from the transformations of the demand, derived from the new tourist demands.

The traditional way of making tourism has evolved reaching all tourist areas, generating new specific segments of the market where the tourist is no longer willing to carry out an unjustified expense. It takes more and more seriously the role of preserving the environment, and grants bigger attributions to the experiences generated of the interactions with other people.

The changes experienced in the tourist phenomenon have radically transformed what could be glimpsed as the traditional tourist system, under the new perspectives, composed by the demands, the knowledge, and forms of making tourism in the contemporary world. The evolution that is presented in the tourist system emanates of its central element, the tourist that when acquiring new experiences, in different environments, creates entropy that when being absorbed by the remaining elements of the system, is used to propitiate haemostasis contributing to its evolution and transcendence.

The tourist system as such has been transformed in different action fronts that show the evolution of the commercialization relationships expressed in the use of the web (internet) that allows the direct interaction between the tourists and the providers of services, the approach of the tourists to know the places, regions, communities and tourist spaces to visit, allowing to compare prices, qualities, and even to try to make a judge on the degree of experiences that will have.

The evolution of the tourist system, toward the conformation of the alternative tourism (process that promotes a fair way of travelling among the members of different communities), it pursues the mutual understanding, the solidarity and the equality among the participants.

The tourist comes off of his elitist character and congregates a renovating environment and social activity, promoted by the consumers themselves, as a result of their evolutionary process where the tourists request, without any imposition, to be given the opportunity to participate in the conservation, development and improvement of the social and environmental atmospheres that surround the tourist activity. In its new placement the tourism creates job positions, protects the natural and cultural resources, at the same time that promotes human understanding.

In accordance with Barreto (1996), the tourists should not carry out lucrative functions, what leaves the concept of business tourism in a difficult position since although tourists services are being used, and they can behave as tourists in their free time they cannot be considered as such, because they don't fulfil the requirement of being travelling for pleasure, they are not owners of their time and they present burden attitudes due to the pressures of the work.

The tourist concept should not come from their motivations, behaviour and attitudes since these are centred in the subjective area, which would not help to dismember its concept because we would already have so many definitions as approaches for its analysis.

The concept of tourist should come from a holistic perspective that will allow us to use a rational valuation for its conception. The tourist is the main element of the tourist system that generates negative entropy that comes from their diversification, necessities, expectations and attitudes, reason why its conceptual treatment should be approached not by the causes of its displacements but for the effects that generates inside the tourist system.

The tourist like the main entropy element of the system may be specified based on their participation inside the tourist system, considering that people have the ability to belong or to stop belonging to the systems, what takes us to the following view. The tourist is that person that belongs to the tourist system and alters its operation, by means of the entropy, independently of the activities, attitudes, or perceptions that they present, tourists generate changes inside the other elements that try to understand to be coupled to its considerations, and in turn it is influenced by the other elements, for the determination of decisions in the tourist system.

Evolution of the Tourism's Conceptual System

Design Of The Model

The general postulates of the Systems Method and its methodologies, as well as the Domain of Science Model by John' Warfield were considered for the design of the model. In a summarized form, the steps and development of the methodology are shown next:

1. Object of study or problem: To outline the elements of the tourist system.
2. To visualize the concepts like a mental representation of the reality inside the psychological Cosmo vision: We can understand this stage like the part of the interaction and mental construction on the study concepts, enlarging our understanding of reality. This happens when we interact and think of such concepts and we relate them with our cosmo vision.
3. Importance or value for humanity. For this work the importance resides in establishing the elements of the tourist system.
4. Systemic Cosmo vision: The reconstruction of the concepts is given in this stage until reaching an approach to a theory with a holistic vision. A way to reconstruct the concepts is changing some original attributes. Changing some original attributes of the existent tourist systems, their order and disorder elements are established.

Evolution of the Tourism's Conceptual System

Considerations of the model

According to the elements and their interrelations the following principles are proposed: The tourist system has entropic elements defined by the vulnerability of the phenomenon to the social, political and economic events. The personal and social security constitutes the bases on which the tourist makes a purchase election. The tourist system, finds its balance in the destinations that try to clean up their image as safe destinations.

In tourism free time is valued in terms of knowledge, experiences, and satisfactions, what determines in turn how they will decide to spend the new free time. The Tourist is the main entropic element of the tourist system whose participation favours changes in the other elements at the same time that it is influenced by them. The elements of negentropy of the tourist system produce information, and structuring of the system, that are useful to propitiate firstly its survival and invoke its development. The handling of electronic information systems (Tic´s), creates negentropy at the time that the options, of making and consuming the tourism are considerably increased.

Evolution of the Tourism's Conceptual System

The identification of the tourist segments and the determination of activities according to their necessities, cooperate to balance the tourist system. The knowledge of the socio cultural environment to visit, favours positive information to the system. The stationary demand, generates fluctuations in the prices, therefore the stability of the system depends on the capacity and sustentation of the linking elements (tourist companies). The elements of tourist linkage (tourist companies) are able to create like every organisation, elements of entropy and negentropy by their own, therefore they are considered as direct modifiers of the tourist satisfaction, haemostasis creator.

The linking elements need to improve their goods and services with the purpose of directing their product to create positive entropy reflected in the increase of their revenues and quality of services. The elements of tourist interactions include the crisscross environments that are considered, to the moment of the tourist experience, and that in general determine the behaviour and evolution of the system.

The regulators conform the supra system, able to implement the changes according to the evolutionary aspects of the tourist system in legal, productive, social, cultural matters and in the generation of new knowledge. Each element of the tourist system is subordinate to a regulator.

The evolutionary element of tourism is the one of greater transcendence to consider its future states and conditions. The main element of the tourist evolution this constituted by the tourists that when returning to their origin place, evolves and influences in the evolution of the remaining elements, presenting bigger impact in the linking elements (tourist companies) and in the regulating elements, (unions, organisations, governments and institutions) tourist.

Next, in a synthetic way, some of the discoveries that have been found in the course of research are described, as well as some preliminary conclusions: The tourism is an open system, customizable, and dynamic integrated by entropic, negentropic and homeostatic elements that determine its condition in an evolutionary phase.

The tourist system is conformed by all the elements that are presented in its manifestation, they create alteration situations in its interior, and aim to establish a balance, while the consideration of tourism like a series of isolated knowledge, a group of dismembered policies, or a group of diffuse procedures, they belong to a social, economic or managerial part different from the one constituted by the tourist system.

The tourism seems to evolve toward the social, environmental, and economic reconciliation, manifested in its sustainable considerations and reflected in the demands of the tourists to respect those environments. Therefore it is a suitable tool to propitiate the social, and economic development, the care for the environment and the cultural invigoration. The linking elements (tourist companies) have the internal capacity of being self regulated, and of balancing the tourist system, at least in terms of what the satisfaction of goods and services concerns, the levels of worldwide competition cause the necessity to respond favourably to the tourist evolution captured in the reference frame.

The tourist companies should consider the role that the human element plays in the process of tourist conomic transformation, reason why they should be focused in the creation of real scenarios, to satisfy their demand, since the human factor is considered to be the essential element of the tourist system. The objective of the tourist system is to provide visitors with the suitable conditions to take a trip, in consequence the reconciliation in the actions of the regulating elements, meaning the participation of the governments, the unions, the institutions and tourist organisations, should result in combined efforts to develop the tourist system, and not in disperse actions that hinder its development. The main mission of the tourist regulators responds to propitiate favourable homeostatic changes, developers of the system, in legal, productive, environmental, social, cultural and educational matters whose commercial, economic bureaucratic barriers or of different nature hinder its function to the degree that their lack of actions have a negative impact in the tourist system. The governments, unions, organisations, and institutions of quick answer, generate favourable conditions for their internal tourist environments, due to their quick action to identify the elements of improvement and to carry out their developing function of the tourist system.

The tourist evolution allows glimpsing the integration of the economic, political environmental and social environments of the tourist issue through its manifestations, generated trough the history of its conformation.

The documented applications of the Science of Systems in tourism that have been found have been incongruous with the advances that this science has had. Prove of it is the categorization of tourism using primarily the cybernetic model of first level of the 50´s or incomplete or mistaken approaches to propose tourist systems. This obeys the lack of a modernized and deep knowledge of this Science. The Systemic Science provides a new research method, and useful tools for the theoretical and praxiologic study of tourism.

Rules for Successful Tourism Marketing

Tourism is an important economic activity because it brings in dollars from outside the community. It continues to be a fast growing sector and is typically included among the top three industries in the country. In addition, tourism provides a "front-door" to non-tourism economic development efforts such as business recruitment. Roger Brooks, a nationally recognized expert in tourism development spoke about rules for success at the 2004 Wisconsin Governor's Conference on Tourism in Green Bay. Many of his rules apply to the tourism marketing efforts of small city downtowns and business districts. Presented below is a summary of his keynote address titled 15 Immutable Rules of Successful Tourism.

Success Begins With a Good Plan

Creating a Tourism Development & Marketing Plan is the first rule for successful tourism. The plan should include several details like product development, upgrades and improvements, repositioning and/or branding, attractions and events, visitor amenities and services, marketing and public relations, public/private partnerships, recruitment, funding and budgets, and organizational responsibilities. The plan should integrate existing comprehensive plans and economic development and Main Street efforts.

Importance of Front-line Sales

Your front-line employees can be your most valuable sales team. This is because they establish the first contact with the customer. The front-line employees should be knowledgeable about your community and should promote other stores, attractions and amenities to visitors to keep them in the area longer.

Critical Mass: In order to attract and keep visitors in your community, there must be several retail and dining establishments within walking distance. Shopping and dining in a pedestrian setting is one of the top activities for visitors. An average rule of thumb for rural communities is to have nine retail stores and four dining/treats establishments within two or three blocks.

Turn Negatives Into Positives: Almost every community and attraction has its challenges. Think creatively on how to convert these negatives into positives. You can then attract people to your area using clever promotional tactics. For example, when an article in the Washington Post labelled Battle Mountain, Nevada the "Armpit of America", the town took a positive spin on that title by having an annual event sponsored by Old Spice drawing thousands of visitors.

Be Unique: In order to be successful, you must be worth the trip. A visitor must be able to differentiate you from the competition and you must strive to be creative and set yourself apart from others. Being unique will make a visitor travel the extra distance.

Telling Stories: Museums and interpretive centres should always tell stories, not just display artifacts. Stories can keep visitors in the area longer, which means additional spending. Visitors also remember stories, and captivating stories are told and passed on to others. More people pick destinations by word of mouth than any other method.

Four-Times Rule: People are willing to travel a distance if you offer something that appeals to them. There should be enough for visitors to see and do in your area. In general, you should be able to keep visitors busy four times longer than it took them to get there.

Marketing vs. Product Development

Before you market your community, make sure it is appealing to customers. If your product is not of great quality, then your marketing efforts are wasted. Product development should always be a top priority, and it never ends. Having a good mix of product development and marketing is also important.

Selling the Experience

Always sell the experience associated with an activity and not the place. If you are using pictures in your marketing campaign, avoid using scenic images. Scenery lasts in the mind for only a few moments. Instead, use images of people laughing and having fun. Viewers are more likely to remember images that include people's emotions.

Branding: Even at the community level, branding is critical for success in tourism. Branding is much more than just a logo; it is what sets you apart from your competition, it is your image and your value. Do not try to be "all things to all people."

WOW Photography: Nothing sells tourism like great photography. Photographs used for tourism purposes should have a "wow" appeal in the viewer and should make the viewer want to go to the place depicted. As mentioned earlier, you are trying to sell an experience and your photos should evoke emotion in the viewer. Photography should be the key element in brochures, public relation efforts, and especially on the web.

Close the Sale: Most communities and attractions spend a significant amount of money on advertising. The primary "call to action" in advertising is to get the potential customer to call and get a brochure, or for them to visit your web site. If this is the case, the brochure and web site should be good enough to close the sale. Otherwise, your advertising effort is largely wasted. Pay attention to certain small details while advertising. For example, for brochures, the best colours to use are red and yellow as these colours get the viewers attention. In addition, most brochures end up in racks along with scores of other brochures and the top three inches is all that is visible to the potential customer. Keep this in mind when designing brochures.

Public Relations

Even though you need both, publicity is much more important than advertising. Implementing a professional public relations campaign can have several benefits: it will build brand, improve your image, increase credibility and will provide a greater return on investment than advertising alone. Public relation is how you build your brand and advertising is how you maintain your position. Studies show that for every $1 invested into a public relations campaign, you get a $3 return.

Effective Web Sites

According to a Nielsen/Netratings study, nearly 75% of the U.S. population has access to the Internet from home. In addition, 94% of Internet users make travel arrangements using the Web. The Internet is by far the number one resource for planning travel and vacations. If you have a tourism related web site, can your potential customers find you easily on the Web? How does your web site compare with the competition? Make the online experience interactive for the customer and remember to promote attractions, not just the place or your organization. Several thousands of dollars spent on web site development and maintenance is not a waste of money. You can even make sure your web site is displayed at the top of a Web search by paying a fee.

Frequency in Advertising

Frequency is more important than variety in placing advertising. People viewing your advertisement should develop Top of Mind Awareness (TOMA). For example, when the words "fast food" are mentioned, most people think of McDonalds because they make a good use of frequency in advertising.

Successful Budgeting for your Medical Tourism Marketing Campaigns

If marketing can be called the vehicle that brings dreams to reality, a marketing budget can certainly be referred to as the fuel that drives the vehicle. A marketing budget has long since outlived the traditional moniker of being a financial tool that helps an organization assign enough resources to achieve its marketing objectives. Today, a marketing budget is a proud badge of recognition that demonstrates that an organization has purpose in its marketing. It says that an organization knows EXACTLY what marketing it intends to perform and how that marketing is going to help its bottom line.

In order to design a marketing budget, on organization first needs two things; an executive in charge of marketing and a manager in charge of executing the marketing plan. The former petitions the keeper of the funds for enough budget dollars to successfully help the organization, while the latter determines exactly how much resources the former should ask for.

The most successful budget style that I have encountered is the Cost Centre Budget approach. With this approach, Medical Tourism is assigned what we call a cost centre. This puts it on par with all the organization's important strategic and operational departments such as Finance, Accounting, and Sales. More importantly, it means that your organization can now capture ALL the medical tourism costs in one place. This is a very important management tool that will enable senior management to assess the performance of the organization's medical tourism operations. Within this Cost Centre, Medical Tourism Marketing is assigned a Cost Centre Group. This means that all the marketing activities associated with medical tourism can be tracked from a financial perspective. Also, it isolates the marketing expenses from the other medical tourism efforts, such as Customer Service, Information Technology (IT), Sales, Public Relations (PR), Education and Training, and Business Processing.

What are your marketing budget elements? In other words, what goes into your marketing budget? There's the obvious; Salary and Fringe Benefits, IT Expense, Advertising, Event Marketing, and Promotional Merchandise. In addition however, your organization should budget for Professional Services, New Business Promotion, Purchased Services and Travel.

Professional Services will include any expenses that the organization incurs to solicit the services of professionals. Included in this line item are creative design, graphic design and website design. Website design, in my opinion, should always merit its own line item due to its importance and the need to isolate and, therefore, manage its expenses. Website marketing is rapidly becoming the most effective (and cost effective) way to attract customers. However, the costs associated with its design and maintenance can become very complex and easily lost with the other design costs that an organization may incur.

New Business Promotion costs are those costs incurred for new products, new markets or new customers. It's very important for an organization to capture these costs separately from ongoing promotion. Most marketing professionals operate under a timeless adage that it costs seven times as much to capture a new customer as it costs to retain an already existing customer. In my opinion, anything that's costing my organization seven times the cost of anything warrants its own specific attention. Plus, proper capture of these costs enables proper management of them and can provide guidance to actually reducing them, thereby becoming more efficient. ALL costs associated with new products, new markets or new customers should be captured in this bucket.

Purchased Services are those services that an organization elects to "buy" versus "build". These costs can include printing, service measurement (customer surveys), project expenses, mail management, and special promotions not associated with any current product or service, nor with any new product or service, such as an organization's community activities. The key to identifying which costs belong in this bucket is that they are for services (usually professional services) other than those included in the Professional Services bucket.

Travel costs might appear to be obvious and one might wonder why they warrant special attention. In one of my previous organizations, I have direct experience that suggests that excluding travel costs that are incurred because of marketing, from a marketing budget can skew the results of a marketing campaign. Imagine a campaign that involves travel to a particular conference where your organization is a sponsor and has a booth or other display space. The costs for travel, lodging, meals and other related expenses can be appreciable and should be included in the budget in order to determine how successful that event was for your organization. ALL expenses that are incurred to get people somewhere for a special reason, should be included in the marketing travel costs bucket. While this article attempts to simplify the budgeting process somewhat, it should be clear that capturing all your marketing efforts is important for your organization. For a particular campaign like marketing to a specific U.S. state, or a particular U.S. ethnic sector, or for a specific purpose in the U.S., the campaign should be set up to capture all the aforementioned costs.

You can never have too many campaigns; each unique in its cost collection efforts so that the success of each can be uniquely and separately assessed. In order to accomplish this goal successfully, the marketing manager and marketing department should know EXACTLY what each campaign involves. This can be achieved by creating a communications plan for your campaign.

The Marketing Manager should be responsible to ensure that all the costs are properly captured and reported up to the executive responsible for marketing. Also, the marketing manager should be responsible for determining what results are expected. How many new customers? How many referrals? How much sales? What incremental sales are expected? By balancing the expected results against the cost, an organization can establish an expected Return on Investment (ROI). And, by balancing the actual results against the cost, an organization can establish an actual ROI. Does your actual medical tourism marketing campaign ROI meet or exceed your expected ROI?

When I was in charge of marketing at a previous employer, I created a campaign for every promotion. We tracked every campaign. We were able to identify and continue successful campaigns and actually improve them. We were also able to discontinue unsuccessful campaigns so they didn't drain much needed resources. That particular product achieved $40 million in revenues in the first year and a retention ratio of almost 80% in the second year. Both achievements are considered excellent for the competitive market of the product. We are so committed to the concept of using marketing budgets, that we have created a presentation that demonstrates how to create a medical tourism marketing budget. Make sure your organization has a budget method that enables it to capture all medical tourism marketing costs. Make sure that you establish expected results, against which actual results can be compared. Using a marketing budget for each campaign will help you achieve this. It will help you demonstrate the success of your Medical Tourism Marketing Program.

9

Marketing Tourism Services

There is an interrelationship between the nature or characteristics of the tourism services and the marketing mix. Hence, there is a need to take into consideration the 7 key issues while determining the criteria of the Marketing Mix (4 Ps).

The Marketing Mix

The most important factor is consumer perception of price

- o Consumer may choose not to buy when offering is perceived to be of lesser value than the asking price. Hence, bookings or visits will decline.
- o If price is low in relation to value offered, then demand will be difficult to manage and revenue loss could be substantial.

The marketer's task is to maintain a balance between; Value Perceived (Quality) & Price.

Price and Demand

- o Price has little to do with cost, and far more to do with what customer arc prepared to pay for a product.
- o How well a changed in price affect a change in total demand—price elasticity of demand.
- o In a market where the product is unique, or without satisfactory substitute, or where-the product is manufactured by a company that enjoys a monopoly or near monopoly, price will be set high.
- o In setting the prices, the company will want to know what levels of demand it is likely to experience at different prices.

For a new product this is hard to gauge. The

- two most common methods of assessing demand are:
- Asking potential customers what they would be willing to pay for service
- Test marketing the product at different prices in different regions.

How can price be used to control consumer demand?

- o Maximize access.
- o Restrict access.
- o Control demand in time.
- o Control demand in space.

Pricing Methods

Cost-plus Pricing

- o A standard mark-up is added to the cost of the product.
- o E.g. A bottle of wine that costs $14 may sell for $28, a 100% mark-up on cost.

Going Rate Pricing

- A strategy of going-rate pricing is the establishment of price based largely on those of competitors, with less attention paid to costs or demand.
- The firm might charge the same, more, or less than its major competitors. Some firm might charge a bit more or less, but they hold the amount of difference constant.

Skimming Pricing

- Price skimming is setting a high price when the market is price insensitive. (Higher-end market).
- To be used when:
  - o Highly differentiated product.
  - o Inelastic demand.
  - o Maximize short-run profit when product has short life cycle or demand exceeds supply over a short time period.
  - o Premium product with added value.

Penetration Pricing

- o Companies set a low initial price to penetrate the market quickly and deeply, attracting many buyers and winning a large market share.
- o To be used when:
  - Little product differentiation.
  - Many competitive substitutes.
  - Inferior product.

Place

- o It is place that represents distribution of and access to the product.
- o In tourism industries, distribution systems are used to move the customer to the product: hotel, restaurant cruise ship or aeroplane.
- o Various distribution channels or intermediaries are used to market tourism services.
- o Distribution channels or Intermediaries are used to describe any dealer who acts as a link in the chain of distribution between the company and its customers.

Distribution Channel Functions

(1) *Information*-gathering and distributing marketing research and intelligence information about the marketing environment.

(2) *Promotion*-developing and spreading persuasive communication about an offer.

(3) *Contact*-finding and communicating with prospective buyers.

(4) *Matching*-shaping and fitting the offer to the buyers' needs.

(5) *Negotiation*-agreeing on price and other terms of the offer so that ownership or possession can be transferred.

(6) *Physical distribution*-transporting and storing goods.

(7) *Financing*-acquiring and using funds to cover the cost of channel work.

(8) *Risk taking*-assuming financial risks, such as the inability to sell inventory at full margin.

Why do companies choose to deal with intermediaries?

(1) It is cheaper for a company to deal through intermediaries than to set up its own network of retail shops or sell its product directly in any other way By paying a commission or other agreed form of financial remuneration to their intermediaries, companies buy the use of distributive network.

(2) The system also acts as a convenience to consumers as they can choose from a range of different products under one roof, instead of having to visit each producer's shop in turn to select their product.

(3) Through their contact, experience and specialization, intermediaries normally offer more than a firm can on its own Managing, Monitoring and Modifying Channels Channel systems will require periodic review and modification to meet changing market needs. Organizations will need to review the success of their channel systems regularly and determine is all the participants are performing at an acceptable level. It may be necessary to:

- Either expand or reduce membership at various levels or drop some existing channel members who are no longer performing.
- Change direction or consider totally new ways of looking at the business.

This is happening as the interest in call centres grows and hotels are reviewing the need for hotel representatives where call centres might be able to achieve the same results more cost effectively. Similarly, major changes are taking place in computer reservations systems with every advance in technology.

Promotion

- o Is an aspect of general marketing that promotion management deals with explicitly.
- o It includes the practices of advertising, personal selling, sales promotion, publicity and point-of-purchase communications.

Why promotional activities are carried out?

All marketing communication efforts are directed at accomplishing one or more of the following objectives:

1. Build product category wants.

2. Create brand awareness.
3. Enhance attitudes and influence intentions.
4. Facilitate purchase.
5. Promotional Mix Strategies.

Most leisure and tourism organisations use a combination of promotional activities including:

1. *Advertising:* the paid-tor sponsorship of a message in a commercially available medium. The media (press, broadcast: television and radio, posters/billboards, cinema) task is essentially to choose and buy the most economical combination of advertising space and/or time to reach defined audiences sufficiently frequently and with sufficient impact to convey the agreed messages effectively.
2. *Sales Promotion:* Those marketing activities other than personal selling and advertising and publicity that stimulate purchasing and dealer effectiveness, such as displays, shows and exhibitions, demonstrations and various non-recurrent selling efforts not in ordinary routine. Sales Promotion can be targeted at consumers, the trade and the company.
3. *Public Relations:* PR in tourism is about how people who matter to a tourism organisation think about it and how their perceptions, attitudes and behaviour can be kept or made positive. *External PR* involves everything an organisation does that impinges on people's perceptions including: its products; its employees; its communication programmes and media coverage, its overall corporate identity; its financial reputation; its promotional activities; the buildings in which it transacts business — in short everything that contributes to the *image* of an organisation. *Internal PR* is used to build and maintain morale within an organisation through such things as good communication practices, incentive benefits, sportsman activity provision, etc.
4. *Direct Marketing:* Tourism organisations make heavy use of promotional materials mailed out or given away to customers or passed on to them by intermediaries Photographs are a crucial element of mass tour brochures. Also, maps, a critical part in tourism promotion in generating interest in a destination.

One of the most difficult things to achieve in brochures aimed at the mass market is competitive differentiation.

5. *Personal Selling:* An interpersonal process whereby the seller ascertains, activates and satisfies the needs and wants of the buyer so that both the seller and buyer benefits. It is a method of influencing the purchase. The selling sequence include prospecting and qualifying, planning and delivering sales presentations, overcoming objections and closing the sale.

Product

Problems in Managing Services

The effectiveness of planning the marketing mix depends as much on the ability to select the right target market as on the skill in devising a product which will generate high levels of satisfaction. Hence, the decision depends very much on the capability of the marketers to tackle the following issues concerning tourism services:

Intangible Nature of Business

Customer cannot physically evaluate or sample most services: they tend to rely on other people's experiences with these services Customers place great value on the advice of hospitality and travel experts, such as travel agents Implications:

- o Tourism marketers tend to 'tangibilize' the tourism offering in brochures and videos-visual displays of the real thing.
- o Marketers tend to generate positive "word-of-mouth" among the customers.

Variability in Production Methods

Quality control of services is neither as precise nor as easy to achieve because of the human factors that are involved in supplying them All staff members cannot consistently provide the same level of service as their colleagues

- * Although standardised service is an admirable target that all organisations should try to achieve it is unrealistic.
- * The same standardisation cannot be provided since the actions of service staff, other+customers and the customers themselves make the experience more variable.
- * Hotels, restaurants, airlines, theme parks and travel agencies

are some of the 'factories' in the business. Behaviour of one customer can ruin the service experience of others.

* Implications:
  - o Tourism marketer design processes to minimise differences in service encounters and provision between different outlets or between different shifts at a hotel. Example: Provision of uniforms and of similar physical surroundings illustrates evidence of standardisation.

Perishability

* Service is highly perishable-"like a running tap in a sink with no plug".
* An unoccupied seat on a train or bed in a guesthouse is lost forever.
* Services and the time available to experience them cannot be stored.
* Implications:
  - o The management task emphasises managing demand and capacity to a degree of time tuning. Example: Airlines offer stand by fares to those willing to fill unexpected empty seats at short notice.

Distribution Channels

There is no physical distribution system in tourism industry. Instead, there are many intermediaries in the hospitality and travel industry where the items are being purchased.

Cost Determination

Services are both variable and intangible. Some customers might require more attention than others.

Relationship of Services to Providers

* Some services are inseparable from the individuals who provide them.
* Example: Restaurant-whose chefs or owners have developed unique reputations for their food, personalities or both.
* Implications:
  - o Marketers attempt to devise delivery systems which ease interaction and invest in campaigns to educate staff and consumers as to how to get the best from the interaction.

o Training in hotels emphasises how staff can manage the interaction.

Target Marketing

- o In tourism industry, we need to acknowledge that not all individuals would want to buy from us.
- o ;e might not have the services that they may be looking for.
- o And hence, it is important to consider targeting the right market to ensure success of our business.
- o Marketing is about developing the right product/service to the right market/people so that they will be satisfied with what they receive.
- o Target marketing can be defined as:
  - Seller identifies market segments (groups), selects one or more and develops products and marketing mixes tailored to each selected segmentx.

Market Segmention

- o Involves dividing market into distinct groups of buyers who requires different products or marketing mixes.
- o There is no single way to segment a market o MaNor variables include.
  - (a) Geographic Segmentation divide market according to location e.g. nations, regions, states, countries, cities.
  - (b) Demographic Segmentation divide market into groups, based on demographic variables e.g. age, gender, family life cycle, income, occupation, education, religion, race/culture, nationality.
  - (c) psychographic Segmentation divide buyers into different groups, based on social class, lifestyle, and personality characteristics.
  - (d) Behaviour Segmentation buyer is divided into groups, based on knowledge, attitude, usage rate, and response.

Refers to the buying behaviour of final customers (individuals and households) to buy goods and services for personal consumption MaNor factors influencing buying behaviour include.

E 'Ypxyvi Jegxsvw

Culture comprise of the basic values, perceptions, want and behaviour that a person learns continuously in a society Culture is expressed through tangible items such as food, buildings, clothing and art. e.g. the culture shift toward greater concern about health and fitness has resulted in many hotels adding exercise rooms/health clubs. e.g. KFC, piazza and Burger King in Israel adapted their menus to make them kosher for Passover (.ewish) Subculture groups of population with shared value system base oncommon experiences and situations Social classesare relatively permanent and ordered divisions in a society whose members share similar values, interests and behaviours e.g. income, occupation, education, wealth Social classes show distinct product and brand preferences in such areas as food, travel and leisure activity. e.g. CE3, managers and directors organizations often indulge in golfing activities.

Reference Group

A personvs refer group consists of all the groups that have a direct/indirect influence on the personvs attitude/behaviour e.g. artist, idol Family Marketers have examined the role and influence of the husband, wife and children on the purchase of different products and services.

Roles and Status: A person position in each group can be defined in terms of role and status a role consists of the activities that a person is expected to perform each role carried a status e.g. pinna parents z daughter Family z wife/mother Company staff.

G 4IVWSREP JEGXSVW

Age and Life Cycle Stage

The types of goods and services people buy changes during their lifetimes. Consumption is also shaped by family life cycle (i.e. number of family members and who they are#) e.g. big family (nuclear family) z high consumption medium/small family z smaller consumption.

B9=ER DECISI32 4R3CESS

This model emphasizes that the buying process starts long before and continues long after the actual purchases It encourages marketer to focus on the entire buying process rather than Nust the purchasing decision.

Problem recognition

The buying process starts when the buyer recognizes a problem or need.

The need can be triggered by internal and external stimuli. They should research customers to find out what kinds of needs/problems, led them to purchase an items, what brought these needs about, and how they led consumers to choose a particular product. E.g. SPA Travel relaxation/need to get out of city life.

Information Search

1. The strength of drive.
2. The amount of initial information.
3. The ease of obtaining the information.
4. The value placed on additional information.
5. The satisfaction one gets from search.

Consumer can obtain information from several sources personal sources family, friends, neighbours, acquaintances Commercial sources z sales person, packaging, advertising, dealers, displays public sources z restaurant reviews, editorials in the travel section Therefore, a company must design its marketing mix to make prospects aware of and knowledgeable about the features and benefits of its products/brands.

E.g. TRA:E0 Fair

(1) promote in newspaper (create awareness).
(2) initial information (from newspaper or a call to travel agent).
(3) obtain information from internet, visit travel agents.
(4) value (are the information of high quality trustworthy).
(5) satisfaction (are consumers happy with the search).

Evaluation of Alternatives

- This is the stage where consumer makes an assessment of the goods/services offered and is considering the alternatives.
- The marketer must ensure that his product/service is on the list of alternatives.
- The buyer must be convinced of its suitability before the buyer can proceed to the buying/purchase decision.
- The product/service must be readily available to the consumer.

Purchase Decision

- o The buyer would have made a decision by now as to which product/service is suitable to fulfil his/her needs.
- o The ideal product would have all the attributes/characteristics that the customer is looking for:
  - Then the decision to purchase is made, the product that is thought to be most suitable will be selected.
  - However, 2 factors can influence the purchase intention and the purchase decision.
    - (i) Attitudes of others (getting information from relatives/family members).
    - (ii) Unexpected situational factors (e.g. earthquakes, flood, SARS, effect of tsunami).

Post Purchase Behaviour

- o Feelings felt by the buyer towards the product offer that has been purchased.
- o To avoid post purchase dissonance, there must be no gap between the expectations of the buyer and the actual product performance.
- o The buyervs decision to buy the product again later will depend on the buyervs satisfaction with the product performance.

Paper on Community Travel and Tourism Marketing

Every community if affected by visitors. While many communities recognize opportunities for growth in the tourism industry, options at the local level expand when travellers are included. Travellers are people away from home temporarily. In collecting data, sometimes "more than miles away from home" further defines a traveller.

This travel may result from a variety of sources: a pleasure vacation, business and convention purposes, friends and relatives, special events and festivals, sport recreation, historic sites, specific attractions, or when people pass-through headed for another destination. The cash register doesn't sort out travel purchases this way, and in reality it is impractical to separate tourists from travellers. All visitors are important to the travel and tourism industry.

Minnesota is experiencing a boom in communities organizing to attract and host visitors as a way to diversify and boost economies. The impact of travel and tourism on the local economy goes beyond first level expenditures at food, lodging, gas, entertainment, and retail establishments. Travel spending brings in outside dollars that "turn over" in the community. Even if you do not have direct contact with travellers, the money filters through the entire economy as residents re-spend travel dollars. But the increased interest in tourism translates to fierce competition in the marketplace.

Key to gaining the attention of potential tourists is development of a community marketing, not a selling approach. Marketing is a continuous, coordinated set of activities associated with efficiently distributing products to high potential markets. It involves making decisions about product, price, promotion, and distribution. Marketing focuses on providing customer benefits and satisfying needs better than the competition. It is based on the principle that consumer buying resistance will be overcome if the product satisfies buyer needs.

In contrast, selling focuses on the product offered rather than satisfying customer needs. It assumes that the main thing necessary to sell the product is to overcome purchase resistance. A statement reflecting the selling approach is "we will attract tourists to Our City because we want tourists and everyone would want to visit. Selling is only a small part of marketing. The formal marketing process involves six steps:

- Analyse your current situation.
- Identify product(s).
- Select target market(s).
- Set objectives.
- Carry out promotion strategies.
- Evaluate results.

When the structure to support tourism is in place-1) attractions, 2) services and facilities, 3) an information/direction/interpretive system, and 4) transportation linkages-communities can move to market their unique tourist and travel experiences. This publication outlines one approach for preparing a marketing that describes how you will get visitors to stop, to stay, to tell others, and to return.

Analyse your Current Situation

What does your community have that travellers want? The first step in the marketing process is to conduct an inventory and analysis of the travel and tourism industry and its potential within your area. Tourism isn't just a community or collection of small businesses with an interest in attracting visitors. Tourism is an entire "region" organizing to draw and host travellers-it's an overall view with a wide angle lens. Analysis answers the question "what is?" As a basis for "what could be?" Ten crucial questions for a community to answer on a regular basis include:

1. What attractions exist that will entice people to stop and visit?
2. What hospitality services and facilities are available?
3. What experiences are visitors having in the community?
4. What promotion methods are used? How well do they work?
5. What are the current markets?
6. What is the competition for your community?
7. How is tourism related to the community lifestyle and goals?"
8. What roles do community organizations play in tourism development?
9. What are trends that affect the tourism industry?
10. What are the community strengths and weaknesses, problems and opportunities in serving visitors?

Attractions (Question 1)

Through fate or creativity, most communities have tourist attractions that draw visitors. A community's basic assets may include:

- Natural resources, or a scenic setting;
- Human-made attractions such as racetracks, museums, or resorts;
- Historical sites;
- Cultural and ethnic resources;
- Recreation opportunities;
- Special events and festivals;
- Availability of high quality personal services such as shopping, medical care and education; or
- Local industries and economic base.

Describe each attraction, including quality. How many of each type of attraction are there? Look forward and list potential visitor resources that could be enhanced or used more fully. The Minnesota Extension

Service publication "So Community Wants Tourism" outlines the range of travel attractors that determine a community's capability to bring travellers.

As you develop a community tourism campaign, it is useful to separate "core" attractions that are a prime reason for travel, from secondary "supporting" attractions that enhance a visitor's experience once they are there. There are infinite reasons to visit Minneapolis and St. Paul, but Twin Cities Attractions Council is organized to promote the plus theatres, museums, special events, and other core attractions that draw large audiences. This distinction is useful when you are selecting an image for your marketing program. The Spicer area tourism committee has developed a four-tier list of tourism assets: most important (includes Green Lake, resorts, 2 hours to Twin Cities); important (Sibley State Park, fishing, golf course); significant (fall colours, hunting, July 4 celebration); and contributing(antique shops, sailing regattas, farm tours). Spicer's marketing theme reflects this ranking.

Hospitality Services (Question 2)

The economic impact of tourism largely comes from spending in the hospitality sector primarily composed of private commercial businesses. The U.S. Travel Data Centre estimates tourist dollar expenditures on a state wide basis by category (1985):

* Food $0.26,
* Public transportation.25,
* Auto transportation.17,
* Lodging.15,
* Entertainment & recreation.09,
* Retail and other.08,
* $1.00.

In nonmetropolitan areas these figures would shift; for example, the public transportation component would drop significantly. It is useful to have local or regional expenditure data to track the travel industry and develop public support for this economic sector. However, data collection requires a visitor survey, and study and questionnaire design are complex. Seek assistance from industry professionals in developing a data base that accurately represents spending patterns.

Good restaurants and sufficient overnight lodging capacity are essential. Describe the mix of establishments, their occupancy, and their services. For example, do motels have facilities for families such as pools and playgrounds, or are they positioned to attract business meetings where evening entertainment may be a factor in the decision to make reservations? Grocery stores, specialty retail shops, entertainment and service stations also support the visitor industry.

Questions about the adequacy of public services come into play. Transportation issues such as roadway congestion, parking and signing, restroom availability, and utilities (sewage and trash disposal) assume importance as the industry expands. Plans for a proposed megamall in the Twin include construction to widen roads in the area.

Tourism Today (Questions 3, 4, and 5)

The tourism experience your community promotes now, whether or accidental, is generally a good indicator for the future. It is often easier to modify and market a travel experience that has evolved over time and is built on local flavour, than Do introduce and develop a new form of tourism that does not match local culture, environment, and heritage. Mississippi Rivertown Rendezvous, an organization promoting the towns along the river corridor from Hastings to Winona, builds upon a common heritage and landscape.

Describe the visitor experience your community offers both in terms of tangibles: the resorts, the boating, the location, as well as the intangibles. Talk about customer benefits when you think about intangibles: rest and relaxation, friendliness, excitement. Then outline and valuate promotion strategies now in use to envision future options. Through survey or observation, determine who is buying your community's experience now. Customers who have visited (even though there may have been no major promotion campaign) are a good clue about the target market your community naturally appeals to.

Outside Influences (Questions 6 through 9)

Tourism marketing occurs within a competitive marketplace that goes well beyond the community boundaries. There are many forms of competition for your customers and their dollars-but neighbouring communities generally are not one of them. A number of strong travel-oriented communities, working together on regional promotion, results in a stronger destination image, a greater variety of attractions and facilities, wider market exposure, and a healthy degree of competition that spurs improvements. The Land of Legends group-a ring of communities within 60 miles of Itasca State Park could not promote itself as a major destination without the involvement of many Chambers of Commerce. This "critical mass" of diverse attractions and quality services also enables the Land of Legends area to attract and host "fam" (familiarization) tours for travel writers and tour brokers as part of an overall marketing program.

More important, there is competition for how consumers spend their discretionary dollar. The purchase of a VCR, buying a more expensive car, or saving for a college education means less money is available for leisure and travel. You also have to be concerned with other destination areas on a national level. Consumers have worldwide choices today; you must understand your competition and their strategies to market your competitive advantages.

In promoting certain visitor experiences, assess what type of tourism is compatible with local lifestyles. For example, many residents of northwestern Minnesota enjoy the hunting opportunities. They use the same resource nonlocal hunters use. Conflicts over resource use must be negotiated before hunting is promoted as a primary visitor attraction. In other areas, emphasis on scattered small town activities is more appropriate than major new construction and facility development. The latest brochure for Southeastern Minnesota Historic Bluff Country emphasizes small-scale tourism businesses such as canoe rental, locally made arts and crafts, bed and breakfasts, and a lefsa factory tour. It is a format designed to encourage travellers to wander and explore the area, rather than directing everyone to a few major sites. In addition, specify the roles various community organizations play in development and promotion, and understand social trends that influence your market position. React quickly when they occur. For example, the move toward shorter getaway mini-vacations is radically changing travel industry strategies.

Where are We Now? (Question 10)

Summarize findings on community attractions, services and facilities, the current travel industry and outside influences in a Written summary statement. Combine relevant in an outline of community strengths and weaknesses, problem opportunities for tourism. Spend sufficient time on this step: analysis is the basis for subsequent decisions about marketing your community's unique visitor experiences.

Identify Product

What is your community marketing? One main reason people travel is to experience a new and different environment. After the situation analysis, most communities find they are faced with multiple options for attracting tourists. The challenge is to choose one dominant identity among all these alternatives. You can not and should not promote all of the community attributes equally. In a tourism marketplace where consumers are faced with diverse choices, need an "edge" to set yourself apart from the competition. You need to create a unique product with a theme or identity that characterizes major promotion efforts. Red Lake Riverlands-Red Lake Falls, Thief River Falls, Crookston, East Grand Forks-features river uses like tubing and boat tours, and nearby food and lodging services. The thirteen Iron Trail United Communities capitalize on the unique mining characteristics and strong ethnic heritage of the Range. Iron world, with its train and festival series, Hill Annex Mine and Tower-Soudan State Park are the core attractions that support the mining theme. A region-wide visitor newspaper and radio information network are part of this cooperative marketing approach.

An example from the private sector is three ski resorts that offer the same hills, the same snow, and the same lift equipment. One business bills itself as a "mountain of hospitality," another is a family resort and the third sells serious, technical skiing.

A marketing theme is the one main idea or message you want to communicate. It should be based on satisfying visitor needs. Theme development requires creativity, and there are advertising agencies that specialize in "positioning" a product in the marketplace and developing a parallel marketing campaign. Consult the Minnesota Extension Service sheet "Creating a Tourism Promotional Theme.

Select Target Markets

Who will buy the product your community is marketing? One certain way to fail is to try to please everyone. A target market is a group of individuals sharing common characteristics, toward whom marketing efforts will be directed. The process of dividing the total market into high-potential target markets is called market segmentation and involves these steps:

- Identifying and describing the different segments that make up the total market;

- Evaluating the economic potential of each segment;
- Choosing one or more market segments on which to focus.

Current visitors are a good indication of target markets attracted to your community. New prospects are likely to have many of the same characteristics unless you are planning a product shift. Target markets can be defined by several factors: geography, demographics, and behaviour.

Geography refers to potential visitors: where they live and they travel. Negative travel time and positive attraction factors are recognized widely as the two main variables that determine what customers choose to see and where they choose to go. Travel time and distance can be negative factors for potential visitors, but the power of an area's tourist attractions may be a counteracting positive factor. A destination that offers a large variety of interesting attractions has more pull, at an equal distance, than a location that offers only one or a few low interest attractions. This doesn't cancel the fact that travel to and from an area is an important part of the total experience, as "pass-through" communities have discovered. Demographics refers to characteristics like age, sex, marital status, number and ages of children and life stage (young single adult or retired) that have direct and obvious effects on travel patterns. For example, unmarried men and married couples with young children have vastly different spending patterns.

Behaviour refers to how potential tourists act, such as length of stay, new us. Repeat visitors, and skills (novice expert). But market segmentation using behaviour variables also refers to why they behave as they do, their interests, and their values. There are many factors that affect travel by individual consumers: the reasons for travel, activities enjoyed during travel, a person's general interests and opinions about travel, and personal values.

For one person, travel may mean a tour of museums, monuments and other cultural attractions. Another person may travel to a meeting of a professional organization. A third person seeks amusement at a sporting event; another visits a park to fish. For different reasons they engage in different activities while travelling and value different types of attractions.

Information on behaviour can be difficult and expensive to collect. Some details are available from observing visitors analysing existing records, but most knowledge is likely to come from surveys or interviews. Work with a marketing professional about survey design to assure a representative sample if you try this method.

New and even established host communities must evaluate each major target market for its economic potential. Consider your product and estimate the drawing power of the attractions. Think about proximity to metropolitan areas and the quality of the transportation network. Consider the of people travelling near your area; consult Minnesota Department of Transportation records.

Use size and accessibility of the target market as criteria. There must be enough members of the target market justify the investment in reaching them. You must be able to reach the target market through a standard form of promotion. Boaters, runners, and anglers, for example, are very accessible: they belong to organizations and read specialized publications. In contrast, young single parents less accessible market because there is no common affiliation or central source of information.

Finally, select one or more of the target markets. You can concentrate on a single target market to the exclusion of all others, or you can use a strategy where promotion campaigns are developed for two or more markets simultaneously. It is likely you will change market segments during the season in the same way resort operators shift their marketing efforts from anglers (spring) to families (summer) to retired couples (fall).

Most important, a community shouldn't try to be all things to all consumers. Primary destination areas like the Twin Cities, state offices of tourism, and major attractions such as Disneyland have the resources to accomplish that. You are much more likely to be successful if you narrow down the target market you want to reach.

Set Marketing Objectives

Now write down marketing objectives that clearly state what community wants to accomplish in its promotion campaign. Objectives keep energy and action focused on what's important. They help you track your success and judge when it is time to review and shift strategies. A good objective contains four elements:

- A specific action of interest such as increased visitation, sales volume, or awareness;

- A measurable outcome, expressed in dollars, a percentage or numbers for example, that indicates how much change will
- A time frame within which the action should occur; and
- An indication of the target market you are trying to reach. Some poorly stated objectives are "to increase visits," "to midweek business," and "to attract more retired couples." In contrast, some examples of well-written objectives follow:
- In the next year, increase midweek (Monday-Thursday) occupancy to 55 percent by attracting business travellers.
- The Chamber of Commerce will book 500 advance reservations from vacationers travelling the Lake Superior circle route in summer (June 1 through Labour Day).
- Increase phone and mail inquiries by 20 percent from fall magazine advertising between August 15 and October 15.
- Increase retail sales on main street during a summer festival by 25 percent over last year's.

Carry out Promotion Strategies

Many communities and private entrepreneurs mistakenly assume that marketing is just deciding on a promotion strategy. They direct broad appeals to poorly defined markets through a variety of media. You can't afford to spend scarce promotion dollars in appealing to people who are not prospects for purchase of your product. Effective and efficient promotion decisions build from a situation analysis, identifying products, selecting target markets and setting objectives.

The message content comes directly from the product and the associated theme. It emphasizes both tangible and intangible aspects, focusing on customer benefits your product offers.

Carrying out promotion strategies involves taking your message to the consumer through a specific delivery system. Promotion is any attempt to stimulate sales by persuasive or informative communications to current or potential customers. The major types of promotion used to stimulate travel and tourism follow:

Advertising: Any paid form of nonpersonal presentation and promotion of ideas, goods, or services by an identified sponsor using mass media. Television, radio and print media some of the major Minnesota destinations are an example.

Personal Selling: An oral or written presentation to one or prospective customers on a face-to-face basis, including telephone solicitation and direct mail. Attendance at sports shows is a form of personal selling.

Sales Promotions: Activities other than advertising and personal selling that stimulate purchasing or create awareness. Sales promotions, including contests featuring free tickets or trips, may be geared toward the individual visitor, while other promotions may be directed toward organizations selling travel services. The Duluth contest to guess the date the first ship will enter the harbour in spring is an example.

Public Relations: A nonpaid presentation of ideas, goods or services generally using mass media. Unlike advertising there is no identifying sponsor. Travel feature stories written after a "fam" (familiarization) tour are a result of public relations efforts.

These promotional categories are known together as the promotional mix. Strictly speaking, the promotional mix refers to the relative amounts of efforts or dollars put into each major promotional category. To find its optimal tourism promotional mix, your community might look at towns comparable size and attracting power. However, do not copy programs-no two communities will be exactly alike.

Finally, the committee may be drawn from owners. The committee structure is used most often to guide tourism development. There are several ways to organize a tourism promotion committee. Some groups originate within the Chamber of Commerce because of shared goals. Others form freestanding community endeavour; the final plan must represent goals independent committees with community-wide representation.

The Minnesota Extension Service publication "Tourism Advertising: Some Basics" outlines a process for selecting an advertising strategy. The tools discussed include magazines, newspapers, radio, television, direct mail, and outdoor displays.

Evaluate Results

There is no secret promotional formula. Test and evaluate regularly. A community or business must continually monitor evaluate results, and experiment with various types of promotion. Even with an effective promotional mix now, the situation may change. Preferences and characteristics of travellers change: marketing efforts must respond.

Evaluate Results

The Minnesota Extension Service publication "Evaluating Tourism Advertising with Cost-Comparison Methods" describes methods such as cost per inquiry, cost per reservation, and return on investment. The importance of coding advertisements to track results cannot be overemphasized.

The Next Step

Working through the tourism development process is a community endeavour; the final plan must represent goals commonly agreed to by area residents and business owners. The committee is used most often to guide tourism development.

There are several ways to organize a tourism promotion committee. Some groups originate within the Chamber of Commerce because of shared goals. Others form freestanding independent committees with community-wide representation. Finally, the committee may be drawn from current leaders in existing tourism agencies, associations, businesses, and attractions. You know the dynamics of your community best to pull together a core group of individuals make things happen.

There must be periodic feedback between the committee and the community at large. In some locations, the tourism committee begins its task with a community-wide survey (by mail, newspaper, or phone) to solicit opinions about tourism development. The results advise the committee and can create a widespread base of public support early in the process. The other strategy is to be sure there is always an opportunity for community discussion at key decision points. The local media can play a major role in keeping the public informed.

Here are seven steps to get started (from "Developing a Tourism Organization," 1987, a Michigan State University Extension Service booklet):

1. Select a name that creates an image and identifies the group.
2. Develop a policy statement, including a statement of purpose and by-laws.
3. Develop an action program: set goals and methods of accomplishing them.
4. Set up committees and subcommittees as needed. Some of the major tasks relate to community involvement, attractions and support services, promotion, budgets, research, and information.

5. Create community awareness and support for tourism.
6. Establish lines of communication and develop a flow of information.
7. Foster a spirit of close cooperation and coordination among the various communities, agencies, and other organizations.

Where to look for Funding

Often good community marketing plans go unrealized or even unused because financial support could not be obtained. Funding can be a difficult obstacle. Communities that have developed a steady and reliable source of marketing funds generally have the most success. Constant scrambling for marketing funds drains energy away from the original marketing objectives. Some of the basic strategies used to raise money for tourism and travel marketing are a lodging tax, local government sources, internal organizational fundraising, private businesses, foundations, and the Minnesota Office of Tourism. Adapt these standard methods to your local situation. Minnesota Statutes permit the creation of a local option lodging tax. Home rule or statutory cities and townships with elected officials may enact a tax of up to three percent on the proceeds of a lodging facility-with a possible extension to municipal campgrounds. In unorganized townships, county officials may enact a lodging tax. Cities townships can create joint districts to better reflect the local tourism region.

Of the proceeds collected, 95 percent must be used to fund marketing and promotion of the area as a tourism or convention destination. These monies may not be used for capital expenditures such as buildings, parks, and civic centres. Lodging facilities are directly affected by the tax, so any plans for a lodging tax should include early discussions with representatives of overnight accommodations. Some communities have had special legislation passed to help fund tourism programs: two options are expansion of the tax base or increases in the tax ceiling. It is normally difficult to pass special interest legislation, but such authority can prove valuable to communities where tourism is a major industry.

Many local governments recognize the importance of the tourism and travel industry to their economies; a number of provide funding to marketing programs implemented by local groups. Monies can come from the general fund, bonding sources, special assessments, or a variety of other sources. Government support can greatly assist local marketing efforts, but funding is less stable due to changing demands for government funds, the health of the local economy, and the fortunes of local politicians. Tourism organizations typically employ some internal fundraising strategies, in addition to outside sources. Membership dues is the most common method. Set either a standard rate or variable fees based on factors such as business size or number of employees. The organization's ability to attract members then becomes critical. Assessments above and beyond dues are another alternative. Assessments are often based on percent of gross revenue or business size. These may help to fund an overall marketing program, but are also used to pay for specific promotional efforts. Tourism organizations can also sell products, services, and activities directly to the public for income. Examples are publications, souvenirs and merchandise, tours and tour guides, and operation of attractions, special events, festivals or auctions. Major businesses operating in the community and benefitting from travel and tourism sometimes make substantial contributions to a marketing program. An important element in obtaining this support is to thoroughly identify the benefits of such a contribution, both to the marketing program and the contributor. Direct benefits-increased sales-as well as secondary benefits-general expansion of the local economy-are important. Tax benefits may be an issue. Do not overlook the potential to build goodwill in the community.

There are opportunities to obtain project-specific grants through organizations such as foundations, the Minnesota Office of Tourism and nonlocal private businesses that will fund ongoing expenses for tourism marketing. Projects that provide promotion to an expanded region or attempt to market an area with an innovative approach are more likely to attract a foundation grant. The Minnesota Office of Tourism administers a joint venture marketing program that allocates matching funds on a competitive basis for advertising, creative marketing, and new brochure development. Private businesses beyond the specific area might also sponsor an activity if there is a connection between their product and the focus of the event. For example, dog food manufacturers could be approached for national sponsorship of a sled dog race.

Travel and Tourism Resources

Tourism USA: Guidelines for Tourism Development. 1986.

University of Missouri, Dept. of Recreation and Park Administration, University Extension. Prepared for the U.S. of Commerce.

- Excellent "how to" handbook with sections on) appraising potential; 2) planning for tourism; 3) assessing product and market; 4) marketing tourism; visitor services; sources of assistance. Single copies are available for $3.00 from U.S. Dept. of Commerce, 1 4th & Constitution, Room 1 865, Washington, D.C. 20030, 202-377-0140. Managing Small Resorts for Profit. 1 985. Minnesota Extension Service, University of Minnesota.
- Contains a marketing section with articles on the market planning process, brochure development, advertising, positioning and package tours. Available for $20.00 from Bud Crewdson, Small Business Development Centre, Minnesota Extension Service, 248 Classroom Office Building, University of Minnesota, St. Paul, MN 551 08, 61 2-625-31 Minnesota Office of Tourism, 250 Skyway Level, 375 Jackson Street, St. Paul, MN 551 0 1,-800-652-9141, 6 1 2-296-Contact for information on a joint venture marketing program. Marketing activities may be eligible for matching funds allocated on a competitive basis to any local, regional, or statewide nonprofit organization formed to promote tourism. Tourism Centre, Minnesota Extension Service, University of Minnesota, 240 Coffey Hall, 1420 Eckles Avenue, St. Paul, MN 55108.
- Offers educational programs and materials for the visitor industry on community tourism development and small business management. Contact your local county extension agent for copies of the extension publications listed in the folder. So Your Community Wants Tourism: Guidelines for Developing Income from Tourism in Your Community (CD-FO-0679, Available 1988) Creating a Tourism Promotional Theme Tourism Advertising: Some Basics (CD-FO-331 1) "Evaluating Tourism Advertising with Cost Comparison Methods" (CD-FO-3372) Tourism Brochures to Boost Business (CD-FO-3273)

Community Improvement Resources

Tourism development depends on citizen cooperation to accomplish community goals and improve the local environment. The Minnesota

Department of Trade and Economic development administers four such programs that give residents an opportunity to develop expertise in identifying and using community resources-the Minnesota Community Improvement Program, the Governor's Design Team, Minnesota Main Street, and Minnesota Beautiful. Program coordinators can be reached at the Department of Trade and Economic Development, 900 American Centre Building, 1 50 East Kellogg Blvd., St. Paul, MN 551 01. The general office number is 612-297-3190.

The Minnesota Community Improvement Program (MCIP) is a community (or county) revitalization and recognition program. Citizens conduct a community analysis and set goals. They build broad support networks and document the improvement process so that MCIP judges can evaluate annual progress. The Minnesota Extension Service provides educational and technical support. Involvement in MCIP can build the skills and coalitions necessary to accomplish other specific tasks such as economic development, downtown revitalization and design, and beautification.

The Governor's Design Team calls on architects, landscape designers, urban planners, artists, and other professionals volunteer their time and services and virtually descend on a community for a two-to three-day intensive design consultation and work session. Communities want the team to a fresh look and new ideas in such areas a downtown revitalized town image, and development potential. Before applying for a visit, the community should focus on specific issues and areas of need. During a visit, broad-based active citizen support and involvement is expected.

Minnesota Main Street encourages revitalization of downtowns in small and midsize cities, working with assets already inherent in the downtown tradition. Rebuilding main street's image depends on improvements in organization, promotion, design, and economic restructuring, made in operation with downtown groups.

Minnesota Beautiful supports activities that help keep Minnesota a clean and quality place to live, work, and visit. Projects include recycling, landscaping, general cleanup of waste materials and unsightly areas, tree planting, and mineland reclamation. Minnesota Beautiful offers educational materials to communities undertaking these projects, and organizes an annual conference to recognize significant progress.

Cultural Tourism Promotion and policy in Malaysia

Malaysia is experiencing a tremendous pace of tourism development. Tourism sector has been recognized by Malaysian government as a major source of revenue and catalyst to the Malaysian economic renaissance. Tourist arrivals to Malaysia for the last ten years have shown a significant rise. In the year 2004, this country attracted 15.7 million foreign tourists generating around RM29.7 billion into the company. Major tourist market for Malaysia has been the neighbouring ASEAN nations especially Singapore, Thailand, Indonesia and Brunei. Other main traditional foreign markets include China, Japan, Taiwan and India.

Coupled with the growth in tourism is a booming interest in the 'new tourism'. Cultural tourism has emerged as a potential form of alternative tourism among both international tourists as well as Malaysian domestic travellers. Cultural tourism in Malaysia attracted great publicities with the increase in the number of incoming tourists annually. Malaysia has marvelous cultural tourism resources that are readily available to be explored such as the existence of multi-cultural, historical buildings, colorful lifestyles and friendly atmosphere. The purpose of this paper is to give an overview of the promotion of culture and heritage in Malaysia as well as the related strategies and policies that support the measure. It also discusses several underlying issues pertaining the cultural management in Malaysia.

Table 1: Tourist arrivals and receipts to Malaysia

Year	*Arrivals (million)*	*Receipts (RM millions)*
1995	7.46	9,174.9
1996	7.14	10,354.1
1997	6.21	9,699.6
1998	5.55	8,580.4
1999	7.93	12,321.3
2000	10.22	17,335.4
2001	12.78	24,221.5
2002	13.29	25,781.1
2003	10.58	21,291.1
2004	15.70	29,651.4

Source: Tourism Malaysia, 2005

Defining Cultural Tourism

Culture in tourism is an important issue. The relationship between tourism and culture can take many forms and the outcome can be viewed as negative and positive when meeting of hosts and visitors occurs and possibly leads to the transformation of the hosts' culture. The destruction of local culture as a result of tourism is well documented. However, studies by researchers' consider this as a lopsided view of the impact of tourism. Studies have shown that tourism have lead to the strengthening of local culture. Culture is defined broadly as quoted in Meethan (2001:117), "*.....as a set of practices, based on forms of knowledge, which encapsulate common values and act as general guiding principles. It is through these forms of knowledge that distinctions are created and maintained, so that, for example, one culture is marked off as different from another*"

World Tourism Organization (1985) defines cultural tourism as the movements of persons for essentially cultural motivations such as study tours, performing arts and cultural tours; travel to festivals and other related events. Essentially, cultural tourism is based on the mosaic of places, traditions, art forms, celebrations and experiences that portray ones nation and its people.

Meethan (2001:128) rightly observed that there are array of tourist activities that come under the heading of cultural tourism. However, he argues for a distinct demarcation of cultural tourism and hence a distinct profile of cultural tourists quotes,

"*....the cultural tourists are those who go about their leisure in a more serious frame of mind. To be a cultural tourist.....is to go beyond idle leisure and to return enriched with knowledge of other places and other people even if this involves 'gazing' at or collecting in some way, the commodation essences of otherness*"

Studies of western culture by Richard (1994) described the cultural tourists were *'a high socioeconomic status, high level of educational attainment, adequate leisure time, and often having occupations related to the culture industries'*. It must be borne in mind that culture is not static but one that is dynamic and evolving. Meethan (2001: 127) draw attention to globalization of culture and also the mobilization of culture for internal and external purposes. Yamashita, Kadir and Eades (1997: 29-30) further illustrates the processes that transform culture.

Heritage tourism can be classified as a subclass of cultural tourism. Both cultural and heritage tourism become a growing segment of the tourism marketplace. Cultural tourists appear to be motivated for different reasons than do traditional tourists. Some tourism destinations see cultural tourism as a promotion for tourism products, and this has been lamented. Millar (1989) and others suggest that heritage tourism is "about the cultural traditions, places and values that... groups throughout the world are proud to conserve." Cultural traditions such as family patterns, religious practices, folklore traditions, and social customs attract individuals interested in heritage as do monuments, museums, battlefields, historic structures, and landmarks.

Cultural Tourism in Malaysia and its Management

In Malaysia, heritage and culture has also been identified as new niche products to be developed extensively in tourism development. Cultural vibrancy is clearly manifested in the ongoing and successful "Malaysia: Truly Asia" promotional drive by the country's promotion arm, Tourism Malaysia. In this promotion, Malaysia boasts to host a wide variety of Asian ethnic groups that making it into a little Asia. Malaysia also has distinctive multicultural architectural heritage with strong Islamic, Chinese and Western influences; all of which have been portrayed in the heritage buildings.

The major heritage elements; historic building, historical sites and unique local cultures are commonly found in many historic cities throughout Malaysia. An inventory has revealed that 30,000 heritage buildings are located in 162 cities throughout Malaysia. From this figure, 69.6% are shop houses and dwellings built before World War II. The unique colonial architectural styles of buildings have played major role in the creation of historic cities such as George Town, Ipoh, Malacca, Tapping, Koala Lumpur and Kuching.

Table 2 Distributions of Pre-War Buildings in Selected States in Malaysia

States in Malaysia	*Number of Pre-War Buildings*	*Percentage (%)*
Penang	5057	24.3
Perak	3351	16.1
Johor	2323	11.2
Malacca	2177	10.5
Koala Lumpur	1763	8.4

The management of culture and heritage in Malaysia was put under the Ministry of Tourism and Culture, established on the 20th of May 1987, combining Department of Culture from the Ministry of Culture, Youths and Sports with the Malaysian Tourism Development Corporation from the Ministry of Trade and Industries. On 22nd October 1992, the ministry was renamed into Ministry of Culture, Arts and Tourism.

This ministry was later divided in Mac 2004, into two ministries, namely the Tourism Ministry and Ministry of Culture, Arts and Heritage. This separation is seen as recognition of tourism as a potential number one sector of the country and a move to appreciate the value of heritage of the country.

Agencies under this ministry are the National Archives, the National Art and Gallery, the Department of Museum and Antiquities, Malaysian Handicrafts (Kraftangan Malaysia), the National Film Development Corporation (Finas), the National Art Academy, the National Library and the Istana Budaya (the Culture Palace).

Despite the move to strengthen the ministries, the separation of the cultural elements from the Tourism Ministry can give impacts on the direction of 'cultural and heritage tourism', leaving this niche area as an no-man's land!

The Formulation of National Cultural Policy

At a national conference organized by Malaysia's Ministry of Culture, Youth and Sports in 1971, the Malaysian government formulated what was to become a national cultural policy based on the following principles:

(i) The national culture of Malaysia must henceforth be based on the cultures of the people indigenous to the region.

(ii) Elements from other cultures which are judged suitable and reasonable may be incorporated into Malaysia's national culture.

(iii) Islam will be an important element in the national culture.

In the period since its implementation, Malaysia's national culture policy has become one important point of vigorous debate and political conflict. In the years since the formulation of a National Cultural Policy, and particularly in the late 1980's, the Malaysian government has been concerned to implement its basic principles by intervening directly and across the board in the cultural field. Not surprisingly, and perhaps because it has not been altogether clear and efficient about its task, government intervention in the cultural field has produced a response on the part of a variety of non-Malaya groups who feel that their cultural freedom has been curtailed.

For example, at a meeting of the Chinese guild and associations of Malaysia held in March, 1983, delegates passed a series of resolutions that were compiled in a joint memorandum to the Ministry of Culture, Youth and Sports.

In April 1984, a group of the best-known Indian cultural, social and religious organizations submitted a similar memorandum. Both memoranda accused the government of having formulated a cultural policy which was Malaya-centric and undemocratic, and requested that a new policy on national culture be established which was more clearly multi-ethnic and democratic.

Law and Legislations on Cultural and Heritage Properties

The legal foundations of the Malaysian cultural policy are derived from the following acts and regulations:

i) Antiquities Act 1976 (Act 168).

ii) National Art Gallery Act, 1958.

iii) Legal Deposit of Library Material Act, 1986 (Act A667).

iv) National Library Act, 1972; The National Library (Amendment) Act, 1987.

v) National Archive Act, 1966 (Act 44), (Revised 1971), (Act A85), (Revised 1993), (Act 511).

vi) Tourist Development Corporation of Malaysia Act 1972 (Act 1972).

vii) Broadcasting Act 1988 (Act 338), Broadcasting (Amendment) Act, 1997 (Act A977).

viii) Cinematography Film-Hire Duty Act 1965 (Revised 1990), (Act 434).

ix) (Perbadanan Kemajuan File Nasional Malaysia Act 1981 (Act 244), Perbadanan Kemajuan File Nasional Malaysia (Amendment) Act, 1984 (Act 589).

x) Perbadanan Kemajuan Kraftangan Malaysia Act 1979 (Act 222).

xi) Theatres & Places of Public Amusement (Federal Territory) Act 1988 (Act 182).

xii) Bernama Act, 1967 (Revised 1990), (Act 449).

xiii) Entertainment Duty Act 1953 (Revised 1973) (Act 103).

Efforts to preserve the heritage buildings in Malaysia are supported by various acts and legislations. The prominent acts have been the Town and Country Planning Act of 1976 or the 172 Act, The National Land Code (Kanun Tanah Negara), the Street, Drainage and Building Act 133, the Antiquities Act 1976, as well as local legislations such as the Malacca Enactment No. 6 (1988). Act 133 for instance stipulates that "No person shall erect any building without a prior written permission of the local authority".

This provision is supported by Section 18 of Act 172 which states "All land/building use shall comply with the local plans (structure and local plans). Any development shall obtain planning permission. And if there is no development plan prepared for the area, the owner/developer of the land shall inform their plan to the adjoining landowners (Act 172,).

To date, a guidelines on the Guidelines on the Conservation of George Town Inner City details out specific recommendations pertaining extensions, renovations, revitalizations of heritage buildings within the prescribed zones.

At present, any erection of buildings is loosely bonded by both Acts (133 and 172). Section 16 of 133 defines erections of building includes 'renews or repairs of any existing buildings in such a manner as to involve a renewal, reconstruction or erection of any portion of an outer or party wall to the extent of one storey height". Further, all building that fall within the definition of development, stipulated in Act 172 also requires planning permission.

The Guidelines is in concordant with Part Vll of Act 133 that gives the State Authority to make by-laws or in respect of every purpose which is deemed by him necessary. In regards to the preservation of buildings, the State Authority, among other things, has the right to make by laws in:-

(i) The construction, paving, width and level of arcades and footways;

(ii) The construction, alteration and demolition of buildings and the methods and materials to be used in connection therewith;

(iii) The minimum timber or other building material content in any building.

Issues

The promotion of culture and heritage in Malaysia faces several underlying issues that both are related to the complexity of the society living in Malaysia. Among the issues are:-

Whose Culture?

Despite the fact that Malaysia is proud of its multiculturalism, promoted worldwide as the 'Truly Asia', the question remains on whose culture should be promoted at the forefront. As discussed above, Chinese and Indians have continuously felt that their cultures are not well represented in the tourism brochures produced by the government.

Similar sentiment was raised up during the nomination process for the listing of Penang and Melaka into the world heritage city. Malays in Penang especially feel that the listing do not benefit them and the island's Malaya history is not taken into consideration.

Some also feel that the listing of the 12000 heritage buildings where many of them are colonial buildings—is just another post colonization of the country, lamented on why we have to glorify the colonial past!

Authentic Versus Staged Culture

Tourism has evolved to become a significant factor in the development of culture in two ways: as a support and as a threat. The converse is also possible– culture can support or inhibit the growth of tourism. In the Malaysian context, there has so far been no specific attempt to study the value of cultural attractions from the point of view of the tourists.

Tourism authorities and promotional consultants simply assume that the cultural elements of a plural society are attractive. Further questions can be raised as to whether it is the 'staged culture' or the 'street culture' that is more appealing to outsiders. According to Kadir Din (1997), 'street culture' depicts the scenes of everyday life that can be readily observed by tourists in their natural setting, as opposed to 'staged culture' which refers to contrived staged presentations, which are specifically prepared for the tourist.

He concludes that in terms of government allocations of funds for tourism, and of coverage by the promotional media, there seems to be a belief that staged culture contributes more to tourism than street culture. To complicate things, as mentioned above, the nomination of Penang and Melaka includes the conservation of cultural elements of the society.

However, with so much pressure and development that have taken place, one may wonder how this society can conserve its cultural elements to remain authentic. Or perhaps, one may also wonder whether what is left is still authentic? A similar comment can be made on the staging of the massive festival of 'Citrawarna'—a cultural parade of various ethnic groups in Malaysia. Perhaps copying the success of the Samba Festival in Brazil or the New Orleans Parade or perhaps the Gion Matsuri (festival) in Kyoto Japan, the Citrawarna Malaysia has a lot of colours but lack authenticity and also history!

Metro Achievers

These households are among the most educated and affluent in the country, with the heads tending to be the elite in their professions or businesses. The families in the clusters comprising this target market live overwhelmingly in the suburbs of major metropolitan cities or "second" cities. In 2002, Metro Achievers represented 20% of households making one or more trips to Vermont. With the clusters comprising the Metro Achievers target market accounting for 14% of all households nationally, such households exhibited a 47% greater likelihood of making one or more trips to Vermont than the average U.S. household. Given their affluence, the propensity of Metro Achievers households to travel to Vermont makes them a highly desirable target market.

Small Town Movers

These are households that live in neighbourhoods well outside the metropolitan beltways, in some cases in relatively remote country towns and villages. However, while residing in less densely populated areas (in some cases perhaps a deliberate choice to exchange a high profile, high-income urban job and lifestyle for a less complex and stressful way of life), many of the individuals in the clusters comprising this target are well educated, and incomes are relatively high. These households tend to be among the most influential in their communities. In 2002, Small Town Movers represented 13% of the households making one or more trips to Vermont. Since the clusters comprising the Small Town Movers target market accounted for 7% of all households nationally, these households were 79% more likely to make one or more trips to Vermont than the average U.S. household.

Small Town Rustic

These households tend to be located in less populated towns and villages, and generally have lower incomes and/or educational attainment compared to Small Town Movers. In 2002, Small Town Rustic households represented 13% of the households making one or more trips to Vermont. With the clusters comprising this target market accounting for 10% of all households nationally, Small Town Rustic households exhibited a 23% greater likelihood of travelling to Vermont than the average U.S. household.

New Eco-topia

New Eco-topia households represent a unique target market. These households tend to live in sparsely populated areas and have moderate incomes. The educational profile of this cluster is heterogeneous, ranging from high school to college graduate. The socioeconomic ranking of New Eco-topia households places them between Small Town Movers and Small Town Rustics. In 2002, these households, which represented 2% of the households making one or more trips to Vermont, exhibited a high propensity to travel to Vermont, with a 62% greater likelihood than the average U.S. household.

Table 1. Prizm-Based Target Markets for Vermont

Prizm Cluster Number	*Cluster Name*	*2002 U.S. Percent*	*2002 Vermont Percent*	*2002 Vermont Index*
	Metro Achievers	13.60%	19.98%	147
4	Pools & Patios	1.80%	3.51%	195
7	Money & Brains	1.00%	1.57%	157
2	Winner's Circle	2.20%	3.58%	163
19	New Empty Nests	2.30%	3.44%	150
5	Kids & Cul-de-Sacs	3.10%	3.80%	123
11	Second City Elite	1.90%	2.56%	135
3	Executive Suites	1.30%	1.52%	117
	Small Town Movers	7.40%	13.21%	179
14	Country Squires	1.50%	2.95%	197
16	Big Fish, Small Pond	1.40%	2.28%	163
15	God's Country	2.90%	4.91%	169
17	Greenbelt Families	1.60%	3.07%	192
	Small Town Rustic	10.20%	12.51%	123
52	Golden Ponds	1.60%	2.01%	126
37	New Homesteaders	1.70%	1.94%	114
41	Big Sky Families	1.60%	2.38%	149
43	River City, USA	1.80%	2.08%	116
58	Blue Highways	1.80%	1.98%	110
39	Red, White & Blues	1.70%	2.12%	125
	New Eco-topia	1.00%	1.62%	162
42	New Eco-topia	1.00%	1.62%	162

Note: that the percentages do not add to 100 because only the top 18 PRIZM profiles are listed here, out of the 62 total PRIZM profiles identified by Claritas, Inc. The 18 PRIZM profiles reported here represent those most likely to visit

Vermont and buy Vermont products. They do not represent all visitors to Vermont. Based on this prior research on Vermont visitors and Olallie Daylily Gardens' interest in marketing using mailings, we designed a study that examines the effectiveness of PRIZM coding as well as current marketing methods already in use by Olallie Daylily Gardens.

Research Methods

The study compared marketing methods and assessed their usefulness in bringing in new business. Olallie Daylily Gardens previously used ads (magazine, newspaper, and radio), a Web site, rack cards, and postcard and catalogue mailings as their primary means of marketing. With the help of the University of Vermont, Olallie also used PRIZM coded mailings and a control mailing to a random sample. The first step of the research was to learn more about Olallie's current customers. Olallie sent Claritas, Inc. A list of over 9,000 household addresses from their database of customers. Results revealed that New Eco-topians made up over 40% of the drive-market customer base. No one PRIZM code dominated the mail-order customer list. The next step was to send a mailing to a sample of potential customers based on their PRIZM category and a random sample as a control. We purchased 10,000 mailing labels (names and addresses) from Claritas, with half of the mailing labels targeted to reach potential mail-order market customers. The remaining 5,000 mailing labels were selected to reach drive-market customer targets. The exact breakdown of the mailing list was as follows.

* South-Central Vermont, excluding zip 05301, (17% or 1700 addresses) of which 850 addresses are randomly selected (no PRIZM), balance of 850 addresses would be PRIZM code #42 (New Eco-topians).
* Southwestern New Hampshire (8%) 400 random, balance PRIZM code #42.
* Northern Massachusetts (17%) 850 random, balance PRIZM code #42.
* Southwestern Connecticut (8%) 400 random, balance PRIZM code #42.
* Minnesota (13%) 650 random, balance with an even distribution of PRIZM codes #42, 41, 15, 1, 2, 14 and 37.
* Wisconsin (13%) 650 random, balance with an even distribution of PRIZM codes #42, 41, 15, 1, 2, 14 and 37.

* Michigan (12%) 600 random, balance with an even distribution of PRIZM codes #42, 41, 15, 1, 2, 14 and 37.
* Illinois (12%) 600 random, balance with an even distribution of PRIZM codes #42, 41, 15, 1, 2, 14 and 37.

The mailing labels were affixed to postcards, and the postcards were marked with codes so we could keep track of responses. Olallie's employees were trained to ask how new customers heard about the farm and check postcards for specific codes. The mailings were conducted during the summer of 2003.

Research Results

During the winter, the Darrows counted the tally of responses for the 2003 season, which runs from May to September. For bringing in new catalogue requests, advertising in *Fine Gardening Magazine* was responsible for the greatest response, leading to 407 catalogue requests. Web searches were second, with 270 catalogue requests. In third place was an advertisement in *Horticulture Magazine*, with 123 catalogue requests. Word-of-mouth came next with 100 catalogue requests. Other forms of advertising ranked lower, including the mailings.

Table 2. Marketing Methods Used by Olallie Daylily Gardens and Percentage of Catalogue Requests and Farm Visits

Marketing Method	*Catalogue Requestsn = 1092*	*Farm Visitsn = 201*
Horticulture Magazine	11.3%	2.0%
Fine Gardening Magazine	37.3%	4.0%
Local Magazines	4.6%	16.9%
Newspaper Ads	0.7%	6.5%
Brochures	0.1%	5.5%
Radio and TV	0.5%	2.0%
Map/Book Listing	0.3%	9.0%
Sign/Poster	0.0%	9.0%
Web Search	24.7%	12.4%
Web Link	4.6%	2.0%
Word of Mouth	9.2%	23.9%
Mailings	1.0%	2.0%
Other	5.9%	5.0%

Word of mouth was the most effective way to bring in new farm visits. Advertising in a local magazine ranked second, and Web searches ranked third. In contrast to catalogue requests, posters, signs, maps, and book listings were effective means of generating farm visits. Similar to catalogue requests, mailings generated a low percentage of farm visits.

Implications

The low response to the mailings combined with high responses to other kinds of targeted marketing methods led us to develop the Niche Products hypothesis. At the bottom of the pyramid are products with broad appeal, such as credit cards. Mass mailings are an effective way to reach new credit card customers for generic cards. Moving up the pyramid, products become more specialized, appealing only to select customers. For example, specialized credit cards target specific markets (e.g., the L.L. Bean credit card for L.L. Bean customers). Products such as those produced by Olallie Daylily Gardens—high-quality, field-grown, hand-dug daylilies—are toward the top of the pyramid, requiring finely targeted marketing techniques such as word of mouth and advertisements in magazines geared toward a select audience. PRIZM code classifications are an improvement on mailings to random samples, but, as we learned from the research, they are not finely targeted enough for such a specialized product as high-quality daylilies.

Conclusions

The next phase of the research project is to fill in the blank spaces on the pyramid and improve Extension's understanding of the marketing methods that work best for different products. Beef, for example, can fit in many places on the pyramid depending on how it is produced, packaged, branded, and marketed. No-name hamburger is toward the bottom of the pyramid, while grass-fed, hormone-free, premium-priced tenderloin raised in Vermont is toward the top of the pyramid. Extension specialists can use this pyramid to help them and their audience make informed decisions about appropriate marketing methods, keeping in mind that the more specialized a product, the more targeted the marketing methods need to be.

Acknowledgements

The research was supported by the Vermont Tourism Data Centre (a partnership between the University of Vermont Rubenstein School of Environment and Natural Resources and the Vermont Department of Tourism and Marketing), University of Vermont Extension, and Olallie Daylily Gardens. I'm grateful to Amelia Darrow, Gary Deziel, Tom Noordewier, and Wendy Wilson for helpful comments on earlier drafts.

Sustainable Development and Tourism: Towards Quality Growth

Europe is the world's most visited region. As mobility and affordability of travel increase with globalization, visitor flows will intensify. There is a real risk of overcrowding, congestion, strain on natural and cultural resources and stress to local communities beyond acceptable levels at major tourism hotspots across Europe. Moreover, large seasonal and geographical fluctuations erode employment conditions. At the same time, developing tourism in Europe's disadvantaged regions – off the beaten track – could bring more local prosperity, especially at times of painful economic restructuring.

Ensuring balanced development is both a challenge and an opportunity for European countries if they want to stay competitive long-term in the global race for welfare gains through tourism. They should therefore tourism, with emphasis on value rather than volume. Sustainable development, which relies on a synergy of economic, social, environmental and cultural goals, offers a way forward whereby growth and quality become mutually reinforcing. A long-term vision and a holistic approach to development are necessary for Europe to lead the way not only as the most popular but also the most successful tourist destination. The report underscores the importance of authenticity and diversity as sources of quality growth in European tourism. It pleads for greater attention to be paid by European policy makers to the issues of safety and security, congestion management, the threat of climate change, accessibility and hospitality problems, as well as dialogue with the private sector, while proposing a series of targeted measures at pan-European, national, regional and local levels. Europe can either reap vast benefits from the sustainable development of tourism or face the consequences of unbridled growth.

Draft Recommendation

Europe has a long and successful history of attracting visitors: it remains the world's most visited region offering a wealth of experiences in distinct history, scenery, culture and lifestyles. Seven European countries– France, Spain, Italy, the United Kingdom, Germany, Austria and the Russian Federation – are among the world's ten most visited destinations. Overall, nearly half of all visitors globally (478 million) travelled in European countries in 2007, and tourist flows in Europe are expected to double in the next two decades as mobility and the affordability of travel increase with globalization. This is both a development challenge and an opportunity, if European countries want to stay competitive in the global race for welfare gains through tourism.

People-to-people contacts generated through travel and tourism can facilitate mutual understanding and international diplomacy. They help to build a community of values in Europe which stands out as an example on the global scene. European countries, as represented by the Council of Europe, should put human beings and sustainability at the heart of their development policies, not least as regards tourism. A long-term vision and a holistic approach to development are necessary for Europe to lead the way as the most popular and successful tourist destination.

Expanding on average by 3-4% every year, tourism has grown into a major economic activity in Europe, directly accounting for some 24 million jobs, 4% of cumulative GDP and US$ 374 billion in annual revenue. A quarter of all tourism is linked to business travel in support of wealth creation, skills and technology transfer, entrepreneurship and connections between markets. In the last few years, tourism development has been particularly dynamic, though uneven, in central and eastern Europe, enabling the region's countries to catch up with western Europe in terms of economic development and living standards but also leading to major socioeconomic pressures due to swelling visitor flows. It is essential to concentrate efforts on promoting the development of *quality* tourism in these states and across all Europe to allow tourism to make a substantial and lasting contribution to overall balanced and sustainable development while avoiding the excesses seen at some mass tourism destinations.

The quantitative and qualitative aspects can and should be reconciled through the sustainable development of tourism based on a synergy of economic, social, environmental and cultural benchmarks. Promoting diversity, authenticity and quality in tourism is a key to lasting success. Thus economic viability, local prosperity, employment quality, social equity, visitor fulfilment, local control, community wellbeing, cultural richness, physical integrity, biological diversity, resource efficiency and environmental purity are imperatives that should be taken into account for shaping a long-term development vision and strategies.

Safety and security are major prerequisites for tourism and travel to prosper. Although Europe has a good reputation for safety, it is not immune to security threats. Council of Europe member states must stay vigilant and reflect on how security could further be upgraded at all levels in a discreet way and in full respect for human rights, ethical values and the rule of law. It is necessary for the Council of Europe member states to review their alert and crisis management systems, including evacuation plans, security communication with the public and cross-border cooperation arrangements. The Council of Europe and its Parliamentary Assembly should also study more closely the legitimacy of new security demands for transatlantic travel recently presented by the US Administration vis-a-vis European states.

With new technologies, evolving consumer behaviour and simplified travel planning, congestion is increasingly frequent in transport, accommodation and tourist sites in many European holiday destinations and business hubs while many peripheral or secondary locations, on the contrary, suffer from the lack of visitors' attention. The congestion causes stress to visitors, disruption to local communities and often a degradation of tourist sites and services. There is an urgent need to better manage tourist flows in order to optimise the use of facilities and resources geographically and time-wise.

Our lifestyles, wellbeing and economies will be gradually affected by climate change. In Europe, northern and southern regions and mountain, island and coastal areas likely to suffer the worst effects but all countries will have to face more intense and frequent climatic disorders and extremes, such as heat waves, droughts, heavy precipitation or storms, as well as related problems, such as forest fires, floods, effects on wildlife and biodiversity, coastal erosion, infrastructure damage, infectious diseases, water levels and lack of resources. As a highly climate-sensitive sector – like agriculture, energy, insurance and transport – tourism needs to adapt and contribute to global efforts to tackle climate change, essentially through cuts in greenhouse gas emissions from transport and accommodation.

Although holidays, and by extension travel, are a right, about 40%

of Europeans do not leave on holidays owing to various forms of deprivation or disability. Families, senior citizens, immigrants, the young and people with disabilities are particularly concerned. Greater attention to the social aspects of tourism could help reduce the seasonality of demand and excessive geographical concentrations of travellers, as well as supporting more stable year-round employment and the development of disadvantaged regions, especially if more travellers could be persuaded to travel outside the main season and/or the busiest areas. Several important issues should be addressed: the physical accessibility of tourist destinations and sites, the economic affordability of holiday travel and better information on travel options for potential travellers with special needs.

Tourism enriches when it takes place in a balanced way resulting in a win-win situation for both visitors and hosts. If state authorities and international institutions are primarily responsible for providing political commitment and policies conducive to sustainability in tourism, the contribution of the private sector is critical to yielding results on the ground and providing feedback to policy makers. Public and private actors should work together to agree, implement and monitor the integrated quality management approach respectful of reference quality standards for tourism services and products.

Whilst tourism and sectoral associations can act as information relays between state authorities and local actors, public-private partnerships might serve to realise pilot projects, promote corporate social responsibility and implement equitable employment schemes, improved pricing models, innovative destination marketing and investment planning compatible with environmental, cultural and social imperatives.

Tourism is first and foremost about people of all ages, interests and skills. Quality tourist services require dedicated and competent people involved as local inhabitants or tourism professionals. Hospitality, with a caring attitude towards people, traditions and heritage, and knowledge of foreign languages, plays an increasingly prominent role. It goes together with sustainability based on responsible consumption and production patterns to minimise resource waste and pollution, and emphasis on value rather than volume. These notions should be taught early at schools. A fair share of revenue from tourism should be reinvested in local development.

Sustainable development of tourism holds much promise for Europe and beyond. Growth and sustainability are compatible targets when properly managed. Development challenges, that stem from evolving lifestyles, economic growth and restructuring, demographic trends and globalization, call for calibrated national, regional and local but also collective – pan-European – responses. In this context, the Assembly underlines the importance of studying the implications of tourism growth on infrastructure development in Council of Europe member states.

The Parliamentary Assembly therefore asks the Committee of Ministers to:

* To incite national governments of the Council of Europe member states to:
    - Ally long-term thinking, best practices and a sum of ambitious economic, social, environmental and cultural benchmarks for shaping national tourism development policies;
    - Screen the compatibility of national tourism legislation and policies with the principles of sustainable development and relevant Council of Europe conventions in the environmental and cultural fields;
    - Involve tourism in the implementation of existing commitments under the UN Framework Convention on Climate Change with its Kyoto Protocol and contribute to the preparation of the new package of measures for the post-2012 period;
    - Support the implementation of international co-development policies, including the Millennium Development Goals, environmental agreements, the UNWTO's Global Code of Ethics for Tourism, the Clean Development Mechanism, multilateral and bilateral aid programmes, in order to help the emerging economies to match their development needs with the drive for more tourism;
    - Promote domestic – intra-country and intra-European – tourism whereby distances travelled are shorter and means used can rely more on public transport;

- Mitigate the impact of carbon emissions due to long-haul travel and transport, not least through the 'polluter pays' principle and a greater participation of European airlines in the EU Emissions Trading System, as well as via tax incentives encouraging a shift from road to rail in goods transport on major European transit corridors;
- Encourage responsible consumption and production patterns minimising resource waste and pollution (especially as regards water and energy use, recycling, waste management, forward planning, etc.) and propagating meaningful alternatives (such as greater recourse to renewable resources, public transport, sustainable construction, etc.) in providing tourism services;
- Promote the sharing of knowledge and good practice on sustainable tourism development with other countries and regions;
- Consider restructuring national tourism organisations to work as public-private partnerships;
- Support the development of family-friendly travel and accommodation options;
- Accelerate the implementation of the Council of Europe Disability Action Plan 2006-2015;
- To encourage and facilitate travel to various European destinations by niche travellers (the young, the elderly, families, the disabled and repeat/experienced visitors) as a means of ensuring a more even geographical and seasonal spread of visitor flows across European regions;
- Carry out regular national and enterprise security audits;
- Establish or designate, as may be appropriate, multilingual national tourist safety focal points and emergency call centres;
- Reassess their alert and crisis management systems, including evacuation plans, security communication with the public and cross-border cooperation arrangements;
- Make better use of new security and defence technologies for civil protection, including in the tourism sector;

- Set up regulatory incentives and binding minimum targets for promoting sustainable construction and renovation of buildings;
- Seek that a fair share of direct and indirect income generated from tourist visits be channelled towards the further development of cultural and natural assets;
- Support the development of tourism as an alternative source of local income and jobs in areas undergoing economic decline and depopulation, especially in rural and mountainous regions;
- Promote quality certification schemes for tourist services and products;
- Study the feasibility of including hospitality and sustainable development concepts into school curricula;
- Ensure the effective protection of tourists' consumer rights;

* Instruct a competent Council of Europe expert committee to study the compatibility of new security demands for transatlantic travel, presented by the United States authorities, with the Council of Europe's values and legal acquis, especially on personal data protection, with a view to presenting recommendations on the matter.

* The Assembly invites the Congress of Local and Regional Authorities to:

- Study the impact and implications of low-cost travel on local development and employment conditions with a view to possibly formulating guidelines on the matter;
- Carry out comparative studies of visitor management frameworks and prepare guidelines on the subject;
- Ensure effective local oversight regarding the implementation of regulations on spatial planning.

* The Assembly invites national parliaments to ensure that national legislation is in place with a view to orienting investors, tourists and other stakeholders and ensuring an appropriate government response to sustainable tourism development issues.

Explanatory Memorandum by Mr. Mendes Bota, Rapporteur

Contents

Europe is the world's most visited region. Its complex history, geographical diversity and cultural riches continue to attract ever more visitors. Out of 898 million tourist arrivals in the world in 2007, about 478 million (48%) were recorded in Europe – an increase of at least 19 million over 2006 as compared to a 52 million increase for the world.

The preliminary data for 2007 shows a steady 4% growth in tourist arrivals in Europe compared to a 6% growth rate for the world. Seven European countries (France, Spain, Italy, United Kingdom, Germany, Austria and the Russian Federation) remain among the world's ten most visited destinations.

Since this trend has been sustained over years and decades, tourism has grown into a major economic activity significantly contributing to welfare gains, cultural exchanges, social cohesion and overall development across Europe.

According to the estimates of the World Tourism Organisation (UNWTO), tourist flows in Europe are expected to double over the next 15 years, accounting for about a half of some 1600 million international arrivals expected worldwide already in 2020.

International tourist arrivals by country of destination (Totals and % change between years)

Country and 2006 ranking	*1995*	*2000*	*2004*	*2005*	*2006*	*04/03*	*05/04*	*06/05*
			In millions				*In %*	
1. France	73.1	77.2	75.1	75.9	79.1	0.1	1.0	4.2
2. Spain	46.8	47.9	52.4	55.9	58.2	3.1	6.6	4.1
3. United States	48.5	51.2	46.1	49.2	51.1	11.8	6.8	3.8
4. China	27.0	31.2	41.8	46.8	49.6	26.7	12.1	6.0
5. Italy	36.5	41.2	37.1	36.5	41.1	-6.4	-1.5	12.4
6. United Kingdom	23.2	23.2	25.7	28.0	30.7	12.7	9.2	9.3
7. Germany	17.1	19.0	20.1	21.5	23.6	9.4	6.8	9.6
8. Mexico	19.0	20.6	20.6	21.9	21.4	10.5	6.3	-2.6
9. Austria	17.5	18.0	19.4	20.0	20.2	-2.7	0.2	1.3
10. Russian Federation	n/a	n/a	19.9	19.9	20.2	-2.7	0.2	1.3
11. Turkey	6.9	9.6	16.8	30.3	18.9	26.1	20.5	-6.7
12. Canada	19.4	19.6	19.1	18.8	18.2	9.2	-2.0	-2.8
13. Ukraine	4.2	6.4	15.6	17.6	n/a	24.9	12.8	n/a
14. Malaysia	7.9	10.2	15.7	16.4	17.5	48.5	4.6	6.8
15. Hong Kong (China)	7.8	8.8	13.7	14.8	15.8	41.1	8.2	7.1
16. Poland	18.0	17.4	14.3	15.2	15.7	4.2	6.4	3.3

Country and 2006 ranking	*1995*	*2000*	*2004*	*2005*	*2006*	*04/03*	*05/04*	*06/05*
			In millions				*In %*	
17. Greece	12.2	13.1	13.3	14.3	16.0	-4.7	10.9	8.6
18. Thailand	8.7	9.6	11.7	11.6	13.9	16.4	-1.4	20.0
19. Portugal	11.6	12.1	10.6	10.6	11.3	-9.1	-0.3	6.3
20. Netherlands	9.9	10.0	9.6	10.0	10.7	5.1	3.8	7.3
22. Hungary	2.8	n/a	12.2	10.0	9.3	n/a	-183	-7.2
23. Croatia	3.8	5.8	7.9	8.5	8.7	6.8	7.0	2.3
26. Ireland	6.4	6.6	7.0	7.3	8.0	2.8	5.5	9.1
28. Switzerland	7.2	7.8	n/a	7.2	7.9	n/a	n/a	8.8
30. Japan	4.4	4.8	6.1	6.7	7.3	17.8	9.6	9.0
31. Belgium	6.4	6.5	6.7	6.7	7.0	0.3	0.6	3.7
34. Czech Republic	5.6	4.8	6.1	6.3	6.4	19.4	4.5	1.6
36. Bulgaria	2.5	2.8	4.6	4.8	5.2	14.4	4.5	6.6
40. Denmark	2.0	3.5	4.4	4.7	n/a	27.3	6.3	n/a
46. Norway	3.2	3.1	3.6	3.8	3.9	11.0	5.4	3.2
50. Finland	2.5	2.7	2.8	3.1	3.4	3.0	10.6	7.5
Other countries in Europe	2.3	2.7	3.0	3.1	3.3	1.7	4.3	4.4
Sweden	2.1	2.7	2.3	2.5	2.4	2.0	5.2	-2.8
Cyprus	.	2.9	2.8	2.4	2.23	-11.0	-13.4	-7.9
Andorra	0.7	1.1	1.8	2.0	2.2	20.7	11.1	9.0
Lithuania	0.5	1.2	1.75	1.92	1.94	19.7	9.5	1.2
Estonia	0.7	1.1	1.5	1.55	1.62	9.2	3.7	4.0
Slovenia	0.9	1.1	1.4	1.5	1.61	1.0	8.1	6.4
Slovakia	0.5	1.5	1.08	1.12	1.54	11.2	3.4	4.3
Latvia	0.8	0.9	1.36	1.43	1.38	23.0	5.0	-2.4
Romania	0.1	0.7	1.35	1.18	1.2	33.0	-12.7	1.4
Azerbaijan	1.1	1.2	1.2	1.17	1.12	3.4	1.3	-4.0
Malta	0.2	0.6	0.83	0.87	0.97	8.4	4.2	11.4
Iceland	0.8	0.8	0.87	0.91	0.91	1.2	4.0	-5.0
Luxembourg	0.2	0.2	0.6	0.73	0.5+0.4	20.5	25.0	3.5+39
Serbia & Montenegro Georgia	0.1	0.4	0.4	0.54	n/a	17.5	48.8	n/a
Europe	**312**	**390**	**419**	**436**	**459**	**4.3**	**4.0**	**4.4**
World	**536**	**684**	**761**	**802**	**846**	**10.1**	**5.4**	**5.5**

Source: UNWTO World Tourism Barometer 2007 and Tourism Market Trends 2006 Edition.

Viewed narrowly, tourism is often seen in terms of tour operators, guides, travel agencies, recreation facilities, entertainment, food, transport and accommodation services. However, from a broader perspective tourism appears as a cross-cutting activity that affects many other sectors ranging from regional and local planning to retail trade. Globally, tourism represents some € 2.9 trillion (US$ 4.2 trillion), or 10.4%, of cumulative GDP. In the European Union, tourism accounts *directly* for over 4% of GDP (ranging, in 2006, from 1.3% of GDP in Latvia to 13.2% of GDP in Malta) and about 11% of GDP if links with other sectors are considered. For non-EU European countries, tourism represents from 1.3% of GDP in Serbia and Montenegro[1] to 6.3% in Iceland and 6.2% in Switzerland. It involves directly some 1.4 million enterprises, essentially SMEs, and generates about 24.3 million jobs as one out of eight working Europeans is employed in the tourism sector and jobs in tourism-related sectors are created faster than the average for the European economy. Tourism jobs are particularly important for the employment of young people who account for twice the share of the labour force in tourism than in any other sector. European tourism still accounts for a half of the global market well ahead of Asian countries (19.3%) and the Americas (16.5%), but global competition is stiffening and capacity problems are increasingly felt in a number of popular European destinations.

At the same time, tourism is penetrating central and eastern European countries and legitimate expectations are growing on the part of both visitors and host communities. Although the region's performance in terms of tourism growth is very uneven, several countries (such as Croatia and the Czech Republic) already face major socioeconomic pressures due to rapidly swelling visitor flows. Special thought should be given to promoting the development of *quality* tourism in these states and across all Europe so that tourism could make a substantial and lasting contribution to overall development. Lessons should be drawn from the experience of highly popular tourist destinations with regard to mass tourism, management skills and tourist services. Your Rapporteur will therefore argue in this report that a long-term vision and a holistic approach are necessary for Europe to lead the way not only as the most popular but also the most successful tourist destination.

In the framework of the preparation of this report, the Sub-Committee on Tourism Development (of the Committee on Economic

Affairs and Development) held extensive consultations with senior representatives of European, national and regional tourism authorities, as well as delegates of this Assembly's Committees on the Environment and on Culture, notably during its meeting in Almancil. This was an excellent opportunity to gauge the importance of tourism to the development of regions not only in Portugal but also in many other European countries. In particular, the role of tourism in stimulating local infrastructure improvements and the preservation of employment in areas of rural decline or undergoing rural regeneration was stressed. Moreover, with globalization regions are becoming rather autonomous actors and have to compete more actively. Sustainable development offers a forward looking approach that can help local communities to make the best of tourism and development.

Reconciling Quantity and Quality Aspects through Sustainable Development of Tourism

Tourism development can be a powerful drive in overall development and many European regions have a large untapped growth potential. However, this does not mean that 'business as usual' or unbridled expansion to become a mass tourism destination is a viable option. Many 'sun, sea and sand' tourism hotspots in Europe already find it increasingly difficult to keep their market shares as visitors become more demanding and new destinations spring up elsewhere in the world. Crowds of visitors and significant fluctuations in visitor flows throughout a year may cause a non-negligible stress to local communities and deplete local resources, thus undermining the structure on which tourism rests. As earlier Assembly reports have rightly pointed out, too much tourism can kill tourism. Moreover, unbalanced or chaotic tourism development is not compatible with a long-term development vision for any community. The responsibility of policy makers therefore is to ensure strong affirmative action in favour of sustainable development, including for tourism.

The very concept of sustainable development aims to reconcile quantity and quality aspects of growth, as growth per se is no longer seen as a panacea or an aim in itself. Since the 1992 Rio Declaration on Environment and Development setting out Agenda 21, there has been a growing public awareness and adherence to the principles of sustainable development that seeks to preserve the planet's capacity to support life in all its diversity. This embraces broad concerns for environmental protection, social equity, the quality of life, cultural diversity and, of course, a dynamic vibrant economy that brings prosperity for all.

Economic, environmental, social and cultural benchmarks for balanced tourism growth

Tourism can serve to enhance the quality of life of visitors and host communities alike; making it more sustainable will boost the sustainability and cohesion of European society. The World Tourism Organisation (UNWTO) and the United Nations Environment Programme (UNEP) identified twelve benchmarks for sustainable tourism as follows:

- Economic viability (tourism destinations and enterprises need to be viable and competitive in order to continue to prosper and yield benefits long-term);
- Local prosperity (tourism should contribute as much as possible to the prosperity of the host community, including a fair share of tourist-generated revenue);
- Employment quality (the number and quality of tourism-supported local jobs must be strengthened, including remuneration, skills and terms of employment);
- Social equity (economic and social benefits from tourism should be widely spread through the recipient community);
- Visitor fulfilment (visitors should have a safe, satisfying and fulfilling experience);
- Local control (local communities need to be fully engaged and empowered in planning and decision making about the management and development of tourism in their area);
- Community wellbeing (quality of life in local communities should be preserved and strengthened, notably as regards social structures and access to resources, facilities and essential services);
- Cultural richness (cultural heritage and authentic traditions of host communities should be respected and preserved);
- Physical integrity (landscapes, both urban and rural, have to be preserved against physical and visual degradation);

- Biological diversity (natural areas, habitats and wildlife must be used in a way that minimises damage to them);
- Resource efficiency (scarce and non-renewable resources must be handled parsimoniously in tourism facilities);
- Environmental purity (air, water and land pollution, as well as waste generation, should be minimised).

In short, economic, social, environmental and cultural concerns need to guide sustainable tourism development policies. A full range of parameters, impacts and interactions between human activities and the environment should be taken into account for a balanced and integrated approach to tourism development and relevant action must be sustained over time. In this context, we wish to strongly recommend that all who care about this issue read the report of the Tourism Sustainability Group, *Action for more sustainable European tourism*, published in February 2007.

The report lists key challenges for the sustainability of European tourism (reducing the seasonality of demand, mitigating the impact of tourism transport, improving the quality of tourism jobs, enhancing community prosperity and quality of life in the face of change, minimising resource use and waste production, conserving and giving value to natural and cultural heritage, making holidays available to all, and using tourism as a tool in global sustainable development) and reviews stakeholder responsibilities for action to meet these challenges. The action framework of the report advocates networking between different players, efforts to promote certification schemes and corporate social responsibility, advisory support services for policy development, national pro-sustainability campaigns, research on good practice, sustainability training for managers, improved land use planning and control, and profiling better targeted information. for tourists. These measures were agreed to underpin the European Commission's position, as stated in its renewed Tourism Policy, in favour of "improving the competitiveness of the European tourism industry and creating more and better jobs through the sustainable growth of tourism in Europe and globally".

Personal and Collective Security as a Top Challenge for the Tourism sector

Tourism is a major contributor to peace, freedom and international understanding: it brings people and countries closer together. At the same time, safety and security are major prerequisites for tourism and development as modern travellers are ever better informed and more demanding. Tourism and travel are the first economic activities to suffer when personal and collective security is perceived as deficient. Health crises, natural disasters and acts of terrorism, as well as problems of personal, legal and criminal insecurity have rapid and lasting consequences on travel choices and by extension can seriously hurt the prosperity of communities strongly dependent on tourism. The aftermath of 9/11 and the 2005 Bali attacks, the Middle East and Asian tsunami crises or criminal outbreaks in individual countries – all this illustrates the powerful negative effects of the fear factor on tourism even if a rebound in activity may be rapid when calm returns.

Although Europe has a good reputation for safety, it is not immune to security threats. It needs to stay on its guard and to reflect on how security could further be upgraded at all levels in a discreet and acceptable way. Facing up to global, regional, national and local security challenges requires drawing lessons from past experiences. A quick look at some salient events of the last few years offers valuable insight. Due to fear of travelling and drastic security measures in the US after 9/11, visitor flows to the US in 2002-2003 shrank by at least 20% and revenues from tourism fell over 25%. Outbound trips by air went down significantly with scores of cancellations in corporate, personal and convention travel, and there ensued a chain of bankruptcies among travel-related businesses. The disruption hit many sectors most severely in the three months after the attacks and growth in the US tourism sector returned slowly only from 2004, reaching pre-2001 level of arrivals in 2006. Globally, in 2001, international arrivals fell by 0.5% and receipts were down by 2% (or US$10 billion), while domestic tourism increased in all countries. The following year global tourism was back to growth with a 3% increase in international arrivals.

Then the US-led prolonged war in Iraq plunged the Middle East region into a security nightmare. A study by the World Travel and Tourism Council (WTTC) showed that this war threatened over 3 million tourism and travel related jobs and billions of dollars worth of economic value, including in the tourism sector. The combined impact with the SARS scare temporarily depressed global travel (although world trade and economy resisted well), with major losses incurred in China, Taiwan, Hong Kong, Canada and Singapore but spillovers also to European countries. To some extent, the Americans' travel intentions to Europe, especially France and Germany, were negatively affected by political disagreements over Iraq and the strengthening of the euro against the dollar.

Additional tensions currently stem from the pressure of the US Administration on the EU governments to accept new security measures for transatlantic travel. This includes the supply of personal data on all passengers over flying but not landing in the US so as to allow them gain or retain visa-free travel to the US and the demand to put armed guards on all flights between Europe and the US by American airlines. The US Department of Homeland Security is also pressing for a new permit system for Europeans flying to the US, which would compel all potential passengers to apply online for permission to enter the US before even booking a ticket, with procedure lasting several days. Moreover, the US Administration is asking European airlines to provide personal data on non-travellers assisting elderly, young or ill passengers to board US-bound flights. This is in addition to 19 items of information on every traveller from the EU to the US that EU countries have already accepted to supply. Not surprisingly, EU officials have qualified the US demands as 'controversial', 'difficult', 'absurd', 'fully unjustified' and 'blackmail'. These somewhat excessive security demands by the US raise legal problems in Europe over data protection and risk complicating transatlantic travel. This Assembly and the Council of Europe must study the problem more closely with a view to seeking a common European position on the matter.

Environmental security came to the forefront with the December 2004 Asian tsunami which killed 225 000 people, including nearly two thousand European travellers, and devastated infrastructure in eleven countries. Despite heavy initial psychological shock on the victims' families, activities in the region, with the help of the international community, recovered to normal rather rapidly and so did visitor flows since the disaster was viewed as a one-off event. Repeated hurricanes take deadly tolls and cause massive infrastructure damage in the Americas. In 2005, Hurricane Katrina, the worst natural disaster in the history of the United States, caused direct economic damage of over $81 billion and huge environmental losses, especially in coastal areas, thus undercutting tourism in otherwise very frequented regions.

In summer 2007, Greek authorities were criticised over their efforts to deal with massive forest fires; entire villages and landscapes were ravaged and the local population, as well as visitors, had to desert them. In fact, forest fires particularly affect the Mediterranean countries where 380 000 to 1 million hectares of landscape burn every year, according to the European Forest Fire Information System. All these disasters highlight the importance of alert and crisis management systems (including evacuation plans) which are in need of urgent and substantive upgrades or complete restructuring in many countries. They also expose policy failures in the strategic management of the delicate balance between the built-up and green areas. Environmental experts warn that climatic disorders and ensuing disasters, such as storms, fires and floods, may be related to global warming and could thus hit more frequently in future.

Unfortunately, security crises come, go and come again: the travel and tourism sector therefore has to constantly adjust and develop ways to minimise these threats and their knock-on effects. Although governments bear primary responsibility for security in guiding various actors, international organisations also have a role to play, especially as regards communication and cooperation. As part of its work on enhancing safety and security in tourism, the UNWTO has sought to launch an international network featuring basic safety information and contact points on countries and emergencies. But this network needs to be further developed and better furnished with country profiles. The British "Know Before You Go" travel safety campaign launched in 2001 and run by the Foreign and Commonwealth Office together with travel industry partners provides a wealth of valuable advice to travellers. Structured by risk-themes, countries and travel formalities, it is a highly recommended site for use by all English-speaking travellers and could be emulated by other countries in Europe.

Pan-European efforts for information exchange, surveillance, risk assessment, crisis management, response coordination and preventive action are paramount and hinge on effective cross-border cooperation, including through European and international institutions such as the Council of Europe. In the area of personal safety, national and sometimes individual responsibility is crucial. From the Council of Europe perspective, concerted and focused action to fight violence and extremism of all sorts should go hand in hand with the work to uphold human rights, ethical values and the rule of law. The Council of Europe antiterrorist treaties, such as the Convention on the Prevention of Terrorism and the Convention on the Financing of Terrorism, but also efforts to ensure parliamentary oversight of security services pursue this goal and deserve full support by member states.

It is reassuring that safety standards in various domains are being developed, harmonised and ever more vigorously implemented in many European countries. It is particularly important that enhanced safety be ensured for public areas, gatherings and cultural events, tourist sites, facilities and services, as well as transport networks. One hundred percent security is hardly feasible but one hundred percent effort and care should be devoted to this end. We have to ensure that a multilingual Europe does not become a 'tower of Babel' when it comes to agreeing safety standards and moving from voluntary to binding safety arrangements, as is more or less the case regarding fire safety.

On the practical side, the Rapporteur wishes to recall proposals voiced at the Almancil meeting of the Assembly's Sub-Committee on Tourism Development regarding possible improvements in local arrangements for visitor safety. They refer to fundamental communication between visitors, host communities, public authorities and private sector enterprises. Thus region-specific security policies, regular and independent security audits, crisis management strategies, clearer sign-posting for tourists, better lighting of public areas and round-the-clock multilingual police service should be considered as priority measures and a vital and urgent public investment. Special tourism police forces trained to offer assistance in several languages successfully operate in Argentina, the Dominican Republic, Egypt, Greece, Malaysia and Mexico, while some countries run call centres with multilingual operators to handle emergencies which involve visitors.

Defining "Carrying Capacity" of Tourist Sites, Especially in Protected Areas and Coastal Zones

With new technologies, evolving consumption patterns and simplified travel planning, visitor flows are not only growing but also become less predictable and hence more difficult to cope with. Crowding and congestion – in transport, accommodation and tourist sites – are more and more frequent, causing the disappointment of visitors, increased business costs, disruption to the local community and often a degradation of tourist sites and services, as well as possibly reduced earnings. Managing tourist flows to optimise the use of facilities and resources requires pro-active policy steps meant to define the carrying capacity of tourist sites and a set of measures and incentives designed to result in a more even spread of visitors – geographically and time-wise. This should be a prime task of tourism authorities and other stakeholders in mass tourism destinations.

Minimising the adverse effects of visitor flows requires an accurate assessment of the upper limits to the acceptable number of visitors and a subsequent monitoring of data on real visitor flows. We should distinguish between visitor and host destination perceptions of what is 'acceptable'. As it were, for certain places, such as landscapes of great natural beauty, sites with rich wildlife or places of worship, most visitors seek 'peace and quiet'; while for other places, for instance markets, festivals, sporting events or public squares, some crowding is expected and even desired. Local people might resent large and noisy traveller groups, especially when these outnumber the local population; local officials will get worried about the impact on traffic, infrastructure and public spaces; and local companies might lose control of their ability to meet excessive short-term demand. All these perceptions and expectations have to be weighed against potential benefits and threats in order to devise appropriate management solutions.

In practical terms, carrying capacity in tourism can be evaluated for the ecological, sociocultural, psychological, infrastructural and management domains. It has been studied in a number of countries and proved very useful for subsequent policy adjustments, such as in the case of Malta where a carrying capacity assessment and a resulting policy line have remained the cornerstone of the country's tourism strategy and are now used for the application of European Structural Funds to improve the quality of tourism facilities and the conservation of heritage. An alternative approach to manageable growth in tourism is expressed in the 'Limits of Acceptable Change' concept which is more flexible and is based on a real assessment of impacts of concern, but is also more permissive and reactive rather than pro-active.

If all natural and cultural sites are precious tourism assets, then protected areas, unique monuments, islands and coastal zones can be likened to 'crown jewels' that have to be handled with special care. In fact, about 63% of holiday makers tend to choose coastal areas, compared with 25% who would choose mountains, cities or countryside. In some countries (Croatia, Greece and Cyprus) coastal tourism dominates the tourism offer and generates the majority of tourism spending. National strategies with regard to special treatment of vulnerable sites have to be adopted, allowing tourism to be incorporated in the picture via the integrated management of protected sites, enforcing stricter spatial planning controls and systematic impact assessment and promoting sustainable development principles across different sectors of human activity. As a source of practical advice we could recommend the know-how compiled in *Sustainable Tourism in Protected Areas: Guidelines for Planning and Management* published by the World Commission on Protected Areas (WCPA) together with the UNWTO and the UNEP. These guidelines promote a long-term vision with short and medium-term goals that seek to optimise economic benefits from tourism in protected areas while ensuring sufficient returns and incentives for conservation purposes. Over 200 natural habitats in Europe are targeted for protection. Many of them are too fragile to be open to tourism but those that are have experienced rapid increases in visitor numbers in the last two decades. It is the primary responsibility of national authorities to determine, through appropriate legislation, the degree of protection sought and the extent of economic activities, including housing and tourism, permitted in protected areas. Research proves that site-specific environmental protection measures and regulations designed to discipline visitors and service providers do not constitute a constraint on tourism. For instance, Switzerland, where nearly 30% of the territory counts as protected areas, has environmental regulation that is among the toughest and most effective in the world but it also ranks as the most competitive country according to the global Travel and Tourism Competitiveness Index elaborated by the World Economic Forum:

Many countries in central and eastern Europe have highly attractive but underdeveloped natural and cultural resources which come increasingly under pressure from economic expansion. They need to secure sufficient funds, consistent regulations and unfailing enforcement in the effective protection of strategic natural and cultural sites, and their good use for tourism purposes. Illegal constructions must be immediately stopped and removed, including when they are a consequence of unethical behaviour by some officials exercising oversight functions (the Rapporteur is aware of many such cases in Albania, Bulgaria, Lithuania, Poland, Romania, etc.).

Mass Tourism – A Threat and an Opportunity?

Mass tourism is often criticised and stereotyped as the extreme form of tourism. However we should recall that, in its early days, it was cherished for the multiple socioeconomic benefits it brought to society at large and was perceived as a sign of the democratisation of travel and holidays. Clearly, the growth of tourism is a natural development as more people accede to higher living standards and can thus more easily afford to travel. This trend is welcome but it also creates new challenges for the tourism sector in order to avoid a suicidal expansion. It is precisely in mass tourism destinations that sustainable development strategies can make the most spectacular and sizeable contribution to progress.

We should bear in mind numerous examples in southern Europe where a critical level of development has been reached such as in many Spanish, Portuguese, Greek and Cypriot Mediterranean 'holiday clusters'. Torrevieja in Spain, for instance, had a stable population of 9200 inhabitants in 1960 which grew to 70 000 in 2001 and reaches about 400 000 in August with a peak of holiday-makers. Urban sprawl added some 90 000 buildings of which 75 000 are used exclusively as summer homes, leading to increased but fluctuating demand for employment, goods and services, as well as massive speculation in real estate and a huge pressure for new construction. Additional income was used to enhance water systems and cultural services but scores of poor architectural quality buildings have radically transformed the local scenery. Local authorities are now looking into ways to promote more value-added investment that would foster competitiveness through quality, diversification and environmental sustainability. Determined to move from mass tourism to more high-end development, the Bulgarian Government has devised an ambitious investment strategy, worth € 3.3 billion, to improve transport infrastructure and waste treatment facilities – in partnership with the European Investment Bank and multiple public and private entities.

The World Tourism Organisation forecasts that most of the increase in European tourism receipts over the next decade will come from alternative forms of travel that do not involve standard 'sun, sand and sea' stays. Market surveys show that travellers are becoming more selective and searching for new experiences; they are more mobile and active, take shorter but more frequent holidays throughout the year, live longer and are increasingly concerned about the environment. Scenery, climate, cost, historical interest, environment, a complete change and gastronomic discovery are what motivate a modern traveller. Looking from an entrepreneurial position, this is an opportunity that calls for more diversified tourism offer but also a challenge because investment planning becomes more complex.

Even when local development relies exclusively on mass tourism, efforts to diversify the local economy should be made in order to attenuate problems linked with seasonal fluctuations in visitor flows and the related pressure on local resources, infrastructure and employment. This requires policy-and decision-making structures bringing together tourism, environment, community and national interests. Commitment to sustainability and a regulated quality-oriented approach should guide long-term infrastructure planning in particular: the potential impact of tourism growth on infrastructure should be studied and policy strategies should link tourism with overall development. The Rapporteur wishes, in this context, to underscore the importance of sustainable (re)construction, as described in the next section, and the need to pursue it more vigorously through affirmative action.

The low-cost flight boom has opened up new travelling opportunities but also created new problems for air traffic control and capacity management in transport and accommodation. The phenomenon of 'overbooking' that originally emerged in air travel is now spreading to the hotel sector, especially in popular urban and holiday destinations or during major public events. While adding extra capacity in hotels may prove difficult and economically irrational, local tourism authorities should explore options for 'emergency' accommodation and put in place customer help-lines. All officially licensed hotels must honour their booking commitments or provide adequate assistance and financial compensation to customers in cases where the original contract cannot be fulfilled.

An Integrated Approach to Congestion Management and Spatial Planning

Avoiding excessive and counterproductive concentrations of tourists requires early and well thought-out action. When permanent congestion occurs, it is a sign of failure in forward planning and the damage caused may be irreversible while fluctuating congestion may be slightly easier to tackle. However the market alone cannot solve the problem that needs a creative local approach and involvement of multiple actors from both the private and public sectors. The UNWTO's *Guidebook on Tourism Congestion Management at Natural and Cultural Sites* offers a most comprehensive and useful insight into the issue.

Permanent congestion occurs in tourist destinations and sites due to large and continuing levels of visitors. To alleviate the situation, major upgrades may be required on various aspects of the site itself and surrounding infrastructures. This includes access, parking and arrival areas, entry and ticketing, public spaces and viewing sites, interpretation and visitor facilities, as well as improvements in management, staff training, information flow and financial back-up.

Fluctuating congestion is mostly seen at well-marketed periodical events (such as school holidays, weekends, festivals, celebrations, sport competitions, etc.) that generate massive visitor flows within relatively short periods of the year. Although additional staff, transport, security, food, beverage, sanitary services and extended working hours are required occasionally, these are nonetheless critical to meeting the expectations of visitors and sustaining the attractiveness of sites. Temporary or permanent pricing incentives can be helpful as a means of regulating seasonal visitor flows if visitors can be informed early and holiday-taking outside the 'high season' should be encouraged. The hosting of the 2012 Olympic Games in London represents a huge investment, sustainable development and security challenge for both the local authorities and the private sector. It will also test the creativity of tourism officials in appealing to visitors with a view to luring them to come again to discover the country as a whole beyond Greater London.

A hotel performance study by Deloitte shows that hotel occupancy rates in the major cities of Europe are improving but remain on average considerably lower than in other parts of the world. Hotel performance in other towns and especially in rural areas could be as low as 20%, essentially due to seasonality and geographical factors. The European Parliament report on the new European tourism policy also reiterated the need to implement a dedicated European tourism programme for retired people in low season which could improve the quality of life of senior citizens, job creation, demand management and prospects for economic growth.

Sustainable tourism development practices combining environmental, sociocultural and economic parameters are applicable to all forms of tourism in all types of destinations, including mass tourism and niche segments. As a continuous process with constant monitoring of impacts and implementation of preventive or corrective measures, it constitutes a global tool for balanced development. Popular tourism destinations like the Russian Federation and Ukraine currently face hotel capacity constraints and need to invest urgently in quality accommodation.

Throughout Europe, especially countries of central and eastern Europe, rapid economic growth, urban development and real estate speculation have led to extreme pressures on landscape planning and often unsustainable construction decisions akin to architectural pollution. It is becoming urgent for local authorities to review policies with regard to the scale, density and design of new buildings. From a sustainable tourism point of view, traditional designs and local building materials should be used as much as possible so as to preserve authenticity and attractiveness of sites.

Moreover, there is growing public concern over the degradation of their living environment and the need for change in the direction of responsible consumption. The sustainable construction, use and management of buildings are especially important for our lifestyles in general and tourism in particular. As the 'polluter pays' principle is more systematically taken into account, "smart" buildings make increasingly more economic and environmental sense. A *sustainable construction* approach aims to adapt buildings to use low-environmental-impact materials and less energy, cause less pollution and less waste (with better heating, insulation, aeration, lighting and water systems), minimise running costs and optimise comfort and benefits to the community. While new buildings in Europe tend to be more efficient, the adjustment-renewal rate (at some 1% a year) of older ones is far too slow to expect massive improvements anytime soon – unless our governments put in place the right incentives towards that end.

European countries could also make better use of the European Landscape Convention (which came into force on 1 March 2004) designed to promote landscape protection, management and planning, and the organisation of European cooperation in this area. The Convention is the first international treaty to be exclusively concerned with all aspects of European landscape. It can also be used for enhancing rural heritage and facilitating the development of green tourism. A number of popular European destinations are currently testing the European Eco Management and Audit Scheme to improve their land use planning. Some countries (Bulgaria, the United Kingdom, Italy, Spain and others) are experimenting with various eco-tax, congestion charging, differentiated payment, eco-certification and 'green grants' assistance schemes to influence consumption patters and consumer choices. Moreover, Austria, Denmark, France, Italy, Latvia, Luxembourg, the Netherlands, Spain, Switzerland and the Nordic countries are participating in the EU-funded VISIT initiative linking 12 eco-labelling schemes for tourism enterprises. Since 2002, sustainability reporting is mandatory for the largest companies in France and efforts are underway to implement the Tourism Quality Plan for improving tourism supply and marketing of tourism services. The Hungarian tourism authorities have introduced the national Tourism Quality Award – a voluntary system aiming to increase the quality of services and the competitiveness of the industry.

Improving Accessibility of Tourist Destinations, Sites and Facilities

The social dimension of tourism is a major factor for sustainable development as social inclusion and equity are important goals. Although holidays are a right thanks to a generalisation of paid leave, making holidays available to all is an important challenge-and opportunity-for the tourism sector. Expert studies show that about 40% of European citizens do not leave on holidays, mainly due to various forms of deprivation or disability (families, pensioners, immigrants, the young and people with disabilities are particularly concerned).

This implies a broader strategic aim for sustainable tourism: development policies seeking to maximise revenues from the sector with moderate or no increases in volume should go hand-in-hand with social inclusion principles. Moreover, greater attention to the social aspects of tourism could help reduce the seasonality of demand and excessive geographical concentrations of travellers, as well as support more stable year-round employment and the development of disadvantaged regions, especially if more travellers could be persuaded to travel outside the main season and/or the busiest areas. The "Bavaria in all seasons" campaign, for instance, pursues multiple objectives in seeking to support family travel, solidarity schemes sponsored by the public and private sectors, as well as resource efficiency, off-peak travel and the 'rain or snow experience' to visitors from extremely dry and hot countries.For all people to have access to tourism, two important issues should be addressed: the physical accessibility of tourist destinations and sites and the economic affordability of travelling on holidays. A relevant priority action should therefore focus on better designed and adapted tourism facilities to meet the requirements of travellers with special needs (such as amenities for families with children, senior travellers and those with disabilities); improving the frequency, inter-modality and comfort of public transport links; encouraging price and tax incentives and related information for travel outside the high season and crowded destinations; pursuing policies to facilitate holiday-taking by people with low income, including through holiday voucher schemes (such as those run in France and Hungary) and other solidarity operations; and, importantly, aiming to earmark part of the income from tourism (via specific charges on tourists and tourism enterprises or voluntary arrangements) to tackle social issues.

Tourism and Climate Change

Climate change is now widely recognised as a major global issue, with a series of implications for economic activities in general and more specifically tourism. Because climate and nature are essential resources for tourism, changing climate patterns and landscapes will inevitably have an impact on travel choices, tourism businesses and host societies, including significant side effects on related sectors (such as agriculture, crafts, construction, etc.) as well as on public health. The phenomenon cannot be considered as a distant occurrence as it already affects the sector, notably certain destinations, for instance mountain, island and coastal regions. In the longer term, changing climate patterns might considerably alter major tourism flows, notably in northern Europe and the Mediterranean.

The UNWTO estimates that tourism contributes about 5% of global man-made greenhouse gas emissions, essentially through transport (90% share of the total contribution). With the explosion of low-cost air travel in recent years, some 43% of travellers worldwide use air transport. This trend is amplifying and air travel remains one of the fastest growing sources of emissions (up by 4% a year). We should also note that 44% of travellers use road transport but road use is growing on average more slowly than air travel, respectively by 2.3% and 3.3% each year. It is hoped that a recently signed US-EU 'open skies' agreement will improve transatlantic air traffic while the arrival on the market of new generation aircraft – the Airbus A380 and Boeing 787 Dreamliner– will generate less pollution and noise due to higher fuel efficiency, multiple technological improvements, higher capacity and lighter weight.

With the liberalisation of European air policies in the 1990s, low-cost airlines brought a near-revolution in travel by putting cheap flights and multiple destinations within reach of most holiday makers or even job seekers. Peripheral locations in Europe have thus become more or less popular tourism destinations, yielding new prosperity to local communities and more variety to travellers. Low-cost companies now carry over 100 million passengers a year and account for a third of all flights. Lately, their expansion has been particularly strong in eastern Europe where cities like Prague, Sofia, Villains and Warsaw have opened new terminals to cope with the soaring passenger flows. It is estimated that every additional million travellers in the air generates some 3000 jobs on the ground. However the large flows of state subsidies needed to prop up secondary airports could be questioned from the point of view of fair competition.

Moreover, busier skies in Europe also mean more noise for local inhabitants and, according to the 'green' parties, more pollution. Luckily, the security of flying in Europe is not yet affected by soaring air traffic but air control capacity problems may soon appear. The apparent cheapness of low cost flights can be challenged on the basis of the 'polluter pays' principle: so far, European airlines have been exempt from the 'carbon tax' through the EU emissions trading scheme and have no obvious incentive to lower their greenhouse emissions. Factoring all the relevant environmental costs into air travel prices could well mean that many low cost operators might run out of business and generate negative reactions down the chain in the localities that rely heavily on low-cost travel for their development. The real cost of no-frills travel should be weighed against the tangible benefits to medium-term local development.

The sustainable tourism concept translates long-term environmental and development concerns into policy objectives aimed at concerted action on the part of national authorities but also competent international institutions. The main challenges include the need to:

- Involve tourism in the implementation of existing commitments under the UN Framework Convention on Climate Change (UNFCCC) with its Kyoto Protocol and contribute to the preparation of the new package of measures for the post-2012 period;

- Mitigate the impact of long-haul travel and transport emissions (In Europe, tourism transport currently accounts for about 8% of CO_2-equivalent emissions, with air transport generating half of that amount and cars about 41% of those emissions), not least through a 'polluter pays' principle and a greater participation of European airlines in the EU Emissions Trading System;
- Encourage responsible consumption and production patterns minimising resource waste (tourists tend to use several times more water than local inhabitants) and pollution (especially as regards water and energy use, recycling, waste management, forward planning, etc.) and propagating meaningful alternatives (such as greater recourse to renewable resources, public transport, sustainable construction, etc.) in providing tourism services, notably accommodation;
- Support the implementation of international co-development policies, including the Millennium Development Goals, environmental agreements, the UNWTO's Global Code of Ethics for Tourism, the Clean Development Mechanism, multilateral and bilateral aid programmes, as Europe has a moral duty to assist the emerging economies to match their development needs and the drive for more tourism;
- Promote the sharing of knowledge and good practice on sustainable tourism development with other countries and regions.

Just as the problem transcends the borders of different human activities, practical solutions will require cross-sector action plans and sector-specific action programmes. Today's politicians have a key responsibility for developing and implementing strategies to attenuate future disorders due to climate change.

Part of the answer could come also through a greater attention to promoting domestic – intra-country and intra-European – tourism whereby distances travelled are shorter and means used can rely more on public transport. Regional tourism promotion schemes, such as "the theme beats the destination" in Bavaria or the "European Destinations of Excellence" (EDEN) pilot project of the European Commission, reflect the willingness to combine proximity tourism with quality and sustainability.

The Role of Public-private Partnerships in Promoting Sustainable Tourism

If state authorities and international institutions are primarily responsible for providing political commitment and policies conducive to sustainability in tourism, the contribution of the private sector is critical to the achievement of results on the ground and providing feedback to policy makers. Public and private actors should work together to agree, implement and monitor the integrated quality management approach respectful of reference standards and quality labels for tourism services and products. Whilst tourism and sectoral associations can act as relays of information between state authorities and local actors, public-private partnerships might be considered for the realisation of pilot projects, the promotion of corporate social responsibility and the development of equitable employment schemes, improved pricing models and investment planning compatible with environmental and social imperatives.

Research shows that there are many cases where large investments in tourism infrastructure and marketing have not translated into desired and sustainable growth. The key finding is that most difficulties stem from the shortcomings in collaboration of the public and private sectors in identifying target population groups and tailoring effective communication to reach them. It is therefore particularly important to use the synergies of public and private institutions for innovative destination marketing. Turkey, Croatia and the Czech Republic are among the countries that have succeeded very well in this respect. OECD research shows that tourism is increasingly seen as a sector in which public investment can be particularly relevant, such as for infrastructure development, SME support, programmes underpinning quality improvements in tourism facilities and services, and licensing schemes for tourism professionals.

Hospitality: The Importance of Skills and Communication

Tourism is first and foremost about people of all ages, interests and skills. For some it means job opportunities and sustainable livelihoods, for others it represents contacts, cultural exchanges, learning experience or recreation. As a customer-minded service industry, it is increasingly subject to global and local competition pressures and labour mobility that call for enhanced attention to competences and added value orientation. To put it simply, when we travel, we want to feel welcome wherever we go; we count on quality experience and hospitality to match our expectations.

Quality services require good infrastructure but especially dedicated and competent people involved in tourism as hosts, be they local inhabitants or tourism professionals. Hospitality needs a smiling and caring attitude and, inevitably, some linguistic skills. The latter is becoming a particularly relevant professional requirement for many jobs and careers. Hospitality could be included in school curricula already at primary level and tourism should be viewed as a means of providing essential learning experience. Facilities for language teaching should be provided and promoted to meet the needs of people of different ages, backgrounds and interests. Public support schemes, such as the 'language-cheque' system successfully used in Belgium, may prove helpful in underpinning both language learning and employability. Tourism companies, sites and facilities should seek appropriate levels of staff qualification and training, including on sustainability issues. Motivating staff to perform at their best implies also an effort on the part of employers to provide good employment conditions, including sufficient salary levels, social security provision, long-term contracts, flexible but consistent working hours and career development.

The spread of the low-cost phenomenon has affected not only tourism-related travel and accommodation but also jobs. Downward pressure on remuneration and working conditions in the tourism sector is leading to situations where, despite higher demand, tourism companies find it increasingly difficult to recruit suitably qualified staff. Quality tourism requires quality staff, and human resources are not just a cost but also a vital investment. Your Rapporteur believes that tourism authorities and professionals should bear this important consideration in mind when adjusting their strategic development plans. Stringent security requirements at visitor arrival points should not serve as an excuse for failures in hospitality and welcome, as has been the case for a number of years in the United States after the 9/11 events. Visitor flows and income from tourism fell not only because of the fear of flying which was short-lived; an unsmiling attitude of immigration officials caused lasting damages to US-bound tourism. Whereas people-to-people contacts generated through travelling are one of the best marketing and diplomacy tools, the recent Visit USA programme consisting of promotion committees in selected countries (UK, Canada, Mexico, Germany and Japan) and a website (currently under development) is a surprisingly meagre effort to win the hearts and minds of the people around the world. This gives some food for thought also to European countries, especially in eastern Europe, that could unleash their largely untapped potential for tourism development with a caring attitude. Russia, for instance, could become one of the world's leading tourism economies over the next decade, according to the WTTC,-provided the country modernises its infrastructures, hospitability services and human resource management.

Promoting Diversity, Authenticity and Quality in Tourism as a Key to Long-term Success

Lessons to be Learned from National Successes and Failures

We have seen that tourism has considerable power to influence the identity and prosperity of the areas where it unfolds. Such changes affect both established European tourism destinations and emerging ones, with the advantage for the latter that they are able to draw lessons from the former in order to avoid or at least minimise mistakes. Multiple development pressures stem from evolving lifestyles, economic growth and restructuring, demographic trends and globalization. They call for measured national, regional and local but also collective – pan-European–responses. The rise of tourism as a principle economic activity for vast areas and regions in Europe involves ever more people and makes the well-planned development of tourism a precondition for its lasting success. The economic, social, cultural and environmental pillars of tourism fit together through sustainable development whereby they become mutually reinforcing. Any excess, especially in economic expansion, risks exacerbating the cost of tourism to society at large and ultimately undermining the benefits. We should view sustainability as a means of improving the competitiveness of the tourism sector and a source of quality growth. The Spanish example is often cited to illustrate the excesses caused by mass tourism in coastal areas. In the last decades, many coastal strips have thus experienced rapid urbanisation often associated with over exploitation of land space and resources, visual pollution and disturbed social balance. Similar examples can be found in Italy and other Mediterranean countries while many other resort areas in Europe (including urban destinations and mountain areas) are increasingly confronted with massive visitor inflows, poorly managed spatial planning and the related consequences.

Luckily, it is also in Spain that we have some good examples of how tourism-related socioeconomic and environmental decline can be reversed. For instance, in Calvià, a major coastal resort area of Mallorca Island, local authorities undertook a major policy shift in the mid-1990s towards a more balanced tourism model based on restoration, contained growth and sustainability. Their action programme centred on spatial planning, quality infrastructure and services, cultural and natural heritage, resource management review and investment. The quality of life of local people was put forward as an overarching objective resulting in a win-win situation for both visitors and host community.

Another interesting case comes from Croatia, whose tourism policies were discussed by the members of our Sub-Committee on Tourism Development with Croatia's Secretary of State for Tourism in May 2007. This country has seen a rapid resurgence of tourism since the end of the war that followed independence. Tourism now accounts for 23% of GDP and is essentially concentrated in coastal zones. Confronted with a major challenge of urbanisation on the coast, driven by a booming real estate market, Croatia opted for sustainability in its tourism strategy with emphasis on value rather than volume. Strict spatial and investment planning regulations were introduced in 2004 for zones within one kilometre of the coast, 300 metres offshore and all islands. Scores of illegal construction sites were demolished, existing ports, facilities and camp sites were modernised, water management systems were upgraded and the state-sponsored programme 'new life for old buildings' assisted the creation of family-run heritage hotels, reducing the environmental impact and improving services offered to visitors. "The Mediterranean as it once was" – the logo chosen – illustrates well the aspiration to excel. Further attention is now given to the conversion of underdeveloped regions and abandoned industrial sites into high-value tourism destinations.

The dynamism of tourism is not hurt but rather stimulated by policy indications to orient investors. The aim being to optimise benefits for visitors, host communities and entrepreneurs, all stakeholders need to show a responsible attitude and behaviour. We see a major challenge for tourist authorities across Europe to ensure that sustainability-and quality-oriented strategies for tourism policy, especially as regards spatial development and demand management (seasonality), are in place and duly implemented at national, regional and local levels. Changes stemming from globalization should be accommodated in a way that responds to the need for restructuring in local economies as a result of decline of certain activities whereas properly managed tourism can provide a healthy alternative source of local income and jobs.

Respect for cultural diversity is a key principle of sustainable development and an important opportunity for the tourism sector. As well as providing a source of inspiration for visitors and income to host communities, cultural tourism can serve as a major force for the conservation and rehabilitation of the historic and cultural heritage, underpin artistic events, stimulate local crafts and folklore, promote local traditions and foster an attachment to fundamental cultural values. More than 200 cultural settings across Europe feature as UNESCO World Heritage Sites. Local and regional authorities should seek to safeguard the authenticity of local cultural distinctions in the way these are presented to visitors and to protect cultural sites against any "collateral damage" due to visitor pressure. A fair share of direct and indirect income generated from tourist visits should be channelled towards the further development and interpretation of cultural assets. We should also stress, in this context, the importance of many 'cultural routes' launched in various countries on the Council of Europe's initiative, as well as the designation of 'cultural capitals' under EU auspices.

Moreover, regional cooperation in running joint and targeted tourism promotion campaigns for overseas markets is an effective, rational and commendable course of action. Some examples of this include the joint marketing effort of the Czech Republic, Hungary, Slovakia and Poland vis-a-vis China, Japan, the USA and other countries under the slogan "European Quartet, one melody". In October 2007, Portugal and Spain launched an integrated programme to promote the Iberian Peninsula as "a must see destination" in Europe, insisting on two distinct cultures in one. There is also the Scandinavia Tourist Board promoting Denmark, Norway and Sweden in the Asia-Pacific region and the Scandinavia official website as a gateway to Denmark, Finland, Iceland, Norway and Sweden aimed at North American travellers.

Regulatory Tools, Policies, Cross-sector Coordination and Monitoring

Once the vision and strategic orientations for tourism are defined, important choices have to be made to reflect, via regulatory tools, the level and nature of tourism sought and local specificities. Key reference tools for influencing tourism development are: land use planning and development control through formal regulations (covering physical benchmarks and impact evaluation) and less formal guidelines (including on ethical aspects for tourism authorities, companies and tourists); economic instruments (such as tax incentives and charges, marketing options and certification requirements); capacity building to assist smaller communities and enterprises (sharing experience, knowledge and good practice could be particularly helpful); targeted infrastructure improvements; and continuous monitoring of trends. Effective communication and information services are crucial to ensure broad public awareness and acceptance of sustainability-oriented regulations.

The search for sustainability in tourism would be meaningless without an objective assessment of whether its underlying principles are being respected. Measuring progress is essential and should rely on the use of measurable sustainability indicators. Such 'accountability' can be used to analyse the current state of affairs (e.g. occupancy rates, tourist satisfaction), stresses on the system (e.g. water shortages, crime levels, site rehabilitation needs), the impact of tourism (e.g. variations in income levels, resource allocation and community wellbeing) and management effort (e.g. pollution changes, quality of jobs). Baseline sustainability indicators should be agreed in consultation with stakeholders from various sectors so as to allow for valid cross-sector comparisons and coordination.

There are also several aspects of tourism development that should be subject to obligatory controls. They concern the minimum requirements for the protection of the environment, communities, visitors and businesses. We wish to single out location-specific development regulations, rights and conditions for employees, rights of access to services and infrastructures, visitor health and safety (notably food hygiene and fire safety), fair trading practices, serious environmental impact (including pollution, noise, waste and resource abuse) and ethical misconduct by visitors or hosts (such as child prostitution). Because these concerns are of universal character, they should be covered by a basic legal framework in all countries and should apply to all forms of tourism. The body of legislation relating to sustainability in tourism is thus quite considerable and it would not be feasible, nor desirable, to consolidate it all in a single law. However, a supportive national tourism law with cross-references to other relevant laws is necessary. It should underpin the long-term strategy for sustainable tourism development and enable due controls, coordination and compliance. In some countries, establishing priority development zones may prove useful for promoting tourism in protected areas or underdeveloped regions. This practice is now being tested in the Russian Federation to stimulate tourism development in the Siberian part of the country, notably the Baikal region and the Far East.

Political Responsibilities for Development Options

Wisely managed tourism enriches society in many different ways. It can stimulate the business environment, competitiveness, innovation and investment, thus becoming a gateway to accelerated overall development. Placing sustainability at the centre of tourism development is now widely recognised as the right way towards fully realising the potential of the tourism sector and a key to its long-term success. National authorities have an important role to play in promoting sustainable development in general and that of tourism in particular. To this end, political will, policy coherence and technical competence are necessary at all levels of government. Moreover, governments should work together and facilitate joint approaches whenever possible in order to tackle transboundary, regional and global challenges of sustainability. This is a major field of action for competent international organisations, including the Council of Europe.

As the World Tourism Organisation rightly points out in its Guide for policy makers, sustainability is the responsibility of all those involved in tourism, but governments should lead the process if substantial progress is to be achieved. Parliaments similarly can assist, primarily at national and local levels, in providing a legal environment that orients the private sector, tourists and other stakeholders and fosters their response to sustainability issues. Your Rapporteur hopes that this report will have contributed to demonstrating that a holistic approach to tourism development should be sought, and how various public policies may affect or be affected by tourism.

11

Internet Marketing Destinations in the Global Tourism

Introduction: Importance of Tourism and Online Travel

Tourism is not only the largest industry in the world but also the number one online segment, accounting for 11% of overall sales on the Net in 1998. E-business on tourism accounted for $13 billion in 1999. The online travel market is experiencing explosive growth, and is projected to go to $30 billion this year. It is already estimated that by year 2003 over 30% of online sales will be generated by online travel alone, including actual travel products as well as advertising earned by travel-oriented sites.

The number of travellers who use the Internet for travel-related and other purposes tops 70 million, half of which consult the Internet to get information on destinations or to check prices and schedules. The number of travellers booking online has soared by more than 80 percent to 11 million in the last year. Travel remains one of the most popular e-commerce categories, with 45 percent of online buyers saying they purchased travel online. This is outpaced only by books at 54 percent.

According to a recent survey by Biz Rate.com (1999), 85% of the respondents intend to use the Internet exclusively or in conjunction with off-line resources to schedule airfare (90% of those planning to purchase travel online), hotel (52%), and car rental (42%) reservations for holiday travel. More than 75 percent of respondents indicated that discounts would motivate them to purchase future travel reservations online. Thirty-nine percent said earning frequent flyer miles or points also would be a strong influence. Cyveillance (1999) estimates that the overall universe of travel sites on the Web is 116,000. Based on analysis, it estimates that only approximately 6,500 travel sites (6%) are e-commerce enabled, i.e., offer the ability to execute transactions online. Internet start-up firms working as intermediaries and travel agencies will continue to fuel the online travel market. There is already fierce competition between intermediaries and hotels, airlines, and car rental companies. Traditional offline companies, such as the Hotel Reservation Network (HRN), are shifting their telephone-based reservation system to the Internet to compete. HRN launched its Web site in 1995. In 1998 it booked 45 percent of its business online whereas in 1999 this figure reached 80 percent. Currently, travel agencies and intermediaries account for more than half the online travel revenue: 54% travel agencies, 25% airlines, 13% hotels, 8% car rental companies.

Tourism Destination Portals for Cyber Marketing

The literature suggests that the search for information used to plan travel is likely to take longer and to involve the use of more information sources than the search for information about most other consumer products.

The tourism industry is characterized by offering complementary business. This is similar to the computer industry, where a buyer often buys an assortment of goods made by different companies. For example, the manufacturers of the computer, printer, and software are often different. Similarly, a traveller will use air travel, a rental car, and a hotel room and purchase meals. Different companies provide these services. The goal of the traveller is to have an enjoyable experience. A properly designed Web site can facilitate the travellers' planning, helping to ensure they make the right choices and have an enjoyable experience. It can also serve as the distribution point for all the services they will need as they plan their vacation.

Tourism Destinations emerge as umbrella brands and they will need to be promoted in the global marketplace as one entity for each target market they try to attract. The emerging globalization and concentration of supply increase the level of competition and require new Internet marketing strategies for destinations. Hence, *destination marketing organizations* (DMOs) increasingly have to identify niche markets and develop their interactivity with tourists.

The distribution/allocation strategy of tourism products should follow a customer-oriented approach. A vertical marketing system should be in place bringing together a set of products related with each destination available for selection. This implies that each tourist destination must have a major portal Web site acting as a gateway to the destination rather than relying solely on a fragmented number of individual Web sites put online by the trade. Indeed, customers require one-stop shopping. The tourism destination portal site ought to be developed by the DMOs in partnership with the major market participants, through a contractual or corporate approach. This would have links from and to the Web sites of the other organizations that have business related to the destination. Partnerships are important because by building relationships with other companies the DMOs get access to their consumers while helping those companies expand their product offerings. Moreover, the development of Web sites by main travel intermediary players is also important as these may allow the browser/visitor to access destination information provided by the DMOs' sites and to compare the services offered by competing destinations in order to make his/her travel decision.

A portal site for marketing tourism destinations should provide information on four core areas:

1. How to get there (e.g., air travel).
2. Getting around (e.g., car rental).
3. Places to stay (e.g., hotel accommodation).
4. Things to do (e.g., places to see, dining, shopping, shows and events).

All the items should come with availability and reservation facilities. These may be provided through links to other sites such as HRN, Internet Travel Network, or the World Res Company. The last is essentially a business-to-business site, in that it primarily serves other Internet companies. World Res provides a list of available rooms and prices at its 8,600 partner hotels to about 900 Web sites, including portals like Yahoo! and America Online, but predominantly travel sites. When a consumer visits one of those sites and makes a reservation, the transaction is reported back to World Res and, in turn, to the hotel that was booked. World Res takes a commission of between 3 and 10 percent of the cost of the booked room. The referring site gets up to

30 percent of the transaction fee paid by the hotel to World Res. The investment bank Bear, Stearns Co. Inc. estimates hotel reservations made via the Internet will generate over $3 billion in revenues in 2002. In a recent market research study conducted by the NPD Group, 28 percent of visitors to hotel sites were found to actually book a reservation, and 84 percent of those were satisfied by the experience. Moreover, whereas it costs about 10 cents per dollar in revenue to book a reservation over the phone, a reservation booked online costs only 2 cents per dollar in revenue.

State of the Art in Web Design

The design of the Web site is one of the key issues to consider for achieving success in e-business. Successful sites are designed around the wants and needs of the targeted audiences. The Web presence must be designed not only to be visually appealing and user friendly, but also to be favourably indexed by search engines. According to a 1999 Jupiter Communications' research study, Internet users ranked "searching on the Internet" as their most important activity, rating it 9.1 on a 10 point scale. And most Internet users find information through the use of search engines and online directories.

Web sites have come a long way from the days of "brochure ware," those advertising-filled pages that flooded most organizations' first sites. Functionality has progressed to the point that the latest wave of Web technology even allows for personalization of content. Personalization technology now allows site designers to access demographic and psychographic information from the organization's own customer information files, other marketing data bases, and research derived from tracking the way visitors move around a site. Software automatically analyses the profiles of site visitors, identifies what they are trying to do, and adjusts parts of the interface on the fly in an effort to enhance responsiveness.

But all this functionality comes at a price. As Web sites expand to accommodate additional features, customers may become confused by the plethora of choices and complex screen navigation trails. To avoid customer burnout and defection, managers need to strive for a balance between simplicity and functionality in their Web site designs to serve customers most effectively. The ideal state is referred to as "one and done." Customers visit the site, quickly find what they need, accomplish their tasks, and get out. Providers who cannot meet this standard risk losing business.

Since growth is an important part of the game, the technological underpinnings of the Web site must be set up to handle increasing transaction volume and transaction complexity. Experts advise building the site in a modular fashion so that the system can be expanded without having to change its primary architecture. The mentor for Web designers is "think big, start small, test quickly, and scale fast."

A site must be relatively simple and fast for the consumer to navigate. A site that limits the number of screens a person has to click through to complete and send a booking form is an important part of the equation. Thus, attractiveness, ease of use, and ability for consumers to quickly make a reservation are important Web design features. One of the contributing factors for ease of navigation is a limited number of elements per page.

Tourism organizations use their sites to post basic information — directions, prices, maps, and other brochure-type facts. But with sites evolving quickly, many need to institute truly innovative ideas: daily updates, real-time videos, snippets of music, e-mail feedback, and other interactive features. One major point of discussion is how sophisticated to make a Web site. Not every computer has the power, or the software, to take advantage of spiffy features. Some sites try to stay light on graphics to reduce download time. Others go heavy on graphics, thinking that is what makes the Internet fun and useful. The answer is to customize the Web site to the organization's target markets at the business-to-consumers (namely taking into account their level of sophistication) and business-to-business approaches.

Another important issue is that tourism organizations do not want to replace the experience by providing state-of-the-art Web sites on their destinations. Rather they want people to use their sites to maximize their visit. There are a number of criteria a DMO must take into account when designing its Web site. The home page is the destination's "storefront" on the World Wide Web marketplace. It provides an index to the set of pages that describe the DMO and the tourism destination. The Web site should be organized in several main sections, including:

* *About the DMO* — this section may include a vision or a mission statement.

* *Tourism products/services* — using video-clips, audio, photos, and text to describe the benefits to the visitors of the destination's services. The Web is a great tool for market segmentation. Hence, the Home Page of the DMO's Web site should be utilized to immediately direct visitors to the most appropriate areas of information. An option of sending a CD-ROM through mail for less sophisticated users should be also considered. For example, a CD-ROM virtual tour of Las Vegas was created for the Las Vegas Convention & Visitors Authority (LVCVA) in conjunction with various corporate sponsors. The CD-ROM contains a vast multimedia directory featuring video clips produced by Vegas-area resorts and the LVCVA, stimulating high-resolution graphics, hot links to LVCVA member Web sites, valuable merchant discount coupons and extensive Las Vegas destination information.
* *FAQ* — providing a list of frequently asked questions.
* *Online ordering* — a site must provide, or at least have links to, booking and reservation facilities. In the former, situation shopping cart software has to be available so that people can put multiple items in their cart from any number of product pages.
* *Interactive request form, guest book, or survey* — the DMO needs to connect with its visitors. This may be accomplished by enticing potential tourists to sign the destination's Guest Book and/or to fill out a survey — the DMO thus captures valuable consumer information for database development and later e-mail marketing actions. Getting users to sign up on an e-mailing list is a great way to stay in touch with current and potential clients.
* *What's new* — this section is where the DMO can put updates or new copies of a newsletter.
* *Giveaways* — a site may add further value to the visitor by giving away other free products and services like postcards, wallpaper, and screen savers.

The home page also needs graphics to look inviting. The best combination is a single sparkling *graphic* combined with text making the overall look of the DMO's "storefront" graphically balanced, pleasing, and informative. The *background texture and/or colour* used throughout the site should never overwhelm the text, but subtly complement it. The *page title* that is displayed at the top line of the Web browser is very important because it often shows up in search engines. The title should be descriptive using keywords that people might use to find the DMO page. A small graphic at the top of each page as well as texture and coloured backgrounds helps to unify the Web pages. Inadequate navigation design is probably the main failing of business Web sites. Getting visitors to information quickly and intuitively is the goal of navigation systems. The navigation should be designed from the customer's perspective, providing as many alternate and user-friendly ways to navigate the site as necessary, such as:

* *Menus* — the top-level menu should be kept to seven sections or less to avoid information overload. The use of left-side menus allow the destination's visitors to get deep into the Web site without clicking through a series of hierarchical linking pages, and displays the structure of the site more clearly. Another way to get the DMO's visitors deep into the Web site quickly is to place a drop-down menu in the main page, with sections classified by indentations or spaces.
* *Image maps, buttons, and jump lines* — every page of the Web site must be reachable, either directly or indirectly, by a hyper text link from the main page.
* *Search engine* — installing a search engine in the Web site, offering information on attractions and entertainment, accommodation and transportation availability, so people can find what they are looking for quickly is another important design feature. Data bases are good for maintaining up-to-date information and allow a visitor to search both the static and the dynamic (Web pages built "on-the-fly") with a key word or date.
* *Hyperlinks* — the power of the Web is its ability to link to any other page in the world. Links from related pages as well as from industry index pages are very important. Thus, another key issue is to expand on the number of other Web sites that have hyperlinked with the DMO's site.

One can easily find numerous resources that teach the principles of good Web design. Sometimes, however, it is just as important to learn what not to do. Web designers should avoid making any of the following top 15 mistakes:

* *Using frames* — although users can now navigate through frames with fewer problems than in the past, frames still prevent users from e-mailing the URL (uniform resource locator) to other users and they also make the page more clumsy to interact with.
* *Gratuitous use of bleeding-edge technology* — instead of bragging about use of the latest Web technology, designers must realize that mainstream users care more about useful content and the company's ability to offer good customer service. Users who encounter as much as a single Java Script error usually leave a site immediately.
* *Scrolling text and looping animations* — it is extremely important for any content and navigation elements to look very different from prevailing advertising designs since users tune out anything that they do not think will be relevant to their task. Currently, banner blindness (users never fixate their eyes on anything that looks like a banner ad due to the shape or position on the page) and animation avoidance (users ignore areas with blinking or flashing text or other aggressive animations) are two serious problems.
* *Complex URLs* — a URL should contain human-readable directory and file names that reflect the nature of the information space. Long URLs cause problems when users e-mail page recommendations to each other.
* *Orphan pages* — all pages should have a link up to the home page as well as some indication of where they fit within the structure of the information space.
* *Lack of navigation support* — users need support in the form of a strong sense of structure and place. Web designers should provide a site map to let users know where they are and where they can go, as well as a good search feature. Canonical navigation elements such as a site logo in the upper left corner (linked to the home page) or a clear indication of what part of the site the current page belongs to (linked to the main page for that section) are very useful.

* *Nonstandard link colours* — users rely on the link colours to understand what parts of the site they have visited. Links to pages that have not be seen by the user are blue, whereas links to previously seen pages are purple or red.
* *Outdated information* — with the growth in e-commerce, trust is getting increasingly important, and outdated content is a sure way to lose credibility.
* *Slow download times* — this is a very severe problem. Slow response times are the worst offender against Web usability. They often translate directly into a reduced level of trust and they always cause a loss of traffic as users take their business elsewhere at a distance of a click. Traditional human factor guidelines indicate 10 seconds as the maximum response time before users lose interest. On the Web this limit may be increased to 15 seconds for a few pages.
* *Breaking or slowing down the Back button* — the Back button is the lifeline of the Web user and the second most used navigation feature, after following hyper text links.
* *Opening new browser windows* — this strategy is self-defeating since it disables the back button which is the normal way users return to previous sites.
* *Lack of biographies* — users want to know the people behind information on the Web. In particular, biographies and photographs of the authors help make the Web a less impersonal place and increase trust. For instance, it is particularly bad when a by-line is made into a "mailto:" link instead of a link to the author's biography.
* *Lack of archives* — old information is often good information and can be useful to readers. It is estimated that having archives may add about 10% to the cost of running a site but increase its usefulness by about 50%. Archives are also necessary to encourage other sites to link to the Web site.
* *Moving pages to new URLs* — anytime a page moves, any incoming links from other sites are broken.
* *Headlines that make no sense out of context* — headlines are actionable items that should help users navigate. They are often removed from the context of the full page and used in tables of content and in search engine results.

Design of Web Sites in the Tourism Industry: A Case Study

An in-depth fieldwork study has been conducted focusing on Web tourism marketing activities performed by public organizations, private companies, and dotcoms in Las Vegas. The findings are reported next.

Public Organizations

The Las Vegas Convention and Visitors Authority (LVCA) is the official destination marketing organization of Las Vegas. Went online on August 1997. The site includes information about conventions, lodging, and attractions in Las Vegas. Initially, the purpose was solely one of providing an online brochure containing over 500 pages of information. No e-mail facilities were embedded in the site. In order to respond to a number of requests, these were included at a later stage.

The Web site has been running separately/independently from the overall marketing strategy of LVCA. In other words, it is not integrated within the marketing strategy and communication plan. LVCA's goal in promoting Las Vegas as a tourist destination is to further develop its brand image as the entertainment capital of the world. Thus, this goes beyond gaming, by including other attributes such as dinning, shopping, shows, etc. With the redesign of the Web site currently under way there is also an intention to finally articulate it with advertising actions.

The LVCA collects e-mail addresses from its Web site visitors. It also conducts short online surveys from time to time on visitors' satisfaction with the Web site. It has built data bases for its three targeted segments: meeting planners, travel agents, leisure consumers. The Web site currently experiences over 7,000 daily users. LVCA hasn't developed any demographic profiles for its Web site users. Actually, this is a major concern which is to be put into practice along with the redesign of the site.

LVCA collaborates offline with organizations from other regions, promoting the Southwest United States as a triangle of complementary attractions: Las Vegas, Grand Canyon, and the Southwest Pacific Coast (San Diego, CA). It cooperates online with other organizations within the region through related links with major hotels, tourism agencies, and the Nevada Commission on Tourism. LVCA is also part of a community of 17 partners supporting a profit site operated by the Donrey Media Group which also owns the Las Vegas Review-Journal.

Las Vegas major competitive destinations may be grouped into three categories:

* Leisure — Orlando, San Francisco, Los Angeles, New Orleans.
* Conventions — Chicago, Atlanta, Orlando, New York.
* Gaming — Atlantic City, (and to some extent) Mississippi.

Three entities are involved in the design of the Web site: the LVCA, a Web vendor (which has been changed), and an advertising agency. Most of the data maintenance of the Web site is done in-house by the Web manager. The Web site is updated on a weekly basis, and the site is now being subjected to a major revision by the first time (once every two years). The most important features of a Web site for destination marketing are considered to be user-friendliness and usefulness, i.e., providing a good balance between graphics and functionality. The LVCA's revised Web site will strengthen these characteristics and will be more interactive. The LVCA's site has some unique features, such as:

* Keyword search and calendar search that are used by 75% of the visitors.
* Hotel and motel search that is used by 60% of the visitors.
* Weather page, which is also frequently used.

The Nevada Commission on Tourism (NCOT) is the state agency dedicated to promoting tourism in the Silver State. Its mission is to offer a composite view of the state, to emphasize the promotion of rural areas, underlining Northern Nevada. The official Web site of the NCOT. The purpose is to make available to the traveller an online visitor centre, providing more information and assisting him/her on planning a trip to Nevada. It aims to attract visitors to travel beyond Las Vegas or Reno, enticing them to extend their stay and go to other places.

The Web site has proven to help increase the number of inquiries about the state and to stimulate the growth in requests for the Visitors' Guide Booklet. Moreover, the site helped save some money on tele marketing, but not on print.

A research program for data collection is running which consists of sampling inquirers (telephone survey) in order to assess conversion ratios. Furthermore, the site has taken ongoing online surveys of its users. The NCOT collaborates offline with other organizations in the region as a member of the Western States Policy Tourism Council that gathers 11 western states of the United States.

The major competitive destinations for Nevada are:

* For the pleasure/leisure market — California (Anaheim-Disneyland), Florida (Orlando-Walt Disney World), Hawaii.
* For the gaming market — New Jersey (Atlantic City), Mississippi, other emerging states, including those expanding Indian gaming.
* For the conventions market — New York, Illinois (Chicago), Georgia (Atlanta), Florida (Orlando, Miami).

Both NCOT and an advertising agency have been involved in the design of the Web site. Its maintenance, updating, enhancement, and redesign is conducted through the ad agency. The site is redesigned once a year. This takes place when a new annual Nevada Visitors Guide/ Booklet is published. Moreover, the site's Calendar of Events, which coincides with the publication of the Nevada Magazine, is updated every two months. In addition, there is a new overall theme every month which is also addressed by the Lieu Tenant Counsellor.

The most important feature of a Web site for destination marketing is to have content-rich, updated, and very complete information. NCOT's site provides information on Nevada broken into six territories. It has a comprehensive hotel/motel listing as well as a calendar of events in the state.

Private Companies

The main purpose of conducting Internet/online activity is to provide information on the different properties/resorts, their services, and prices in order to entice users to make reservations and come to the resorts. The major players in Las Vegas are the Mirage Resorts Group (Bellagio, Mirage, Treasure Island, Golden Nugget), Mandalay Bay Group (Mandalay Bay, Luxor, Excalibur), Park Place (Paris Las Vegas, Flamingo Hilton, Las Vegas Hilton, Circus Circus), MGM (MGM Grand, New York New York), Boyd Gaming Corporation (Stardust, Sam's Town, Fremont), and Harrah's. Whereas the Las Vegas Convention and Visitors Authority's promotion gives more weight to conventions, the main resort groups emphasize the gaming/casino activity more.

It is generally agreed that the LVCVA should be the centerpiece of a Web site portal for Las Vegas as a tourist destination. However, in reality two other sites have been in that position — vegas.com and lasvegas.com. The former is part of a large regional media group that includes the Las Vegas Sun newspaper, Showbiz weekly, Las Vegas Life, Las Vegas weekly, and Las Vegas Golfer. The latter is operated by the Donrey Media Group that also owns a major Las Vegas newspaper, the *Las Vegas Review Journal.* This site is run with the support of 17 partners, primarily government agencies, including the LVCVA. Interestingly, vegas.com is given preference and considered more popular than lasvegas.com as a portal site to Las Vegas. The design of the Web sites is usually outsourced. A number of senior executives are also involved. The maintenance and information updating is mostly done in-house.

The most important features of a Web site are considered as:

* Being visually/graphically attractive.
* Providing correct and up-to-date information.
* Being interactive.
* Enabling chat lines and stimulate consumer comments.
* Providing availability and booking online.
* Developing the right promotion online to entice the transient guest by providing attractive offers and interactive tools (e.g., weather information, driving directions, what to do) and using banners for brand image-building.
* Offering a toll-free number.
* Capturing data for conducting direct e-mail campaigns. Retail data bases are built with names and addresses of customers and prospects who visit the sites and inquire about further information.

Dotcoms

They usually receive over 300,000 visitors with more than 4 million page views a month. However, they are facing increasing competition from other sites such as (a Cox Communications interactive media city guide), and Microsoft's Side Walk. Actually, according to a recent research from Media Metrix (1999), a leader in Internet audience and digital media measurement, MSN Side walk has surpassed all competing online city guides in terms of consumer reach, achieving a reach of 7.3 percent, compared with other local guides like Digital Cities, with a reach of 6.3, and City Search, with a reach of 5.5 percent.

The dotcom sites are normally designed and maintained in-house. Major information updating takes place once a week (e.g., entertainment) whereas a lot of news is updated on a daily basis.

The most important features of a Web site for destination marketing are seen as providing quality content/information current and complete on the destination (e.g., resorts, restaurants, show listings, dining weather), ease of navigation/usability, and booking facilities. It is expected that in the near future the latter will be extended to also accommodate e-commerce on shows, restaurants, and sightseeing tours. Frequently asked questions and bulletin boards are also considered important characteristics.

Search Engine Positioning

Due to the clutter of sites available on the World Wide Web, DMOs ought to position themselves as the portals of their destinations. A sample search on the Yahoo! Directory as well as on the other major search engines by typing the name "Las Vegas" as a key word resulted in the following numbers. The Yahoo! Directory found 969 Web sites on Las Vegas. The Northern Light search engine found 1,313,971 pages on Las Vegas. In terms of search engine positioning, lasvegas.com is by far the best positioned. It consistently appears on the top 20 Web sites on Las Vegas: Alta Vista, Excite, HotBot/Lycos, Infoseek, Web Crawler, and Northern Light. Vegas.com comes ahead of lasvegas.com on Hotbot/Lycos and Northern Light but it does not show up on Excite, Web Crawler, and Alta Vista. The official Web site of the LVCVA, is visible only in Alta Vista and Infoseek.

Hyperlinks

Using the Alta Vista search engine the actual number of Web sites hyperlinked with each of the main dotcoms were found as follows: (8,570); (1,938); (1,212); and (1,017). Curiously, some hotel resorts have even more links such as the MGM Grand (1,235). Other national dotcom companies have most of the highest number of links: City Search (8,232), Virtual Cities (4,899), Cimedia (2,438), and MSN Side walk (2,319).

Tourism is one area that can greatly benefit from a city's online presence as out-of-state and foreign residents visit a Web site and decide they want to travel there. Web sites of DMOs will continue to evolve into more marketing tools than just archives or information services.

Their success relies heavily on the organization's ability to design effective Web sites, i.e., implementing the do's and avoiding the don'ts of Web design and Web usability. This paper addresses all these issues within the context of portal sites for marketing tourism destinations in the global market space.

Table 1. Do's & Don'ts of Web Design for Destination Marketing Organizations

Do's	***Don'ts***
* Content/Information	* Content/Information
* About the DMO	* Outdated information
* Tourism Products and Services	* Lack of biographies
* Frequently Asked Questions	* Lack of archives
* Online Ordering	* Headlines that make no sense out of context
* Interactive Request Form, Guest Book, or Survey	* Complex URLs
* What's New	* *Navigation*
* Giveaways	* Using frames
* *Navigation*	* Gratuitous use of bleeding-edge technology
* Menus	* Scrolling text and looping animations
* Image Maps, Buttons, and Jump Lines	* Orphan pages
* Search Engine	* Lack of navigation support
* Hyperlinks	* Nonstandard link colours
	* Slow download times
	* Breaking or slowing down the Back button
	* Opening new browser windows
	* Moving pages to new URLs

Lessons from www Tourism Initiatives in South Africa

In Soweto, Johannesburg, in early December 1999, the South African Minister of Environmental Affairs and Tourism launched the "South Africa Welcome Campaign" as part of the process of educating South Africans about the importance of tourism in the country's economic development. According to Minister Mohammed Vali Moosa:

"Tourism follows manufacturing and mining in its contribution to our country's GDP [gross domestic product] and could quickly overtake mining if we continue to grow tourism both domestically and internationally. It is also the sector identified by the World Economic Forum as capable of rapid job creation." The purpose of the "South Africa Welcome Campaign" is to raise public awareness about the importance of building a culture that welcomes tourists to the country. According to the Minister, World Economic Forum statistics reveal that for every eight tourists that visit South Africa, one permanent job is created. Some of the important statistics which are provided include the following:

* Tourism is the world's largest earner of foreign currency;
* South Africa only attracts 0.2% of the annual estimated 300 million tourists in the world;
* South Africa was ranked 25th in the world's top tourism destinations in 1998 — up 10% on 1997 but was only ranked 42nd when it comes to top tourism earners in the world;
* Tourism brings an estimated 20 billion Rand (R) (US $3.1 billion) into our economy, second only to manufacturing and mining in its contribution to the gross domestic product (GDP); or in other words, it contributed 8.2% to South Africa's GDP in 1998;
* 75% of all South Africa's foreign arrivals are from Africa;
* In 1998 South Africa saw a 24.6% rise in American visitors to the country;
* Foreign tourists stayed 16.9 days on average in our country in 1998 and spent R842 (US $152) per day.

The catalytic role of tourism in South Africa cannot be underestimated. In a country where a significant proportion of the population is unemployed and underemployed, the need for economic transformation is urgent. It seems — at a superficial level — that tourism is the panacea for the country's economic woes. However, South Africa is a very complex country and the role of tourism is slightly more complicated than it seems from the Minister's speeches or World Economic Forum fact sheets. It is also widely recognized that South Africa has not harnessed her full tourism potential and several reasons are offered for this.

The typical one is that crime in South Africa is stifling the tourism industry's growth. Rising violent crime levels may deter many tourists, particularly North American, Asian and European tourists, from visiting the country but there are other less obvious factors that impact equally on the fact that South Africa is not optimizing its real tourist potential.

A less profiled reason is that of xenophobia which has only recently received some attention from the South Africa media and national government. Xenophobia is typically understood to refer to a pathological fear of strangers and strange places. In South Africa, xenophobia assumes a more complex cultural and economic form in South Africa. Earlier in 1999, several African men working in South Africa and travelling on public transport were thrown from the train by an angry mob of supporters of the group known as the Unemployed People of South Africa. It was alleged that the *makwerakwera* (an impolite term for foreigners speaking African languages that sound like chirping crickets) 'stole' employment opportunities from South Africans. South Africa's economic hardships combined with the impact of years of isolation from the rest of the continent leads to a messy mix of distrust and disregard for other people from the African continent.

A third reason, and one with which we are particularly concerned, is that the proliferation of Web-based tourism initiatives in South Africa does not challenge the fundamental economic disparities between the vast majority of impoverished South African communities, the tourists who visit the country, and the tourism service providers.

The central purpose of our paper, therefore, is to look at some key issues of which we have been made aware through initiatives on which we have worked over the last 18 months, and to share these lessons with other developing countries, especially regarding use of tourism Web initiatives, particularly as it relates to commercial and to cultural tourism.

Commercial Tourism: Lessons from the Magic Tour Net Project

The Magic Tour Net project, the first case study to which we refer, is a commercial tourism enablement initiative on the Web and from which we have learned some critically important lessons. The focus of our reflections on this case study is an examination of commercial tourism and the related business implications when applied to the Internet.

The Magic Tour Net project was a European Commission (EC)-funded initiative aimed at addressing some of the concerns through the development of appropriate tools to enable the development and hosting of sophisticated tourism Web sites, supporting development of a tourism portal and addressing the availability of data for tourism Web sites. The development of the technical components was validated through the development of a pilot application focusing on the Western Cape province in South Africa. Details of the technical aspects of the project have been described in another conference paper — *Magic Tour Net: A Web based Multimedia and GIS Authoring System for the Development of Tourism-Oriented Web sites* by Laurens Cloete, Hina Patel, Maria Rita Nazzaralli of CSIR and Intecs Sistemi — and are not repeated here. The project also included a task focusing on the commercial exploitation of the project results, which incorporated a study into possible business models.

A key assumption of the Magic Tour Net project was that the Internet has the potential to overturn conventional business models and, by implication, to redefine the roles of different tourism actors such as travel agents, Tour Operators, and national and regional tourism authorities. As we progressed on this initiative, we had first-hand experience of the reality that new business models require new skills and tools. Theoretically, the Internet should allow tourism service providers such as hotels or restaurants or museums to offer their services directly to consumers.

There were, however, a number of considerations that prevented this from happening to the extent that we initially believed was possible.

The first of these was that the ability to design professional Web sites capable of competing with other distractions on the Web and ensuring Web sites were updated and maintained was (and still is) constituted by skills and resources not available to the majority of South Africans and to tourism service providers. The movement towards designing intuitive and user-friendly tourism applications was one step towards supporting a more dynamic and empowered tourism service sector in South Africa.

The second consideration was the need to stimulate and compel the virtual tourist. It is the case that potential tourists would like to get a sense of the place and the people they are intending to visit. Many tourists tend to use conventional media such as printed travel literature books containing visual images and maps of the places they would like to visit. Integrating images and static maps into Web site content is relatively easy but it offers little value over conventional media, and the Web site content remains essentially static. Overcoming this inertia of visual and other content was therefore an important consideration. During the course of the project, a survey was undertaken and the results confirmed a lack of dynamic, multimedia data that could be used to build tourism applications. We extrapolated further that finding accommodation or other tourism information presents a significant hurdle to the acceptance of the Web as the way to access tourism information.

The solution was able to address these two considerations in the following way. The solution consisted of building a tourism Web site development and use system that would allow novice developers (i.e., the tourism service providers) to develop and publish professional Web sites with sophisticated functionalities that are not available on non-expert applications, and which, in turn, could be accessed effectively and efficiently by tourism users. From the tourist's perspective, it was possible to obtain — from a unique address — a large range of tourist information and to select a series of services to build his/her own tailored package. The added value to the tourist included the following:

* Information was available about an increased number of tourism actors in the tourism supply chain (e.g., service providers, travel agents and tour operators) in the host country thus enhancing the tourist's ability to choose; and
* Reservation and booking functionality was available at a potentially reduced cost to all players in the tourism supply chain.

These benefits are, however, obvious. A less obvious and more radical benefit is that the existence of comprehensive tourism Web sites highlights the changing roles of traditional media in the tourism supply chain. It is often assumed that the Internet is a threat to tourism but in fact, we argue, the Internet highlights the artificial distinction between the roles of Travel Agents and publishers. By combining the very valuable information that publishers own with reservation capabilities of Travel Agents and Tour Operators, a value-added service can be provided to tourists at a reduced cost. Another benefit is related to foreign exchange. Although tourism is an important foreign exchange earner, a significant percentage of the money spent on tourism remains in the tourist's original country. For example, flight bookings are typically made in the tourist's home country and not in the host country. Through use of the Internet, service providers in countries that depend on tourism can offer their service in the tourists' countries and address this problem by offering some of the service over the Internet in the destination country. That assumes a more equitable distribution of the financial benefits across the home and host countries. And for South Africa, it is imperative that this happen.

The Magic Tour Net system was developed in recognition of some of the changes that are taking place in the tourism value chain. It addressed, in part, a third important consideration, namely the impact of the Internet on the whole tourism value chain as it applies to more than just the tourists and the tourism service providers. The Magic Tour Net system does have a potential to address the problem of maintaining up-to-date data about the service or the host country. Through the tools provided by the system, it is possible for data to be maintained by people that have the greatest interest in having their data up-to-date. For example, restaurants may be able to own a part of a larger Web site dedicated to a city or region. A common and professional look of the Web site can be built into the system through the design of templates and style sheets, but data can be maintained by many different entities in whose interest it is to keep their data updated.

What it did not address directly was the impact of the Internet — and related tourism supply chain transformations — on the people of the host country who engage in informal and opportunistic economic activities within the broader tourism supply chain. In a developing country, informal and opportunistic economic activity (e.g., informal traders of crafts or 'car guards') are real and necessary survival strategies for the vast majority of unemployed and underemployed South Africans. The mentor of the Internet Society (ISOC) — the Internet is for Everyone — takes on a more subtle significance than just having all South Africans seated in front of personal computers with modems. Instead, virtual tourism content should be developed in recognition of the fact that the broader tourism supply chain can be transformed and that the benefits of an enhanced tourism supply chain should allow for accrued benefit to the widest range of South Africans, formally and informally employed.

Cultural Tourism: Lessons from the Culture ware Project

The second case study to which we refer in this paper is the culture ware project and our specific focus is on the lessons we have learned about cultural tourism initiatives as applied to the Internet's tourism supply chain. This project is a multi-million rand state-funded project on which we are working within a consortium made up of a historically disadvantaged university, a state tourism marketing body, and a Section 21 Western Cape tourism company. The project has several aims but one of the most important is to develop proof of sustainability of digital multi-cultural consumption in tourism, education and public awareness. The project is currently in its second year.

One of the research activities undertaken within the framework of the culture ware project was the creation of a virtual tourism experience. The chosen environment was a 'non-traditional' tourism and cultural site, namely an informal settlement on the eastern seaboard of South Africa. The virtual environment consisted of, among others, a virtual *shebeen* or a beerhall in which users could interact with a shebeen queen avatar, an interactive radio digital object which allowed users to select music of musicians such as Hugh Masekela and Miriam Makheba, an interactive newspaper digital object which played video clips of shack destruction in the 1950s, and so on. The virtual environment was developed using appropriate virtual reality (VR) and multimedia software, and translated into VRML (Virtual Reality Modelling Language) for distribution on the culture ware project's Web site.

The specific residential site was chosen as a potential tourism experience because it currently is a high-profile presidential project and has several cultural and economic programs under way to reclaim the township's potential and its past. And tourism is regarded as an important enabler of its reconstruction and development. The experience designed consisted of a nostalgic/retrospective experience into the township's vibrant community life of the 1950s. This residential site is part of a larger group of cultural spaces — including Sophia town and District Six — which receive local attention because of South Africa's process of reclamation and political and cultural restitution. A story board was conceptualized in which a narrator (in this case, a nine-year-old boy called Mandla) 'talked' the viewer through the experience to enhance the realism of nostalgia for a potentially 'alien' cultural and historical experience (alien, that is, to the viewer). A list of curatorially and historically authentic artifacts were presented, and the structures and landscape in the environment were closely examined and redesigned to depict textural and historical integrity (e.g., the shack home polygons were re-angled away from 90-degree verticals to 80-degree verticals while roof polygons were manipulated to appear 'mangled').

The development of this virtual tourism experience created several important challenges. Some of these challenges were obviously of a technical nature and included translation of a virtual reality model into suitable format for consumption via the Web. We do not wish to address these here but instead focus on two other challenges — namely, designing culturally sensitive interfaces and Intellectual Property Protection (IPP).

Interfaces are often regarded as technical elements only but there has been a significant rise in awareness of the context and content-specific requirements that impact directly on the conceptualization and design of interfaces, whether they be for the Web or other means of distribution.

We begin our discussion of this issue by referring to an important argument by Barbara Kirshenblatt-Gimblet in *Destination Tourism: Tourism, Museums and Heritage* that had direct relevance to the content and context design issues in our project. Kirshenblatt-Gimblet argues that the current mechanisms we use to display culture and art demand that we ask questions about the meaning behind 'displaying' these items. Her argument is that there is a technology that has developed which guides how we use objects and artifacts to 'display' their meaning to us and to others. The meaning behind design in cultural tourism Web sites is, we argue, of critical importance in a developing economy and there are several reasons for this, which we will examine in turn.

The first is that cultural tourism experiences enabled through Internet technologies and Web-based initiatives are part of a much broader process of commodification of knowledge in society. Jean Francois Lyotard in *The Post Modern Condition: A Report on Knowledge* emphasized this point several years ago when he argued that in an era of rapid growth of computerized information technology, technology is both a product and hastener of change. In the Information Age, knowledge is 'legitimate' because of two things: the effects of that knowledge and the efficiency of the effects of that knowledge. Leotard calls this 'performativity.' Knowledge has become a commodity and can be controlled and sold with the intention of achieving more for the purposes of securing a market edge. Our concern, here, is that in efforts to promote cultural tourism in South Africa, the Internet is obviously increasingly used to attract foreign tourists to South Africa's shores but these efforts often occur outside — or ignorant of — questions about the unintended consequences of this form of commodification of cultural tourism content.

There is, and will continue to be, an inherent triviality to Web content of cultures and people. A Web-mediated or virtual-life experience of a culture is not intended to replace the real-life experience of that culture and place — including the annoyance of long queues or lost passports! However, as Sherry Turkle has argued in *Life on the Screen*, 'we construct our technologies, and our technologies construct us and our times.' According to Turkle, the Internet provides us with opportunities for cultural appropriation through manipulation of specific objects and hence, people's knowledge of cultures develops through those things with which they have become actively involved. Turkle argues that in today's era while we know that computers are not sentient yet, the way in which we interact with them — and through them — blurs the boundaries between things and people. In the age of computer-mediated communication, Turkle asks what impact will this have on our commitment to other people? The Internet, she argues, is a social laboratory for experimentation with self, identity and post modern life. The Internet is an 'easy fix' to providing a substitute to face-to-face interaction. It is part of a move toward virtuality which tends to skew our experience of the real in several ways:

* It makes denatured and artificial experiences seem real (obviously, we build our idea of what is real and what is natural with the cultural materials available);
* It lends itself to what Turkle refers to as the 'artificial crocodile effect,' an effect that makes the fake more compelling than the real; and
* The extent of how compelling it is makes us believe that we have achieved more than we really have.

Cultural tourism experiences consumed via the Internet — unless intentionally designed to do otherwise — run the risk of presenting context and content about a host country, at best, in inherently trivial ways and at worst, in paternalistic ways. Data and information used in a cultural tourism Web site or application are often presented as sufficient unto themselves rather than — as should be the case in South Africa's tourism imperative — as sufficient information to help the virtual tourist transform into a *real tourist.*

Cultural tourism content can also be presented or displayed in such a way that the subject (e.g., an indigenous rural Nguni culture) becomes the object of someone else's gaze. The relationship between tourist and host is a complex one and it should not be the case that cultural tourism Web sites are designed only for the benefit of the tourist or for the service provider. Benefits should accrue, too, to the host, in the broadest sense of that term. And that issue raises directly questions about whether or not the conceptualization of the Web site was sufficiently participative of the people on whom the gaze of the virtual and real tourist will fall. In participative conceptualization and consultation processes with communities, the assumption is that members of that community have an active role in accruing benefit and adding value to the entire supply chain and the relationship with the tourist. In that sense it is possible to argue that cultural tourism Web content will reflect the economic models on which they are based. And if it is the case that tourism is central to the human and economic growth of a developing country, then progressive tourism management approaches are critical considerations in the conceptualization and design of tourism interfaces. The Internet does not, in and of itself, result in these progressive tourism management and transformative economic approaches — instead it reveals the need for them more clearly.

The second lesson learned relates to Intellectual Property. In cultural tourism Web sites, obviously, the cultural artifacts which are on display should be culturally authentic. No cultural tourism initiative — virtual or otherwise — can be sustainable if it is premised on inauthentic content and context. And obviously in Web-based cultural tourism experiences, authenticity is particularly important as a way of making information about a people or a culture sufficiently compelling to get the virtual tourist transformed into a real tourist. However, culturally authentic artifacts — particularly in postcolonial countries — are particularly at risk of exploitation because the resources required to preserve those cultural heritage artifacts are often channelled into more immediate concerns such as housing, health care and (unfortunately) often weapons of war.

IPP should be of higher import to African countries because of the legacies of cultural artifact, natural resource and human plundering that constitute the colonial legacies of those countries. Unfortunately, it does not always and consistently receive the same attention. South Africa, however, has recently developed legislation on cultural heritage resource management and is addressing issues of IPP as it relates to digital facsimiles of those artifacts.

Securing the intellectual property rights of a particular cultural artifact obviously embraces a technical component — and these issues are addressed in another conference paper by culture ware project researchers, Johan Eksteen and Dr. Louis Coetzee — but also legal and curatorial components.

In South Africa, the design imperative to make cultural tourism Web sites compelling and attractive to the virtual tourist has been brought into direct conflict with the IPP imperative and specifically the legal and curatorial aspects of digital reproductions of culturally authentic artifacts. As the virtual cultural tourist's need for heightened and unique stimulation increases, the need for content and context authenticity is enhanced. But this, however, assumes that someone, somewhere, has taken care of the IPP of a digital artifact. South Africa is unique in its dilemma. What we mean is that it has a vast array of multicultural communities and artifacts which when combined with the legacy of cultural hegemony and sophisticated institutionalization and organization of English-and Africans-speaking cultural groups implies that the majority of our cultural artifacts are at risk from a new form of technological colonialism. The Internet ushers in real risks of having the IPP of a digital reproduction of an indigenous South African cultural artifact being held by a non-South African agent. And in that relationship, a South African agent would be expected to, for example, pay for the right to use a digital reproduction of a particular photograph of an indigenous bead work design, on a South African cultural tourism Web site. Obviously, that is not to the economic or cultural benefit of an emerging South African cultural tourism industry.

State intervention may seem anathema to many developed countries which actively support little or no state intervention in the free market global economy but in South Africa, state intervention in matters of this nature is critical. Progressive cultural heritage management legislation as well as provision of support to cultural groups to ensure IP on their own cultural artifacts, whether those artifacts be tactile, oral or foodway artifacts, becomes one of the most important preventative mechanisms against a new era of (technologically enabled) colonialism.

Conclusions

In our paper, we have presented some key lessons that we have learned from two quite different Web-based tourism initiatives in which we have engaged.

The first case study, the Magic Tour Net project, examined the impact of the Internet on more equitable distribution and facilitation of the skills and resources required to develop and publish suitable commercial tourism Web sites. And it also attempted to highlight the importance of developing commercial tourism Web site applications that are cognizant of the obvious and hidden changes that the Internet has upon the tourism supply chain.

We believe that we are only now beginning to understand some of these impacts and are progressing slowly towards being able to ensure that our tourism Web initiatives are able to ensure that tourism enhances the economic and human development imperatives in South Africa. In our second case study, the cultureware project, we have learned some critically important lessons about the impact of the Internet on cultural tourism as a phenomenon and enabler of human and economic development. We highlighted only two issues among the many we encountered. The first was about the consequences of commodification of tourism information in the content and context of these Web sites. And related to that was the second lesson about IPP of postcolonial countries' cultural artifacts in a potentially increasing technologically enabled neo-colonialism.

Our specific country's dynamics and realities require solutions and approaches that may not be appropriate to all countries engaged in Internet-based tourism but we do believe that what we have uncovered will be of increasing importance to other developing countries' increased access to and use of the Internet in their economic activities. We hope not only that the lessons we have learned will enhance the activities in which we engage but also that the application of these lessons will ensure that other members of the developing world engage in Web-based activities in a more empowered way, such that Web-enabled communication and commerce benefits them and their people.

Challenges and Opportunities Facing Canada's Tourism Industry

The world has changed dramatically over the past 10 years, but some of the issues that faced the tourism industry in the early 1990's are still here today. The environment in which the industry operates requires tourism stakeholders to fundamentally shift their strategic approach not only to resolve long-standing issues but more importantly to effectively address current challenges and capitalize on new opportunities.

Changing demographics, shifting travel patterns and volatile economic conditions are increasing the pressure on industry stakeholders to develop effective campaigns and business strategies. More recently, health and safety issues such as pandemics and global security concerns as manifested by WHTI have increased the urgency for industry action.

The challenges facing the tourism industry are complex and numerous. Addressing these challenges will require a high level of coordination and cooperation to marshal resources more effectively. Fiscal pressures and competing priorities among all F/P/T partners and tourism stakeholders will require new and innovative partnership arrangements to respond to growing competition and global opportunities.

Opportunities exist for governments and the private sector to seize the extraordinary opportunity afforded by "mega events" occurring in Canada and abroad. For example, Canada can learn from Australia's experience with the Sydney Games in 2000 as it prepares to host the 2010 Olympics in Vancouver. The Sydney Games demonstrated that strong public/private partnerships and cooperation result in widespread incremental benefits. The challenge confronting governments and tourism stakeholders will be to establish the necessary linkages to ensure the development of collaborative strategies in conjunction with major international or domestic events so that lasting benefits will be created across the country. The analysis of domestic and international arrivals and spending patterns indicates that if Canada is to continue to be a pre-eminent destination for leisure and business travel, investments will have to be made to enhance and tailor tourism products and services according to the needs of a highly competitive marketplace. Further analysis of niche markets and specific strategies to position the industry within those niches will have to be undertaken by both public and private sector tourism stakeholders. It is in this context that Building a National Tourism Strategy will be developed and refined.

The consultations with industry stakeholders confirmed many challenges that were identified in the November 2003 Consultation Framework and the key challenges listed below represent priority areas for collaboration. However, since then, changing circumstances may have altered stakeholder priorities. At the time of the consultations, the U.S. had yet to announce the WHTI. Following the announcement in April 2005, it became increasingly clear that this measure could be highly detrimental to the Canadian tourism industry.

WHTI is a national, industry-wide concern affecting every region and most sectors of the tourism industry. As such, it is an issue that could be effectively addressed in the context of a National Tourism Strategy.

Provincial/territorial governments will continue addressing particular issues and challenges in their jurisdictions but increased collaboration is required so that their strategies and action plans can help strengthen the tourism industry by enhancing its international competitiveness. Whether competing with new and emerging destinations or responding to world "shocks," addressing the challenges facing the industry in a collaborative manner will be key to growing tourism in Canada.

Key challenges raised during industry consultations include:

1. Comprehensive research to better understand the expectations of travellers;
2. More cohesive marketing and promotional campaigns while reflecting provincial/territorial realities and diversity in Canada;
3. Further development of Aboriginal tourism;
4. Human resource strategies to attract and retain employees in the industry;
5. Investments in tourism infrastructure;
6. Efficient and integrated transportation systems; and.
7. Broadening and adopting sustainable tourism and best practices.

Understanding the Expectations of Travellers

Research has shown that as demographics shift so do travel patterns and demand for products and services. The advancement of technology has also had a significant impact on the tourism industry. Continuing to upgrade and modernize visitor information services will be important in providing visitors with quality, user-friendly and consistent year-round information. Being able to understand and adapt to these changes will be increasingly important.

An Aging Population

What was once a relatively homogeneous market for international tourism products is now fragmented into a number of highly specialized niches. As the baby-boom generation advances through middle age, industry stakeholders recognize that customer needs and expectations are changing.

There will be rapid growth in the seniors market segment as the baby-boom generation begins to reach 65 years of age in 2011. It is estimated that seniors will represent 25 percent of Canada's overall population by 2026, compared to the current 12 percent. Similar aging trends are forecasted in most developed countries. Trips by foreign residents in the older segments of the population have been increasing more rapidly than trips taken by other age groups. This slow but steady shift is forcing the industry to adapt its services and products in order to appeal to a growing, mature clientele.

Figure

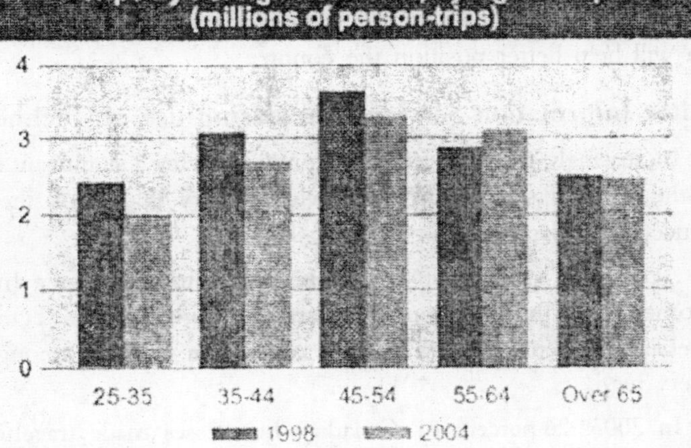

Source: International Travel 2003, Statistics Canada

The Government of Ontario's report "Impacts of Aging the Canadian Market on Tourism in Ontario," states that "if the new generation of [mature] Ontario residents displays similar tourism activity preferences to their 2000 counterparts, the impact of an aging population will result in a shift away from outdoor activity such as canoeing and fishing, towards non-strenuous warm weather activities and indoor cultural events and attractions." This reinforces the importance of conducting research on travel patterns to be able to tailor tourism products, and be more responsive to present and future preferences.

Changing Travel Patterns

According to a survey conducted by the Western Australia Tourism Commission, an emerging market referred to as the "children of the information age" is developing. This segment is characterized by increasingly sophisticated travellers who are experienced, well-educated and discriminating consumers who are more aware of what the competition has to offer.

They are becoming less destination-oriented and more experience-oriented. This transformation into an "experience market" is based on personalized services and customized holidays that allow visitors to play a more active role in their travelling experiences and search continually for new tourism products, such as the increasing variety of spa vacations. The CTC has identified a similar trend in Canada and research in this area will help better position the country.

Visitor Information Services: Increasing use of Technology

Increasingly, the knowledge economy is having a significant impact on the tourism sector and the travel industry is one of the most connected in Canada.

According to the 2004 Conference Board Consumer Internet Barometer, two-thirds of consumers are now using the Internet to make travel arrangements and the level of satisfaction reported among users is very high.

In 2003, 26 percent of Canadian businesses made travel-related purchases online, up 18 percent from 2002. Combined private and public sector online travel sales reached $19.1 billion in 2003, an increase of almost 40 percent on top of a 27 percent jump the previous year. The Economist referred to online travel as being one of the most successful forms of e-commerce.

Americans presently buy 20 percent of their total travel online, but many in the industry believe this proportion could reach 50-60 percent within a decade. The International Federation for Information Technology and Travel and Tourism reported in January 2005 that convergence of the Internet, wireless applications and inter-active objects are increasing the importance of smart business networks.

Additionally, pervasive computing applications will provide new services and greater convenience for customers. The last decade has seen Internet business solutions transform consumer behaviour and business practices resulting in a rapid growth of new business models such as the low-cost airlines and their online reservations systems and 'smart businesses'. Smart businesses are flexible, dynamic, collaborative, and able to move swiftly to leverage market opportunities.

Internet business solutions are not only affecting business models, they are also driving market changes. In 2004, online bookings in Europe increased by more than 50 percent and 10 percent of total revenues in travel and tourism came from online business.

Three consumer trends are e-business driven: readiness to spend more on trips, more frequent vacations but shorter stays, and an increasing importance of the mature segment of the market. Internet business solutions are increasingly used to improve visitor information services but their application to reduce costs and increase operating effectiveness and efficiency can have a substantial impact on business viability.

The F/P/T partners will need to collaborate in working with their tourism industry to ensure that they fully capitalize on the advantages provided by IBS.

Cohesive Marketing Campaigns that Reflect Provincial/Territorial Realities

Canada's cultural, geographical and language landscape makes the country a highly appealing tourist destination. Diversity is one of Canada's major differentiating characteristics and capitalizing on it must become a tourism planning priority. The tourism industry's maturity or level of development varies among provinces and territories. Some areas of Canada are still emerging destinations, while others are better established with thriving tourism businesses.

Southern Canada is characterized by major cities, events and gateways, relative ease of access and a wide variety of well-established and emerging products. Maximizing the potential of festivals and events (i.e., sport, culture, and heritage events) will require new horizontal approaches for the tourism sector.

Northern Canada is characterized by emerging destinations based on nature tourism, niche products, Aboriginal attractions and wilderness. Access to these areas and their sustainable capacity are an on-going challenge facing tourism development. Research requirements and product development and marketing opportunities vary across provinces and territories and among rural and urban areas. The CTC leads Canada's national marketing campaigns in collaboration with those of the provinces/territories.

However, there is a need to keep developing collaborative approaches to increase the cohesion, effectiveness and efficiency of national initiatives, while at the same time, recognizing the different priorities and needs of all provinces and territories. Strengthening the collaboration of tourism marketing between the provinces/territories and the CTC will not only serve to better coordinate existing initiatives but it will improve their complementarity, potentially leading to innovative partnerships.

The F/P/T partners need to collaborate on research initiatives to identify growth opportunities for all provinces and territories of Canada. Improving overall coordination of research, product development and marketing strategies will better enable F/P/T partners to capitalize on new and emerging opportunities both domestically and internationally.

Developing Aboriginal Tourism

Aboriginal tourism is one of Canada's unique strengths, in both the domestic and international markets. However, the growth of this segment of the tourism industry faces significant challenges. Tourism represents about one quarter of the Aboriginal economy in Quebec, the North and the West.

According to the 2003 National Study on Aboriginal Tourism in Canada, demand for Aboriginal tourism is outpacing capacity. There are relatively few market-ready products in the Aboriginal tourism sector, particularly near gateway cities and major tourism routes.

Many businesses do not have sufficient tourism market awareness, business skills, product development and marketing expertise to successfully compete. The Virtual Tour of Aboriginal Canada, a web portal, was developed in response to the perceived need to generate a higher level of public awareness regarding Canada's Aboriginal tourism industry.

There is great potential to increase Aboriginal tourism activities and at the same time contribute to the wealth creation, economic development and self-reliance of Aboriginal people and communities in all provinces/ territories in Canada. The Quebec Declaration clearly recognizes Northern and Aboriginal tourism as an emerging and important sector. Improving partnerships between Aboriginal stakeholders, industry and government will require a better understanding of Aboriginal aspirations and Aboriginal culture in relation to market realities in an effort to evolve the Aboriginal owned product offering.

Developing Northern Tourism

Canada's northern tourism products offer a truly unique experience. While the North is renowned for its nature and wilderness adventures and aurora tourism, it also offers history, distinctive culture and festivals as well as some innovative emerging products such as 'diamond tourism' in the Northwest Territories.

The number of tourists travelling to the North is slowly rising. In 2004, the Yukon had over 250,000 arrivals, an 8 percent increase over 1999. The Northwest Territories saw arrivals increase by almost 4 percent between 2002 and 2004 when the number surpassed 61,000. While Americans represent over three quarters of the Yukon's tourists, more than half of the arrivals in the Northwest Territories are Canadian.

Increasing the number of tourists that visit the North is challenging because it is a product with a narrow market segment. Other issues include access, both in terms of availability and cost, receptive capacity and sustainability. Transportation infrastructure is expensive. Long distances with low traffic result in high costs to individual travellers. These key considerations must be taken into account when endeavouring to develop northern tourism. The northern environment is remote and highly fragile; its natural beauty is part of Canada's heritage and wealth.

Attracting and Retaining a Workforce

The Conference Board of Canada estimates that there will be a shortfall of close to one million workers in the Canadian economy by 2020. According to the Canadian Tourism Human Resource Council, Canada's overall labour force is expected to decline from a growth rate of 1.4 percent in 2005 to 0.4 percent in 2016, due to an aging population and lower birth rates. To compound the problem, labour demand continues to increase across all sectors as a result of strong economic growth.

The tourism labour market is characterized as a seasonal, fragmented, multifaceted service industry, with a large number of entry-level jobs. The seasonal nature of the tourism industry is contributing to the development of dual labour markets, comprised of core workers and peripheral ones. In many cases, employees view tourism as a gateway into the labour market.

Approximately 60 percent of tourism employment is within the food and beverage, and accommodation sectors. These are the areas most in need of a stable and skilled workforce.

Figure

Source: Statistics Canada National Tourism Indicators

In light of potential labour shortages, it has become increasingly important to enhance the quality of jobs in the tourism industry and to facilitate the entry of those who are under-represented in the labour force. Canada needs to study what other countries are doing to address similar challenges.

For example, some Organisation for Economic Cooperation and Development (OECD) countries are currently undertaking efforts to enhance the employability of foreign workers. An opportunity exists to examine how Canada can adjust current immigration policies to better reflect the tourism industry's needs.

Although the tourism industry offers the first work experience for many people, the sector is sometimes ill-perceived as a career choice. At the same time, the ability to attract skilled employees is critical to the industry's growth. There is a need to promote the wide range of long-term career opportunities and prospects that tourism offers, particularly in the operation and management ranks, as well as general hospitality. Attractions, hotels, airlines, auto rentals, and entertainment are but a few areas that offer rewarding, long-term careers.

Investing in Tourism Infrastructure

Typically tourism infrastructure is viewed as consisting of museums, cultural institutions, heritage sites and parks, but the enjoyment and success of tourism experiences also requires quality public infrastructure. All governments are committed to work collaboratively to restore infrastructure in Canada. As such, they have invested more than $30 billion in infrastructure since 1993 in numerous projects across the country.

Despite the substantial investment that governments have made in infrastructure, Statistics Canada reports that the growth in value of public infrastructure assets in Canada has been significantly lagging behind the economy as a whole. In the mid-1970s, public infrastructure as a share of GDP was 23 percent, but declined to 16 percent by 2001.

However all governments are making substantial investments in public infrastructure that benefits the tourism sector directly and indirectly. The significance of tourism interests in infrastructure projects must continue to be communicated to the various jurisdictions responsible for infrastructure development. The strategy will be instrumental in championing coordination and cooperation between governments, particularly in providing policy direction on tourism and related infrastructure projects.

Ensuring an Efficient Transportation System

As the second largest country in the world, Canada's vast territory and diverse geography pose an ongoing transportation challenge for the tourism industry. During the stakeholder consultations, concerns regarding the impact of an inadequate transportation system were raised.

The high cost of air travel in Canada's remote areas and limited transportation options, especially by rail and ferry, affect the ability of tourism operators to promote their products. At the same time, recent shifts and growth in the low-cost carrier segment of the airline industry is helping the domestic tourism market.

The cheaper, more flexible price structure of these airlines has enticed more people to travel. They provide affordable air access to many provinces and territories in Canada that were once considered too costly to serve. In this context, there is a need to continue seeking opportunities to ensure that accessibility, affordability, and service quality are facilitated by a liberalized international air policy, and that tourists' entry into Canada is not impeded. Efforts to seek opportunities for new international bilateral agreements with other countries need to continue.

In addition, the updating of existing agreements, such as the recently concluded liberalization of the Open Skies bilateral agreement with the U.S. should be encouraged. As changes to air liberalization are primarily related to federal transport policy, the CCTM will collaborate with key transportation departments and other stakeholders, as required, in achieving the key results and outcomes.

There is also a need to better integrate the national transportation system to allow passengers to connect easily between modes of transportation, whether they are travelling by bus, boat, plane, train or automobile to or from other points within and outside Canada.

As part of this, particular attention should be paid to ensuring the efficiency and security of the Canada-U.S. Land border, since the U.S. is our main source of international travellers. To this end, Canada and

the U.S. signed the Smart Border Declaration in 2001, agreeing on a 32-point action plan to address border processes, invest in border infrastructure, and identify technological solutions to speed movement across the border while ensuring security.

The Border Infrastructure Fund was established to support border infrastructure projects at Canada's busiest land border ports of entry. Furthermore, as part of the 2005 Security and Prosperity Partnership of North America, Canada, the U.S. and Mexico are committed to a number of initiatives that promote border efficiency and security.

The Government of Canada is committed to pursuing integration of the national transportation system and to investing further in new infrastructure at the border. Budget 2006 provided an unprecedented level of support for infrastructure of various types across Canada. This includes support for small and larger scale municipal infrastructure projects in communities across Canada, and improvements to land border crossings and highways.

The fluidity of our major international gateways and trade corridors is crucial not only for the tourism industry, but for the economy as a whole. Through the Asia-Pacific Gateway and Corridor Initiative, Canada seeks to boost commerce with the Asia-Pacific region to integrate investments in transportation infrastructure and improve the efficiency and reliability of the regional transportation system.

Adopting Sustainable Tourism Development and Quality Practices

Sustainable tourism enhances and preserves our natural and cultural heritage and improves Canadians' quality of life. Tourism development needs to balance economic viability, environmental conservation and social impacts. Sustainable tourism endeavours to minimize environmental and cultural impacts while contributing to economic development. The long-term success of the industry depends on business owners and operators being stewards of the environment and adopting quality practices.

In A Manual for Sustainable Tourism Destination Management by Walter Jamieson and Alex Noble, 2000, it states that increasing evidence shows that an integrated approach to tourism planning and management is now required to achieve sustainable tourism. The document goes on to identify some of the most important principles of sustainable tourism development which include:

* Tourism should be initiated with the help of broad-based input that involves all stakeholders, including the community where the development is taking place, and the stakeholders should maintain control of tourism development.
* Tourism should provide quality local employment and a linkage between the local businesses and tourism should be established.
* A code of practice should be established for tourism at all levels—national, regional, and local—based on internationally accepted standards. Guidelines for tourism operations, impact assessment, monitoring of cumulative impacts and limits to acceptable change should be established.
* Education and training programs to improve and manage heritage and natural resources should be established.

F/P/T governments and the industry must work together to develop a cohesive strategy for tourism sustainability in Canada. In spring 2004, the Tourism Industry Association of Canada (TIAC) undertook an update of the Code of Ethics and Guidelines for Sustainable Tourism developed in 1992. The update, prepared in consultation with industry, was released in February 2005. The Code provides a common basis and framework for the industry to move forward effectively in support of the shared responsibility for sustainable tourism. The aim is to enhance the quality and sustainability of natural and cultural heritage-based experiences. The Code could provide the basis for F/P/T partners to develop a collaborative approach to a sustainable tourism.

Tourism Marketing Strategy

The Accidental Tourist

"For Newfoundland and Labrador, there's no such thing as an accidental tourist. It takes deliberate planning and determined effort to visit here, compelled by curiosity and the promise of what's unique and different in our people, culture, lifestyle, and dramatic scenery."

Barriers & Opportunities

Travel distance, access, and cost continue to be significant barriers for visitors, and a competitive disadvantage for the tourism industry in Newfoundland and Labrador. A short peak season, capacity constraints during peak season, and increasing problems and delays at border crossings and in airports make increasing tourism visitors and revenue even more difficult. Competing with well-known tourism destinations that are well-funded and heavily advertised makes the job even tougher. Despite these barriers, there are opportunities open to Newfoundland and Labrador Tourism.

Baby bloomers are entering the empty nest stage of the family lifestyle. They have money, time, and keen interest to explore destinations that are off the beaten track, unusual and unspoiled places where few have gone before. Places like Newfoundland and Labrador. Ontario, our largest nonresident market, still remains largely underdeveloped for Newfoundland and Labrador tourism. Our greatest opportunity may lay in the launch of the new Tourism brand positioning and personality for Newfoundland and Labrador – and the creative strategy which we use to express it. Our coastline, rich history, unique culture, people, and natural environment remain our key strengths.

Marketing Objectives

The marketing objectives for Newfoundland and Labrador Tourism are to increase nonresident visitation and expenditures from our core markets, thereby increasing the tourism industry's annual contribution to the economy. The strategies and campaigns created to achieve these marketing objectives will also be guided by the desire of government and the Tourism Board to extend the tourism season beyond the core summer season in order to increase the economic benefit and the long-term viability of the industry.

Marketing Strategy

Newfoundland and Labrador Tourism will take a growth-strategy approach to marketing Newfoundland and Labrador as a tourism destination. Advertising will reach and persuade visitors to come to Newfoundland and Labrador, rather than to other destinations in their evoked set. Public and media relations will reinforce the key messages, delivering a consistent and relevant brand image of the province, while sales and online initiatives will "close the loop." The tourism product – in the form of attractions, experiences, and infrastructure – has a larger role to play in increasing length of stay, amount of money spent per trip, and overall tourism revenues. To be successful in attracting customers from competitors, it's essential that we focus and concentrate our resources on the best opportunity – and create programs and campaigns that are fully integrated.

Target Markets

Newfoundland and Labrador Tourism will focus and concentrate its resources against the target audiences and markets which offer the best opportunity and the highest return on investment. The target market is the nonresident touring and explorer market with concentration in Toronto, Ottawa, Calgary, Halifax and Montreal. Additional geographic markets include the Mid-Atlantic Region of the United States, California and the UK. Activity-based markets include Meetings, Convention and Incentive Travel market, the Hunting and Fishing market, the Hiking market and partnerships in Outdoor Adventure and Cruise markets.

Touring & Explorer Market

The touring and explorer group is a broad leisure market seeking sightseeing and soft-adventure experiences – from nature viewing to cultural experiences to hiking, birding, and whale-watching. Demographically, research reveals them to be singles and couples in the pre-and post-full nest stage of the family life cycle. Not surprisingly, they tend to be in two age groups: 25 to 34 and (skewed) 45+ years of age.They also tend to be well-educated and have a higher than average proportion who are university-educated and have higher than average household incomes.

Psychographically, they see themselves as increasingly sophisticated and experienced travellers, seeking more unusual places and experiences 'off the beaten track'. They are looking for an antidote to the stress and plastic composition of urban life and modern times. They're interested in discovering and experiencing the unspoiled natural environment. They are curious people, more interested in unexpected and intriguing experiences than repeat trips to conventional 'tourist' destinations: "been there, done that."

Marketing efforts in the United States will shift from the New England region to the Mid-Atlantic region for Newfoundland and Labrador. These travellers are seeking adventure and cultural experiences in new destinations. To maximize our efforts, Newfoundland and

Labrador works cooperatively with the Atlantic Canada Tourism Partnership (ACTP).

ACTP is a nine-member, pan-Atlantic partnership comprising of the Atlantic Canada Opportunities Agency, the four Atlantic Canada Tourism Industry Associations, and the four provincial departments responsible for tourism. The international market is developmental for Newfoundland and Labrador, with low penetration but with long-term potential and high-spend per visitor. Newfoundland and Labrador Tourism will continue to pursue this market in partnership with its Atlantic Canada Partners (ACTP), with primary focus being on the United States and the United Kingdom.

Marketing activities include travel trade partnerships, familiarization tours, trade shows, media relations, and joint marketing with the Canadian Tourism Commission (CTC). The CTC and its industry partners have launched a new global advertising campaign in the UK, Germany, and France. ACTP is a partner in this UK program to build more consumer awareness of the region.

Meetings, Conventions & Incentive Travel Market

Newfoundland and Labrador Tourism provides consultation, materials support, and mailing assistance to international, national, and regional conference organizers hosting conventions and meetings in Newfoundland and Labrador.

Incentive travel is a global management tool that uses an exceptional travel experience to motivate and/or recognize staff for increased levels of performance in support of organizational goals. Newfoundland and Labrador Tourism provides consultation, marketing, and product development support to industry suppliers in this lucrative market. Trade shows and marketplaces are available through partnership opportunities in North American markets.

Outdoor Adventure Market

Outdoor and nature activities such as hiking, birding and kayaking are core to our tourism experiences. These experiences appeal to outdoor enthusiasts and have a broad appeal to our touring and explorer market. Newfoundland and Labrador Tourism partners with the Newfoundland and Labrador Adventure Tourism Association at consumer and trade shows.

Hunting & Fishing Market

Newfoundland and Labrador offers hunters and sport fish enthusiasts some of the most amazing and rewarding outdoor recreation experiences in the world.

Newfoundland and Labrador Tourism partners with the Newfoundland and Labrador Outfitters Association (NLOA) to develop a fully-integrated marketing program for the hunting and fishing market.

Newfoundland and Labrador Brand

Brand Positioning

Most tourism brands are positioned on tangible products and features. Not surprisingly, most advertising presents an inventory of 'products' – places to go, sights to see, and things to do. But people don't buy 'products', they buy benefits. The real benefit lies several layers below the tangible tourism 'product' – in the emotion of the brand, and the feelings it evokes.

Newfoundland and Labrador will stand for 'creativity'. 'Creativity' is true to the brand of Newfoundland and Labrador. Creativity – natural, spontaneous, and uncomplicated – defines who we are, what we do, and the place around us.

We express it in everything we do and say. It will differentiate the Newfoundland and Labrador brand and become our strongest unique selling point. 'Creativity', as the brand positioning, will be expressed and supported by three pillars:

People: The very real character of our people, their attitude, and way of life. Real, genuine people – warm, friendly, welcoming, uncomplicated, witty, humorous, and fun-loving. All the more powerfully felt because of the historical undercurrent of an unrelenting and unforgiving environment, mastered only through a fierce independence, steeped in self-reliance, quiet pride, and creative ingenuity.

Culture: Our history, heritage, music, art, language, architecture, folklore, traditions, values, and the vitality of colour and texture in everything we touch. It links our past with our present and expresses our spiritual and creative and intellectual qualities.

Natural Environment: This place of fierce beauty that lives by the sea. A rugged land with 29,000 kms of coastline, rich icons of whales and wildlife and icebergs, and a sensuous magic light that pours over the landscape and into the art and culture, and hearts of our people.

Brand Personality

A tourism brand personality is the feeling or image that people have about a place. Newfoundland and Labrador's brand personality will personify the creativity of our people and our culture and guide all marketing programs. The Newfoundland and Labrador Tourism brand personality is the natural and spontaneous expression of who we are:

* Natural and uncomplicated.
* Warm and friendly.
* Genuine and authentic.
* Quietly and proudly independent.
* Spontaneous, rather than practiced or self-conscious.
* Witty and funny, with a natural spontaneity.
* Creative – not only in art and culture, but in our natural ingenuity and inventiveness.
* Comfortable in our own skin.

Touring & Explorer Marketing Activities

Canada Market (Newspaper Campaign)

Online Campaign: A series of online advertising including leader boards, big-box, skyscraper, and banners on a variety of business/news-related websites such as The Globe and Mail, travel-specific websites including Air Canada, Expedia, Travelocity & Yahoo and interest/activity websites dedicated to activities such as birding, hiking, whales, and nature viewing.

Ontario Market (Television Campaign)

Ambient Campaign: Newfoundland and Labrador Tourism is finalizing its ambient marketing activities for the upcoming campaign. Ambient marketing is also called guerilla marketing or place-based marketing; it is marketing or advertising that occurs wherever customers happen to be, it is memorable because it is usually unexpected and unconventional.

Newspaper Campaign: A combination of full-page ads and 4-colour preprinted inserts in Ottawa Citizen.

Radio Campaign: Sponsorship of weather and air quality reports on selected radio stations in Toronto.

United States Market: Marketing efforts in the United States will shift from the New England region to the Mid-Atlantic region for Newfoundland and Labrador.

These travellers are seeking adventure and cultural experiences in new destinations. To maximize our efforts, Newfoundland and Labrador works cooperatively with the Atlantic Canada Tourism Partnership (ACTP).

ACTP is a nine-member, pan-Atlantic partnership comprising of the Atlantic Canada Opportunities Agency, the four Atlantic Canada Tourism Industry Associations, and the four provincial departments responsible for tourism. In 2009, Newfoundland and Labrador will continue to focus its efforts in the United States with an emphasis on the hiking and walking activity markets.

Magazine Campaign: Newfoundland and Labrador Tourism advertisements in Audubon, Harpers, National Geographic Traveller, and Smithsonian.

Online Campaign: A series of online advertising including leader boards, big-box, skyscrapers, and banners on websites such as Audubon, Smithsonian, Yahoo, Google, National Geo and activity websites such as Backpacking Light.

Overview: The international market is developmental for Newfoundland and Labrador, with low penetration but with long-term potential and high-spend per visitor. Newfoundland and Labrador Tourism will continue to pursue this market in partnership with its Atlantic Canada Tourism Partnership (ACTP), with primary focus being on the United Kingdom.

Marketing activities include travel trade partnerships, familiarization tours, trade shows, media relations, and joint marketing agreements with Overseas Tour Operators/Wholesale and with the Canadian Tourism Commission (CTC).

International Travel Media Program

The Travel Media Program plays an integral role in maximizing consumer and trade awareness of Newfoundland and Labrador through unpaid media coverage in key overseas markets. Travel media includes freelance journalists, travel editors, broadcasters, producers, and travel trade media. Newfoundland and Labrador Tourism, along with our International counterparts, estimates editorial value from travel stories is four times that of paid advertising. In 2008-09, Newfoundland and Labrador received in excess of $45 million in media coverage and was featured in numerous international newspapers and magazines.

Editorial

Help us keep media informed of what's new in Newfoundland and Labrador. We welcome your information on new travel products, events, personalities, folklore, and regional descriptions for unique travel story opportunities. The information you give us is used to pitch unique story ideas to media and to initiate and plan media tours to Newfoundland and Labrador for qualified journalists. You are also encouraged to submit articles on new tourism products and attractions for the CTC and various media outlets.

Media Tours and Press Trips

Co-host travel media at your business as they tour Newfoundland and Labrador to experience our tourism products first-hand. You may participate by sharing costs or providing in-kind contributions for these tours.

Sales Activities

Media events, promotions, and sales calls in our key international markets are crucial elements in our travel media program. Many of these activities are undertaken in partnership with the CTC and the Atlantic Canada Tourism Partnership (ACTP).

In-Province Resident Marketing Activities

Newfoundland and Labrador Tourism will continue a season extension program for the in-province market. The program covers all four seasons and provides opportunities for tourism operators to promote seasonal packages and create partnerships with other operators in their region.

The objectives for the program are:

* To increase resident in-province travel and expenditures by motivating residents to travel at home.

* To increase resident knowledge of activities and attractions that occurs during fall, spring, and winter seasons as well as the summer period.
* To increase frequency of travel by motivating residents to take additional and more frequent short trips during the shoulder seasons as well as their annual summer vacation. Increase focus on the shoulder seasons.

Resident Direct-Mail Campaign

The Resident Direct Mail Campaign consists of direct mail brochures and a multimedia advertising campaign. It is an excellent opportunity to get your vacation package delivered to every household in Newfoundland and Labrador through the brochures mailed each summer, fall and winter. Your involvement in the In-Province Direct Mail Campaign is automatic and free when you participate in the Packaging Marketing Program.

Bibliography

Andrew, N; Flanagan, S & Ruddy, J: *Tourism Destination Planning*, Dublin, Dublin Institute of Technology, 2002.

Apostolopous, Y and Leivadi, S: *Sociology of Tourism, The: Theoretical And Empirical Investigations*, London, Retailed, 1996.

Ashworth, G J and Dietvorst, A G J: *Tourism and Spatial Transformations: Implications For Policy and Plan*, Wallingford, CAB International, 1995.

Ashworth, Greg and Larkham, P J: *Building a New Heritage: Tourism, Culture & Identity in the New Europe*, London, Routledge,1994.

Baum, Tom: *We're all Going on a Summer Holiday: Images of Tourism Past and Person*, Buckingham, University of Buckingham, 1995.

Beeho, A & Prentice, R: *Conceptualising The Experiences of Heritage Tourists*, 1997.

Beeton, Sue:: *Film-Induced Tourism*, Clevedon, Channel View, 2005.

Belie et al.: *Tourism and the Inner City: An Evaluation of /Impact of Grant Assist*, London, HMSO, 1990.

Benefice, Brian G, and Cooper, Chris: *Geography of Travel and Tourism*, The, London, Heinemann, 1987.

Bolshevism, Germy: *Coping with Tourists: European Reactions to Mass Tourism*, Oxford, Berghahn Books, 1995.

Boniface, Priscilla and Fowler, Peter: *Heritage and Tourism: In the Global Village*, London, Retailed, 1993.

Bosselman, Fred P: *In The Wake of the Tourist: Managing Special Places in Eight Countries*, Washington, DC, Conservation Foundation, The, 1978.

Briguglio, L and Vella, Leslie: *Competitiveness of the Maltese Islands in Mediterranean in Tourism*, Chichester, John Wiley, 1995.

Brown, Dona: *Inventing New England: Regional Tourism in the Nineteenth Century*, Washington DC, Smithsonian Institution, 1995.

Brunt, Paul: *Market Research in Travel and Tourism*, Oxford, Butterworth Heinemann, 1997.

Burkart, A and Medlik, S: *Management of Tourism*, The, London, Heinemann, 1975.

Chambers, Erve: *Native Tours: The Anthropology of Travel and Tourism*, Prospect Heights, Waveland Press, 2000.

Chandler, Harry and Carter, John: *Chandler's Travels: A Tour of the Life of Harry Chandler*, London, Quiller Press, 1985.

Clark, Colin: *Tourist Services and Guidance: Heritage and Information*, Strasbourg, Council of Europe Press, 1989.

Coccosis, Harry and Nijkamp, Peter: *Sustainable Tourism Development*, Aldershot, Avebury, 1995.

Cohen, Erik: *Towards a Sociology of International Tourism*, 1972.

Dann, Graham M S: *Language of Tourism*, The, Wallingford, CAB International, 1996.

Davidson, R and Maitland, R: *Tourism Destinations, London*, Hodder and Stoughton, 1997.

Davidson, Rob: *Travel and Tourism in Europe*, Harlow, Addison Wesley Longman, 1998.

Ecotec: *Calderdale: Tourism Impact Study*, Calderdale, ECOTEC/Calderdale Council, 1990.

Edensor, Tim: *Tourists at the Taj*, London, Retailed, 1998.

Edgell, David L: *International Tourism Policy, New York*, Van Nostrand and Reinhold, 1990.

Elliott, James: *Tourism: Politics and Public Sector Management*, London, Retailed, 1997.

Fairgrieve, James: *Geography in School*, London, University of London Press, 1926.

Foster, Douglas: *Travel and Tourism Management*, London, Macmillan Educational, 1985.

Frechtling, Douglas C: *Practical Tourism Forecasting*, Oxford, Butterworth Heinemann, 1996.

Gamble, P. R: *The Educational challenge for Hospitality and Tourism Studies*, Tourism Management, 13, 1992.

Ghimire, Krishna: *The Native Tourist*: Mass Tourism within Developing Regions, London, Earthscan, 2001.

Goeldner, C. R: *The Evaluation of Tourism as an Industry and a Discipline, Paper Presented to*, International Conference for Tourism Educators, Guildford, University of Surrey, 1988.

Gunn, Clare and Var, Turgut: *Tourism Planning*, London, Retailed, 2002.

Hall, C Michael *Tourism Planning: Policies, Processes and relationships*, Harlow, Prentice Hall, 2000.

Hall, Colin and Jenkins, John: *Tourism and Public Policy*, London, Retailed, 1995.

Hall, Colin Michael: *Tourism and Politics*: Policy, Power, & Place, Chichester, Wiley, 1994.

Harrison, Lyndon: *Tourism Means Jobs*, Chester, Lyndon Harrison, 1996.

Harron, S and Weiler, B: *Ethnic Tourism*, Belhaven/Wiley, 1992.

Inkpen, G: *Information Technology for Travel and Tourism*, Harlow, Addison Wesley Longman, 1998.

Inskeep, Edward *National and Regal Tourism Planing*: Methodologies & Case Studies, London, Routledge/WTO, 1994.

Irwin, William *The New Niagara*: *Tourism, Technology, And the Landscape of Niagara Fal*, University Park, PA, University of Pennsylvania, 1996.

Jack, G and Phipps, A: *Tourism and Intercultural Exchange*: *Why Tourism Matters*, Clevedon, Channel View, 2005.

Jakle, John: *Tourist, The: Travel in Twentieth Century North America*, University of North Nebraska, 1985.

Jennings, Gayle: *Tourism Research*, Chichester, Wiley, 2001.

Judd, D R: *Promoting Tourism* in US Cities, 1995.

Karski, A: *Urban Tourism* - A Key to Urban Regeneration?, 1990.

Kotler, Philip et al: *Marketing Places*: *Attracting Investment, Industry & Tourism etc*, New York, free press, 1993.

Labarge, Margaret Wade: *Medieval Travellers*: *The Rich and Restless*, London, Hamish Hamilton, 1982.

Laws, Eric: *Tourist Destination Management: Issues, Analysis & Policies*, London, Routledge, 1995.

Leed, Eric J: *Mind of the Traveller, The: From Gilgamesh to Global Tourism*, New York, 1991.

MacCannell, Dean: *Tourist, The: A New Theory of the Leisure Class*, London, Macmillan, 1976.

Machin, Alan: *Retracing the Steps: Tourism as Education, Janus*, Fin, ATLAS / FUNTS, 2001.

Opperman, Martin and Chon, Kye-Sung: *Tourism in Developing Countries, London*, International Thomson Business Press, 1997.

Patullo, Polly: *Last Resorts*: *The Cost of Tourism in the Caribbean*, London, Cassell, 1996.

Pearce, Douglas: *Tourism Today*: *A Geographical Analysis*, Harlow, Longman, 1995.

Pearce, P L: *Social Psychology Of Tourist Behaviour*, The, Oxford, Pergamon, 1982.

Peters, M: *International Tourism*, London, Hutchinson, 1969.

Ringer, Greg: *Destinations: Cultural Landscapes of Tourism*, London, Routledge, 1998.

Ritchie, Brent: *Managing Educational Tourism*, Clevedon, Channel View, 2003.

Robinson, H: *Geography of Tourism*, A, London, Macdonald and Evans, 1976.

Robinson, M, Evans, E & Chalazion, P: *Tourism and Cultural Change, Sunderland*, Business Education Publishers Ltd, 1996.

Rogers, H Anthea and Slinn, Judy A: *Tourism: Management of Facilities*, London, Pitman: M & E, 1993.

Schwaninger, M: *Trends in Leisure and Tourism for 2000 - 2010*, Prentice Hall, 1989.

Scottish Tourist Board: *Visitor Attractions: A Development Guide*, Edinburgh, Scottish Tourist Board, 1991.

Seaton, A V et al: *Tourism: The state of the Art*, Chichester, John Wiley, 1994.

Shaw, G and Williams, A: *Tourism and Tourism Spaces*, London, Sage, 2004.

Stevens, Terry: *Island Tourism*: Malta, , WTO, 1993.

Trench, R: *Travellers in Britain*, London, Aurum, 1990.

Tribe, John *Corporate Strategy for Tourism, London*, International Thomson Business Press, 1997.

Urry, John: *Tourist Gaze*, The, London, Sage, 1990.

Van den Berg et al: *Urban Tourism: Performance and Strategies in Eight European Cities*, Aldershot, Avebury, 1995.

Van Harssel, Jan: *Tourism: An Exploration*, New York, Prentice Hall, 1994.

Veal, A: *Leisure and Tourism*: Policy and Planning, Wallingford, CABI, 2001.

Wahab, S A: *Tourism Management*, Tourism International Press, 1975.

Walle, Alfred H: *Cultural Tourism*: A Strategic Focus, Boulder, Co, Westview Press, 1998.

Wilkinson, Paul: *Tourism Policy and Planning: As Studies from the Caribbean*, Elmsford New York, Cognizant Communications Corporation, 1997.

Yale, Pat: *From Tourist Attractions to Heritage Tourism*, Huntingdon, Elm, 1991.

Zarkia, Cornelia: *Philoxenia: Receiving Tourists*-but *not Guests-on a Greek Island*, Oxford, Berghahn Books, 1996.

Index

A

B

C

D

E

F

G

H

I

L

M

W

□□□